Regulation
of Marketing and
the Public Interest

Pergamon Titles of Related Interest

Balderston/Carman/Nicosia MARKETING AND PUBLIC POLICY
Davis MANAGING AND ORGANIZING MULTINATIONAL
      CORPORATIONS
Liebling U.S. CORPORATE PROFITABILITY
Slappey THE FUTURE OF BUSINESS — ANNUAL REVIEW:
      1980-81
Thorelli/Becker INTERNATIONAL MARKETING STRATEGY
Wang BUSINESS WITH CHINA
Ways THE FUTURE OF BUSINESS

Related Journals*

DESIGN ABSTRACTS INTERNATIONAL
IPRA REVIEW
JOURNAL OF PRODUCTS LIABILITY
LONG RANGE PLANNING
PROGRESS IN PLANNING

*Free specimen copies available upon request.

PERGAMON
POLICY
STUDIES
ON BUSINESS

Regulation of Marketing and the Public Interest

Edited by
Frederick E. Balderston
James M. Carman
Francesco M. Nicosia

Essays in Honor of Ewald T. Grether

Pergamon Press
NEW YORK • OXFORD • TORONTO • SYDNEY • PARIS • FRANKFURT

Pergamon Press Offices:

U.S.A. Pergamon Press Inc., Maxwell House, Fairview Park, Elmsford, New York 10523, U.S.A.

U.K. Pergamon Press Ltd., Headington Hill Hall, Oxford OX3 0BW, England

CANADA Pergamon of Canada, Ltd., Suite 104, 150 Consumers Road, Willowdale, Ontario M2J 1P9, Canada

AUSTRALIA Pergamon Press (Aust.) Pty. Ltd., P.O. Box 544, Potts Point, NSW 2011, Australia

FRANCE Pergamon Press SARL, 24 rue des Ecoles, 75240 Paris, Cedex 05, France

FEDERAL REPUBLIC OF GERMANY Pergamon Press GmbH, Hammerweg 6, Postfach 1305, 6242 Kronberg/Taunus, Federal Republic of Germany

Library of Congress Cataloging in Publication Data

Main entry under title:

Regulation of marketing and the public interest.

  (Pergamon policy studies on business)
  "Grether bibliography": p.
  Includes index.
  1. Marketing—United States—Congresses. 2. Marketing—Social aspects—United States—Congresses.
I. Grether, Ewald Theophilus, 1899-   II. Balderston, Frederick E. III. Carman, James M. IV. Nicosia, Francesco M. V. Series.
HF5415.1.R43 1981   381'.3'0973   80-19731
ISBN 0-08-025563-9

Printed in the United States of America

Contents

Dedication

On the 29th and 30th days of March, 1979, colleagues, students, and friends assembled at Berkeley to honor Ewald T. Grether on the occasion of his eightieth birthday. It is significant to note that this celebration took the form of a scholarly conference.

From that conference came the set of papers contained in this volume. The range of topics is wide. However, all focus on some aspect of marketing and public policy. Both in the range of topics and the variety of intellectual styles whereby these topics are addressed, the volume is hoped to be a fitting celebration of the work of E.T. Grether as scholar and teacher.

The record of Grether's writings (see the special bibliography under his name), beginning in 1927, shows a continual commitment to the development and use of economic analysis for explaining marketing phenomena and for guiding public policy. From an early emphasis on studies of the structure of wholesale and retail distribution, Grether soon developed a vigorous emphasis on pricing and price policies, and published steadily, culminating in Price Control Under Fair Trade Legislation (1939). While this interest continued and, over time, became absorbed in his wider concern for antitrust and for pro-competitive policies generally, Grether also contributed significantly to regional analysis, especially with respect to the prospects for further economic expansion in the Far West, in a series of articles and reports in the period following World War II.

Elsewhere in this volume, Ronald Savitt discusses at length the theory of interregional marketing and the importance of Grether's contributions to that theory.

With Roland S. Vaile and Reavis Cox, Grether participated in the formulation, in Marketing in the American Economy (1952), of the most comprehensive of his contributions to marketing theory and its managerial and public policy applications. While this was a text for marketing courses, it was also fresh and far-ranging in its treatment of concepts of marketing flows and in the economic analysis of the marketing activities and policies of the individual enterprise.

From the mid-1950s on, Grether continued and broadened his attention to antitrust and pro-competitive policy issues. He served on a national committee appointed by the U.S. Attorney General to study the antitrust laws, an episode assessed by Donald Turner in the course of his contribution to this volume. A steady series of articles was followed by the compact and incisive monograph, Marketing and Public Policy (1966).

A trustee of the Marketing Science Institute from 1962 onward, Grether has remained actively involved with that organization, assisting in the formulation of its research agenda and following very closely the development of the "PIMS" project. In June, 1977, the Institute held a symposium in his honor on the topic of Marketing and the Public Interest, and it published a volume in 1978, reporting the papers and discussions of that symposium, including a paper by E.T. Grether on perspectives of the issues of marketing and public policy.

From this account of his research and writing, it might be difficult to believe that E.T. Grether also served for an unbroken span of 20 years, from 1941-1961, first as acting dean and then as dean of the School of Business Administration at Berkeley.

During this period, the business school survived the problems of wartime mobilization and the in-rush of veterans during the postwar years; it expanded its faculty greatly, established a separate Graduate School of Business Administration to serve as administrative domicile of master's programs and established a doctoral program of its own. At the same time, Grether was a power in the Academic Senate of the University of California, on the Berkeley campus. Then, as the multicampus university needed a university-wide Senate structure in parallel with its administrative organization, Grether served from 1964-66 as vice chairman and then chairman of the university-wide Senate. His bibliography includes a number of policy papers written for the Academic Senate, and his office files must contain dozens of internal administrative and Senate memoranda from these years of active, unstinting involvement in the leadership of his university.

Concerning E.T. Grether as teacher, colleague, and friend, there is ample testimony from those for whom he has been a major influence. He has been the source of much inspiration and the friend to several generations of scholars. His work has been the wellspring of great stimulation and his demeanor the role model for appreciating the art and practice of scholarship. His contributions to marketing have been extensive; as one of a small group of scholars, he has carved a place for marketing and he can be considered a founder of an independent discipline. In recognition of this contribution, he was elected to the "Distribution Hall of Fame" in 1953 and is the only scholar to have been awarded the "Paul D. Converse Award for Contribution to the Theory of Marketing" twice: in 1955 and 1975.

On a very personal basis, it is important to note E.T. Grether's unselfishness. Indeed, the time and effort he extended to students and colleagues are reflective of his enormous generosity. He has always been willing to share his ideas, search for new ones, and prod others to do their best. He has been for many of his students and colleagues the prime source of inspiration for understanding the values of an academic career.

It will be ample reward for the authors and editors of this volume if those concerned with marketing and public policy find this volume to be helpful and free-ranging in its ideas. It needs to have both of these qualities to be worthy of E.T. Grether.

Acknowledgments

The authors and editors received valuable help in the preparation of this book from many sources. Some of the people who helped to strengthen the papers are acknowledged in notes at the beginning of chapters. The formal reviewers of the papers, some of whom are listed in the back of the volume, worked hard to provide constructive comments to authors. Similarly the audience at the conference helped to strengthen the papers through the discussion of the papers.

The executive secretary for the conference and for this book was Gwen Cheeseburg. While her devotion to excellence in preparation of all materials is always great, in this case it was a labor of love since she has worked with Dean Grether for about fifteen years.

The conference itself was coordinated by Richard Haber with the assistance of Kim Denison, Mary Dunlavey, Donald Norris and Betty Robinson. Angela Clark, the Editor at Pergamon Press, was always prompt and helpful in working with the editors and in coordinating production of the book. In Berkeley, Patricia Murphy prepared the art work and Josef Chytry did some copy editing and prepared the references. The editors are sincerely grateful to them all.

I
Competitive Behavior

1 Rules Versus Analysis, The Search for a Middle Ground

F.E. Balderston

Part I of this book contains seven papers and a critique. All of the papers deal with the question of how public policy makers can evaluate the welfare implications of a number of typical types of competitive behavior, including price cutting, horizontal mergers, investment in research and development, new product introduction, and product improvements. It is clear that in many situations all of these types of behavior are to be encouraged.

How can we determine when there may be significant negative welfare implications? Some would argue that in the name of efficiency and equity, fairly clear and simple rules should be enunciated – particularly in these areas where behavior is more likely to be pro-competitive than anti-competitive. Wherever a clear-cut prescriptive standard for an important aspect of pro-competitive policy can be agreed upon and enunciated, this will solve many problems. One good effect is prophylactic. Competitors will be able to guide their own behavior to conform to the demands of the standard, knowing that if they do so, they will avoid antitrust prosecution. Potential litigants, as a second benefit, will clarify their positions in legal controversies much more readily by appeal to known standards. Finally, the courts can be expected to develop case law in a much more coherent fashion if there are well-stated prescriptive standards against which to range the nuances of judgment in the particular fact-situation.

Donald Turner initiates this section by discussing the problems of arriving at rules based on sound economic analysis and workable in the legal context. He discusses antitrust rules concerning horizontal merger, predatory pricing in monopoly, and then offers comments on the complications of deregulation. In the predatory pricing discussion, the assumption is that the relevant product and the price at which it is sold are well defined. Those are the usual classical assumptions.

All the other papers in Part I develop analysis and evidence in a way that seems to say, however, that things may fail to be as they neo-

3

classically seem. The first of these, by John Narver, questions the ease with which we can determine what the true price offered in a transaction is.

Narver starts with broadened definitions of the elements of price and cost in a transaction, drawing on the marketing literature to supplement the abstract treatment of price as a single-dimensioned variable in economic theory. Then he shows that "true price" may be different from the nominal dollar price; furthermore, changes in the true price may be in either the same or in the opposite direction to changes in the nominal price.

Narver's analysis carries to the conclusion that if market price appears not to respond to new cost or demand conditions, it is necessary first to examine all the ways whereby both seller and purchaser may be adjusting their behavior. Only after such an examination, and negative findings, would it be correct to infer that non-competitive market power was being exercised to prevent price response.

The rest of the papers in this part of the book are somewhat more concerned with product variation than with price variation. In all cases, the analysis must focus on the market dynamics of a particular competitive approach or policy. David Grether's concern is with the impact on competition of spending for research and development of new products and processes. He first undertakes a comprehensive review of the literature concerning relationships between R & D and the state of competition. He finds disagreements as to the existence of a strong association between R & D and a concentrated market structure.   Further, if an association exists, does high R & D lead to market concentrations or vice versa?

Grether then discusses in thorough fashion the conceptual and technical problems of arriving at measures of R & D input and output and measures of market concentration. Finally, he assesses current knowledge of these relationships with respect to public policy. Do the larger firms undertake disproportionately more R & D? Do concentrated industries spend especially heavily for R & D? Does high R & D spending contribute to high concentration?

Grether suggests that simultaneous-equation models, rather than the usual single equations, would help to resolve these problems.

Having the cash flow required to support a major R & D effort may require first achieving a dominant position in an existing market. One explanation for this is provided by the empirically derived "experience curve" theory that posits that there will be a continuing reduction of unit production costs as cumulative output increases. If so, then the firm which has the dominant market share will have the greatest cumulative production experience, will have the lowest unit costs, and thereby will have the profit margin to support research and development. Donald Thompson investigates the public policy implications of this particular aspect of market dynamics.

Thompson reviews evidence concerning the experience curve and applies this to Canada's public policy problems. How may a nation with a relatively small internal market stimulate the development of efficient, leading sectors? Since a firm having a high market share can capture available cost reductions quickly, especially in a growing market, should such a dominant firm be encouraged for its efficiency despite the dangers of monopolization? Thompson considers several aspects of this important problem.

The papers by Lee Preston and Almarin Phillips return to the issue of predatory marketing behavior by dominant firms. In both papers, the emphasis is on product improvement as a possible technique of predatory conduct. "Predation" is inherently a dynamic phenomenon. A firm makes exceptional price reductions, product changes, terms-of-sale changes, output increases, or other nonprice changes temporarily, expecting to more than recoup the cost of these marketing efforts after competitors have been seriously weakened or eliminated.

Preston assesses the case of IBM as a possible market predator, using the very large evidentiary record available from antitrust litigation involving IBM. Here again, the issues pertain to market dynamics. The dominant firm has available to it a large number of competitive actions in the marketplace for computing equipment. Preston assembles from the record evidence that he is convinced implies a predatory pattern of conduct by IBM in the early 1970s toward several competitors who manufactured "plug-compatible" peripheral machines. IBM was required in legal discovery proceedings to disclose numerous internal company documents, and the record, interestingly, includes some of IBM's own strategy memoranda.

The assessment of the pattern of business conduct has two complicating aspects: First, the business actions of IBM, taken individually, were presumably not illegal acts and might not ordinarily have been destructive of competitors either in intent or effects, but their combined impact is what counted. Second, the same pattern of conduct, had it been undertaken by a firm other than one dominant firm, would probably have not been thought to be exceptional or anti-competitive. In Preston's view, these actions did amount to a predatory pattern of conduct when undertaken by IBM.

Phillips provides an analytical framework for assessing the public policy implications of product improvements by drawing distinctions among quality changes, line extensions, and new product introduction. He then considers the validity of antitrust rules regarding predatory market behavior in application to such cases.

This group of papers, then, provides extensions of economic analysis useful as guides for an antitrust, pro-competitive public policy. In his insightful critique of this section, Roland Artle demonstrates that many unanswered questions remain. Clearly, the distinction between the analysis in these papers and that found in classical price theory and welfare economics is that the addition of marketing variables and theory provides a richness and complexity that is much more reflective of real competitive behavior. Further, it is important to consider that welfare optimization may include political and social objectives beyond those of simply short-run transactional and allocative efficiency. Our body of antitrust law focuses only on the efficiency benefits of competition. It is exactly this breadth, richness, and excitement of the joining of economics, marketing, and public policy that have been central in the work of E.T. Grether throughout his professional life.

2 The Need for Rules and the Difficulty in Formulating Them

Donald Turner

It was my pleasure in March, 1979, to participate in two felicitous events honoring distinguished economists on the occasion of their eightieth birthdays: Harvard honoring Edward S. Mason and California honoring Ewald T. Grether. The similarities in these two men are remarkable. Mason was graduated from the University of Kansas; Grether from the University of Nebraska. Mason is recognized as the founder of the industrial organization field in economics; Grether is the leading authority in public policy toward marketing activities. Dean Grether presented the first paper in the program of the American Economics Association honoring Professor Mason. Both have been leading scholars, Dean Grether being almost unbelievably prolific. Both were outstanding teachers who left a band of devoted students, since distinguished in their own right, whom they have stimulated and inspired. Both made substantial contributions to government in advisory and other capacities. Both devoted a considerable part of their attention to antitrust policy, a commendable choice in my opinion. Mason was godfather to the book on antitrust policy that Carl Kaysen and I wrote (Kaysen & Turner, 1959), and Grether and Kaysen in 1957-58 worked together on a confidential report to persuade the Antitrust Division to a more economically oriented approach to antitrust enforcement – a wise recommendation which I'm afraid did not have a crashing impact – (not untypical of recommendations to government agencies). Finally, both Mason and Grether had a strong interest in the relation of economics to public policy, and a strong sense of the legal, social, and political institutional limitations that the economists making public policy recommendations must reckon with.

This last topic is the one addressed in this paper. Two areas are considered. The first is the problem that a legal scholar like myself encounters in trying to determine what the appropriate antitrust rules should be for various business practices and market structures. I shall then reflect briefly on some of the lessons we have learned from direct government economic regulation of market performance and from recent efforts to dispense with it. I will close with a few recommendations for my economist friends.

ECONOMIC ANALYSIS VERSUS SIMPLE RULES

First, with regard to economics and antitrust laws, I will take it as a premise that the only proper goal of antitrust law is to promote the economic objectives of a pro-competitive policy; that is, to maximize consumer welfare through efficient allocation of resources and through progressiveness and the development of new techniques and new products that put those resources to better use. There are, of course, many other goals that society may seek to promote for various social and political reasons – dispersing wealth, limiting business size, preserving small business units, and providing security. A pro-competitive policy contributes to some of these goals, partially conflicts with others, and in some instances, namely security, is in flat contradiction. In the main, our courts, in interpreting antitrust law, have given primacy to the economic goals of antitrust, and have refused to be drawn into the task of balancing them against other social and political values. The reasons were fully stated in the recent Areeda and Turner treatise (1978). The summary was so well put in that treatise that I cannot improve upon it and I shall simply quote a part of it here.

> First, economic or social objectives which competition either cannot satisfy or may be thought to disserve are typically dealt with directly by a wide variety of other legislative enactments. Competition and efficiency considerations, in short, operate within parameters set by other politically determined public policies. Second, direct legislation is a more effective and appropriate method of promoting such other objectives. Within any plausible bounds of statutory interpretation, antitrust law can at best make only a marginal contribution to those other goals. Moreover, the weighing and resolution of conflicting interests and objectives would involve the courts in essentially political decisions for which there are no workable legal standards, and would often place them in a regulatory or supervisory role for which they are ill equipped. (Section 105)

However, giving economic analysis a primary role in antitrust interpretation, which I think it must have, still leaves proper solutions very hard to come by in many instances. The underlying constraint is that antitrust law, like much other law, cannot possibly be turned into a case-by-case collection and assessment of all the relevant facts. For the law to be reasonably administrable, predictable, and consistently enforced – which are paramount legal considerations – it must commonly rely on relatively simple rules or presumptions that disregard or sharply limit the consideration of some variables that economists deem to be relevant.

The difficulty is that economics and economic prescriptions are often not very helpful in formulating legal rules responsive to this need. Now I do not wish to underestimate what economics has contributed. It has, at the least, pointed out many vulgar errors in past judicial interpretations of antitrust, and it has done much more than that on more sophisticated levels. However, inevitable and pervasive departures from conditions underlying the economist's theoretically perfect competition model greatly complicate the task of formulating reasonable antitrust rules. Economic theory is inadequate in some areas and in serious and continuing conflict in others. Someone once said there are as many definitions of workable competition as there are workable economists. Moreover, the empirical data that are necessary to resolve or determine the relevant theoretical questions are often unavailable or unobtainable within the time and resources that the enforcement mechanism can sensibly devote to the problems.

I will try to illustrate the problems encountered in formulating sensible legal rules by dwelling briefly on two issues: horizontal mergers and predatory pricing.

Horizontal Mergers

The functions of antitrust rules here is to prevent what the economist calls undue concentration. It is generally, though not universally, agreed that this is a worthwhile objective, and it is also usually agreed that the appropriate legal approach is to create presumptions of illegality based on merging firms' market shares, subject to some limited defenses. The larger the market shares, the more that this and similar mergers will increase concentration in an industry. Now all of this, however, raises many vexing questions. How large should the market shares be for presumptive illegality? Should they vary with the present degree of concentration? Should such other factors as barriers to entry, size of buyers, product heterogeneity, and the like affect the size of the critical market share? I can find no clear answers to these questions. There is, first, a serious and ongoing dispute over what degree of concentration is high enough to worry about. I can find reputable economists saying that concentration as low as four firms with 50 percent of the market is worthy of concern; others saying you don't have to worry until it gets to four firms with 80 percent or even higher. The effects of concentration are obviously affected, or would seem to be affected, by entry barriers and the like, but no feasible schemes have been devised for determining their actual impact on particular cases or even for drawing general rules. As recently as two or three years ago, somebody made a study of the effect of concentration in retail grocery markets, where we have supposed that freedom of entry is about as high as in any industry you can think of. Yet this study indicated that as four-firm concentration went from 40 to 70 percent, there was a distinct and substantial increase in prices and profitability. When one sees a study like that, one wonders whether the law should take barriers to entry in account, even apart from the problem that the economists have been unable to measure them to anyone's satisfaction.

Another problem is that all these issues are interrelated. You cannot set appropriate market share figures for making a merger presumably unlawful unless you've decided whether it's feasible to incorporate other market structure characteristics. If it isn't, that's going to affect your general rule. If the cost of overprohibition of mergers was slight, we wouldn't have to worry much about these problems, but that is not so because of the possible loss of economies of scale or other efficiencies that mergers may promote. And here again, the empirical data just don't settle down. Twenty years ago it appeared, or so we were told, that scale economies rarely required a firm with a market share of over 5 percent. Recent studies have cast great doubt on this proposition and, in fact, one leading student of market organization — and not of the Chicago school, I may add — has recently surmised that you need a market share of over 10 percent as often than not. Here again, we might forget about that problem if efficiencies were readily realizable by routes other than merger. There are two alternatives: one is internal expansion, the other is a joint venture. Yet it seems fairly clear that while forestalling mergers may not permanently prevent the attainment of efficiencies through internal growth, it may often delay the process at an aggregate social cost of a magnitude high enough to worry about. Internal expansion is often deterred by the prospect that a substantial addition to the capacity of the market will depress price to the point where expansion will not be profitable. Moreover, the growing economic literature on transaction costs, although primarily focused on the question of vertical integration, suggests that joint ventures may often be an inefficient substitute for full firm integration. The problem would again be eased somewhat if the magnitude of economies could be more or less readily determined. Yet, with the possible exception of plant scale economies, this does not appear to be the case. In sum, in this area economics has seemingly done little more than leave us with a range of plausible administratively feasible solutions, no one of which is clearly superior to the other. We are reduced, pretty much, to relying on educated instinct, which is better than uneducated instinct, but is not as satisfactory as pretty clear proof.

Predatory Pricing

My second example that illustrates the problem of case-by-case economic analysis in antitrust enforcement concerns the enforcement of predatory pricing under Section 2 of the Sherman Act. Until recently, the case law on predatory pricing has been characterized by vagueness and a paucity of economic analysis. Professor Areeda and I proposed that legal tests for predation be based on a limited number of cost-based rules (Areeda and Turner, 1975). This proposal provoked widespread interest and discussion in the scholarly journals. An amplified and slightly modified version of our analysis appears in our antitrust treatise (Areeda and Turner, 1978, Sections 711-722).

Our simple rule deals with the case of a dominant firm that engages in predatory pricing practices to destroy or ward off new entrants. The rule proposes that a prima facie case of predation would be established if it could be shown that the dominant firm's price was below reasonably anticipated average variable cost, and that the firm may not defend on the grounds that the price was "promotional" or merely met an equally low price of a competitor. Promotional spending, as a substitute for a price reduction, should be deemed predatory when timed to coincide with entry or promotion by a rival, and when average variable cost, including the promotional expenditure, exceeds price. Note that this rule avoids placing any limits on investment or on the development of product variation. It also provides a way to avoid the need to measure marginal costs.

Subsequently, Professors R. Posner, F.M. Scherer, and O.E. Williamson raised various objections to our proposed rules. Scherer (1976) raises some technical points regarding our economic analysis, but his principal concern is that our rule may not result in long-run welfare maximization. His conclusion, among others, is that the courts can and must delve into the intent of the dominant firm if it is to determine if a price is predatory. He argues that without a thorough examination of how the firm perceived the probable effects of its behavior and an examination of the long-run effect of that behavior, the courts are likely to reach economically unsound decisions.

Williamson (1977) proposes a temporary output limitation on a monopolist's response to new entry, and extends our analysis to include situations of existing oligopoly in which one competitor is alleged to engage in predatory pricing for the purpose of eliminating one or more competitors, and to firms in the late growth stage of their life cycle. He rises to the challenge of developing rules, but his rules are much more complex than ours. He, like Scherer, believes that to understand the welfare implications of a pricing policy requires an analysis of the dynamic effect of that policy and that our static rule simply will not do.

Our reply to Williamson, in brief, was that his rules raise some theoretical problems of their own and seem less administrable than ours; and our reply, in brief, to Scherer was that his own complex economic analysis proves our point.

There is no way that a monopolist could determine a priori what his proper price floor is, and no realistic way — wholly apart from the unfairness of such an approach — that a court could make such a determination after the fact. How, for example, is a firm to know of its competitors' or new entrants' costs; and how is it to know what will be the future demands (and hence "deadweight" welfare losses) and future costs of capacity to meet those demands? Scherer's constructs for determining what price will maximize long-run welfare have no operational utility for antitrust law purposes. Nor is an inquiry into the monopolist's "intent" likely to provide any illumination. (Areeda and Turner, Reply to Scherer, 1976, p. 897).

In addition to the fairness concerns raised by spongy tests concerning intent and future effects, society cannot afford a legal system that requires costly investigations into economic analysis and forecasts in each antitrust case. While it is certainly possible that the simple rules approach may, in some instances, produce nonoptimal welfare results, we continue to believe that the simple average variable cost rule is the most sensible solution for predatory pricing and the one that will maximize total social welfare.

DIRECT REGULATION OF MARKETING ACTIVITIES

Now let me turn to other forms of direct regulation and recent tendencies toward deregulation. When discussing antitrust law, I was describing an area where, in my view, social and political questions do not seriously impinge on policy formation. It is a matter of statutory interpretation and the courts are going to be primarily occupied with economic issues of competition. Politics should not play any role. It is also an area, however, in which economics often speaks with less than a clear voice. When you move to the area of direct regulation – of airlines, surface transportation, field prices of natural gas, and other price controls – the situation is reversed in both respects. Here, the economic analysis is usually relatively clear and has as good a consensus as you can normally expect. But, since we are dealing with legislation, or repeal of legislation, and not judicial interpretation, political considerations are critical, if not decisive. Notice first that we have substantially deregulated in the airline industry and serious efforts are being made to deregulate surface transport. Why? First, the economic case is reasonably clear for deregulation. Both industries would work fairly well with no direct regulation at all. You may need to retain some maximum rate regulation for monopoly rail services, but that's a detail. Second, and this is of critical importance, the felt political sense is that deregulation will not only promote efficiency, which the general populace may only be dimly aware of, but will lead to lower prices, a particularly delightful prospect in times of inflation. The chief barrier to deregulation has been the disruption to vested interests. Investments and jobs would be threatened by a return to a competitive regime. This will probably make it much more difficult to pass deregulation legislation for surface transportation than it was for air transport because the vested interests are much more pervasive and much stronger. The Teamsters Union, for example, when told that deregulation will produce a more compact, efficient motor carrier industry, knows for whom the bell tolls – efficiency means fewer jobs. But, again, in both of these areas the prospect is for lower prices and increased customer service – a clear consumer benefit.

Look, in contrast, at the problems of getting decontrol of natural gas, oil, and gasoline. Again, the economic analysis seems reasonably clear. Ronald Coase once said that economists may be uncertain as to many things, but one thing they know – at a higher price, less will be demanded and more will be supplied. Hence, maximum price controls on goods in short supply are counter-productive. But here, unlike deregulation in transportation, prices will clearly rise, at least in the short run. This is politically unpalatable. There are vastly more consumer voters with felt vested interests than there are business voters.

Well, this leads me to some simple advice to my economist friends; and I guess, really, I'm an economist too, so I'm advising myself. Like E.T. Grether, you've got to keep doing your scholarly thing, with perhaps a greater focus on the practical limits that law and legal institutions impose on fine-tuned public policy solutions. By and large, I think public policy solutions have to be rather crude. Now, if you're worried that your message may be ill received, you can take comfort in the fact that in this country we may criticize the messenger but we don't shoot him. The scholar must be content with a quite long time horizon. Dean Grether's and Carl Kaysen's recommendations to the Antitrust Division would have necessitated a radical transformation of what had been done for decades — you do not get that done in a short period of time. It takes time for any new insights to filter through the legal and political process. The economists have done very much. Antitrust law, however depressed you may be about some of it and whatever the problems I have described, is much more perceptive in my opinion than it used to be. Further improvements are in the making. That we would have deregulated airlines and may deregulate surface transportation seemed wholly implausible as recently as five years ago. The sustained efforts of economists and others in this area finally bore fruit. Natural gas regulation is being phased out and other price controls may be as well.

What we have to recognize is that the layman, the public, demands too much. When Oscar Wilde was taken to see Niagara Falls, somebody noticed that he didn't say anything and asked him what he had to say. He said, "It would be more impressive if it ran the other way." Unfortunately, we as scholars can't make what we see as facts run the other way.

3 On the Unresponsiveness of Market Price

John C. Narver

The responsiveness of markets to changes in costs and demand is a central analytical and policy issue in a market economy. The conventional benchmark in the analysis of market responsiveness is the purely competitive world of classical economic theory: a model in which impersonal forces of supply and demand relentlessly conduce price adjustments.

To what extent in the contemporary economy is market response to supply and demand changes consistent with the classical model? The Great Depression demonstrated vividly to some economists that not all markets in the United States were dominated by impersonal supply and demand forces. In particular, Gardiner Means, in a well-known paper (1935), introduced what was to become the controversial doctrine of "administered prices," which to him were prices set by administrative action and by the same process held rigid, in contrast to "market determined prices," prices effected by the interaction of buyers and sellers and for that reason necessarily more flexible.

PROBLEMS WITH THE LANGUAGE AND THE MODELS

Whatever the substance of the concept, "administered prices," the semantics themselves have produced difficulties. "Administered prices" implies that only in the case of "market-determined prices" are the concepts of "supply" and "demand" and perhaps even "markets" analytically relevant. Adelman for one has protested that:

> The idea of a price "other than that set by supply and demand" is simply a verbal misunderstanding. Price is always set by supply and demand, but either or both may be under monopoly control (1958, p. 147).

*Comments by William Alberts, Johny Johansson, and Leigh McAlister are gratefully acknowledged.

The years since the "discovery" of administered prices have ushered forth literally tens of thousands of pages of analyses and debate on the alleged aberrant behavior of prices in a substantial subset of markets. In the introduction to its 1963 volume, Administered Prices: A Compendium on Public Policy, the U.S. Senate Antitrust and Monopoly Subcommittee noted that in the preceding six years the subcommittee had published on the subject 26 volumes of hearings numbering over 16,000 pages. If to this total one adds subsequent testimony plus the literally scores of scholarly articles on "administered prices" and derivative ideas such as "administered profits," "target-return pricing," "full-cost pricing," and "cost-push inflation," it is understandable why journal editors, Congressional staffs, the printers' ink and paper industries, as well as Gardiner Means himself all may be smiling, for one reason or another.

The examination of the alleged unresponsiveness of market prices vis-a-vis the classical model is not original to the United States. Alfred Marshall, in a somewhat impatient tone, writes of explaining (once again?) prices whose behavior some observers argued was inconsistent with the classical model:

> Further, there must always be a good many movements of retail price which stand in no relation to changes in the wholesale trade, or are even in opposite directions. . . . But all cases of this kind put together cover a very small part of the transactions of life; and, it would not have been worthwhile to call attention to them at all, were it not that they have furnished sensational material to writers who have argued that retail prices generally are arbitrary and scarcely at all subject to economic law. (Tucker, 1973, p. 23.)

Is there by now a verdict or at least a near-verdict in the debate on the reality of administered prices? In a word, no. The rank of economists affirming both the substance of the concept of administered prices and the empirical substantiation of them is large and prominent, among whom, in addition to Means, are Adams (example 1963), Blair (example 1972), and Weiss (1977). The opposition, ranging in viewpoint from skepticism to outright rejection, is equally numerous and vocal and includes economists such as Stigler (example 1970), Adelman (1963), and Weston (example 1972). Feelings run high. One opponent's annoyance with the term is unequivocal:

> "Administered prices" is a catchy phrase which promises everything, explains nothing, and thereby gets in our way of learning something. . . . To explain why a price and a pattern of output is what it is and not something else takes analysis of supply, demand and market control; setting up models of competition, monopoly, collusion, imperfect collusion, etc., and seeing which best fits. All this labor is saved, and in addition one has the nice feeling of being profound and up to date by saying: "administered prices." (Adelman, 1963, pp. 22, 24)

To make matters worse, if possible, those proclaiming the reality of administered prices disagree among themselves on the determinants of the phenomenon. Means believes there is no necessary relationship between administered prices and monopoly. Weiss disagrees, contending that some market power is necessary for administered prices and that prices should be more rigid the greater the level of concentration (1977, p. 614). However, why firms with market power would as a general rule prefer rigid prices to profit-maximizing prices puzzles, to say the least, Stigler and the entire Chicago School. (Stigler and Kindahl, 1970, p. 15) Indeed, one of the most staunch believers, John Blair, describes administered prices as a phenomenon in search of a theory (1959), though the discussant of his paper prefers to see them as a "theory in search of a phenomenon" (Bailey, 1959, p. 460).

So, administered prices: reality or illusion? The jury is out, and out it most certainly will stay until some different analytical perspectives are adopted. Some argue that the issue of the reality of administered prices is an empirical one (Weston, 1972). However, the present state of the statistical warfare has been summarized incisively by Bock who states that both sides to a major extent traffic in statistical irrelevance. All protagonists use price indices, but indices even at their best simply cannot reveal what must be shown (Bock, 1975).

A MORE ADEQUATE CONCEPT OF PRICE AND FRAMEWORK FOR PRICE ANALYSIS

The motivation for the present paper is that the conceptual framework for both the theoretical analysis and perforce the statistical analysis of "administered prices" is insufficient. The conceptual framework implicit in the majority of the arguments of both sides may be characterized as: (1) a partial model of price; (2) a partial model of demander choice; and (3) a static and partial model of the firm posited in a world of certainty! The debate must be liberated from the constricting clutches of such narrow models out of which can come only an illusion of proof. Alfred North Whitehead's warning of the seductiveness and tenacity of pet theories is worth repeating:

> Every age produces people with clear logical intellects, and with the most praiseworthy grasp of the importance of some sphere of human experience, who have elaborated, or inherited, a scheme of thought which exactly fits those experiences which claim their interest. Such people are apt resolutely to ignore, or to explain away, all evidence which confuses their scheme with contradictory instances. What they cannot fit in is for them nonsense. An unflinching determination to take the whole evidence into account is the only method of preservation against the fluctuating streams of fashionable opinion. This advice seems so easy, and is in fact so difficult to follow. (1967, p. 187)

To "take the whole evidence into account" requires a more comprehensive theoretical framework than has been used in the debate. The purpose of the present paper is: 1. to offer a more comprehensive concept of price and thereby a more realistic framework of the demander-choice process and the market decisions of the firm;(1) and 2. within this framework to interpret various (including allegedly "perverse") behaviors of price.

The implications of this paper extend beyond the administered-prices debate to the empirical analysis of price behavior in general.

Price and Demander(2) Choice: A Suggested Framework

> The real price of everything, what everything really costs the man who wants to acquire it, is the toil and trouble of acquiring it. (Adam Smith, <u>Wealth of Nations</u>, Modern Library Edition, Chapter 5, p. 30.)

To understand supplier behavior in a market, one must understand demander behavior. A demander decides whether to buy a product by comparing what he perceives as the total expected benefits to what he perceives as the total expected costs of attaining the benefits. Therefore, an analyst's model must conceive of both <u>product</u> and <u>price</u> from the perspective of the demander.

The following is a total benefit, total cost, and constraint view of demander choice. Though a highly simplified model, it does illuminate some critical elements of price and demander choice, and hence, supplier behavior.

A demander enters into exchange to satisfy some need or more generally to achieve a desired end state. The desired end state consists of benefits which may extend over more than one period.

One may divide the consumption process conceptually into an "acquisition" (including search) phase and a "use" (including adjustment, maintenance, and disposal) phase. Some of the demander's benefits may occur in the acquisition process, and some of his costs may occur in the use of the product. A model that constricts costs to acquisition and benefits to use, as most do, is of very limited usefulness.

More precisely, the demander's desired state consists of each period's expected benefits, $\bar{B}_t$, cumulated over n periods. The present value of the desired end state, Ψ, is:

$$\Psi = \sum_{t=1}^{n} \frac{\bar{B}_t}{(1+r)^t} \qquad\qquad 1.$$

where: $\bar{B}_t$ = expected benefits to be received in period t

   r   = appropriate risk-adjusted discount rate

Exchange is not free. Every participant, "supplier," or "demander" must perform some work to effect exchange, and his inputs are money, time, and energy (physical and psychic). When these elements have alternative valued uses, their use constitutes sacrifices — which is to say costs.(3)

The total cost or the "effective price" of a desired end state is the sum of the present values of the total net expenditures of money, time, and energy required of a demander to effect the end state.(4) For a given demander, the effective price, π , of a desired end state is:

$$\pi = P + T + E \qquad\qquad 2.$$

where:(5)

$$P = \sum_{t=1}^{n} \frac{\bar{P}_t}{(1+r)^t}$$

the sum of the present values of the demander's expected money costs of attaining a given end state, using an appropriate risk-adjusted discount rate, r.

$$T = \sum_{t=1}^{n} \frac{w\bar{t}_t}{(1 + r)^t}$$

the sum of the present values of the money equivalent of the demander's expected time inputs in attaining the end state. (Expected time inputs, $\bar{t}_t$, are converted to money by multiplying by the per-unit opportunity cost of time, w.)(6)

$$E = \sum_{t=1}^{n} \frac{z\bar{e}_t}{(1 + r)^t}$$

the sum of the present values of the money equivalent of the demander's expected energy (physical and psychic) inputs in attaining the end state. (Expected energy inputs, $\bar{e}_t$, are converted to money by multiplying by the per-unit opportunity cost of energy, z.)(7)

Effective price may consist entirely of any one or any combination of money, time, and energy expenditures. In the case of a "free" service — e.g., a public library — there is a price, but it is one that, aside from taxes, may consist entirely of user sacrifices of time and energy.

Money prices may be negative due to some type of monetary "gift" to the demander that exceeds his money expenditures. Therefore, effective price may be positive, negative, or zero.

There are two sources of the costs comprising the effective price of an end state: (1) costs related to exchange with a particular supplier — "supplier-specific" costs; and (2) costs related to the market in general — "market-general" costs. That is:

$$\pi = (P_s + T_s + E_s + P_m + T_m + E_m) \qquad 3.$$

where:

P_s = the present value of the supplier-specific expected money expenditures incurred in the acquisition and use phases – e.g., the prime costs of the product, adjustment costs, parking costs, etc.

T_s = the present value of the supplier-specific expected time expenditures incurred in the acquisition and use phases – e.g., delays in sales assistance, delivery, etc.

E_s = the present value of the supplier-specific expected energy (physical and psychic) expenditures incurred in the acquisition and use phase – e.g., physical exertion due to location of parking; energy expended in adjustments, psychic costs from, say, insulting behavior by supplier personnel, etc.

P_m = the present value of the market-general expected money expenditures incurred in the acquisition and use phases – e.g., travel expenses to and within the market area, etc.

T_m = the present value of the market-general expected time expenditures incurred in the acquisition and use phases – e.g., search time, traffic delays, etc.

E_m = the present value of the market-general expected energy expenditures incurred in the acquisition and use phases – e.g., anxieties about personal safety, physical effort required to travel to and within the market area, etc.

The demander's supplier-specific money costs, P_s, may be divided into two components:

$$P_s = P_{sd} + P_{so} \qquad 4.$$

where:

P_{sd} = direct money payments to the supplier (the "prime cost" of the product)

P_{so} = other money expenditures traceable to dealing with a specific supplier (e.g., transportation costs, parking fees, etc., traceable to exchange with the particular supplier)

Then per equation 3.

$$\pi = (P_{sd} + P_{so} + T_s + E_s + P_m + T_m + E_m) \qquad 5.$$

Only P_{sd} comprises the source of the supplier's sales revenue. The other six sets of demander expenditures affect, but with the minor exception of P_{so} (for example, parking fees) do not comprise revenue to the supplier. The elasticity of P_{sd} is directly related to the relative magnitude of P_{sd} in   (Narver, 1978). That is:

$$|\eta P_{sd}| = f\left(\frac{P_{sd}}{\pi - P_{sd}}\right) \qquad 6.$$

Necessary and Sufficient Conditions for Exchange

One will engage in exchange only if the present value of the desired end state exceeds the present value of all the costs (not just the money price) required to effect the end state. A demander who does not attempt to compare all expected costs to all expected benefits risks incurring total costs exceeding total benefits, an outcome with presumably limited appeal.

Thus, the necessary condition for exchange is a perceived increase in utility, U:

$$U = \psi - \pi > 0 \qquad 7.$$

Reservation price, $\pi *$, is the maximum effective price one is willing to incur rather than go without the desired end state. The sufficient condition for a demander to engage in exchange is that the effective price is no greater than his reservation price. That is:

$$\pi \leq \pi* \qquad 8.$$

Reservation price is affected by two sets of factors: (1) one's desire to attain a given end state in comparison to alternative end states; and (2) one's money, time, and energy available for attaining the end state. That is:

$$\pi* = f(D, W) \qquad 9.$$

where:

D = one's desire for the given end state
W = one's available wealth in terms of money, time, and energy (physical and psychic)

Either desire or wealth can be binding. Thus, when a demander's desire exceeds his wealth, then wealth, W, is the dominant constraint, and $\pi * = W$.(8)

Clearly, equation 8 is the sufficient condition for exchange to occur. For when equation 8 is true, the demander's desire and ability to expend wealth equal or exceed the total cost of attaining the end state.

Reservation price, $\pi *$, consists of money, time, and energy reservation prices:

$$\pi * = f(P*, T*, E*) \hspace{3cm} 10.$$

As with $\pi *$, each of $P*$, $T*$, and $E*$ is determined by two factors, desire and wealth. For example, $P*$ is determined by the demander's desire, D_p, to expend money to attain the end state, and his money wealth, W_p, available for spending to attain the end state. Accordingly, if with respect to money expenditures his desire exceeds his wealth — i.e., $D_p > W_p$ — then W_p is the binding constraint, and $P* = W_p$. Parallel arguments hold for $T*$ and $E*$.

The Goal of the Firm and Marketing Policies

The argument that managers seek to maximize the market value of the firm is more persuasive theoretically and empirically than any alternative contention (e.g., Sherman, 1974). The present (market) value of the firm may be represented as:

$$V = \sum_{t=1}^{n} \frac{\bar{\pi}_t}{(1+k)^t} \hspace{3cm} 11.$$

where:

$\bar{\pi}_t$ = expected profits in period t

k   = the cost of capital (includes both the risk-free rate and a risk premium)

Thus, the level of expected profits as well as the expected variability of the profit stream affect the value of the firm. To maximize its present value the firm will maximize $\bar{\pi} | k$ or minimize $k | \bar{\pi}$. Managers' perceptions of the expected risk-return relationships lie at the heart of their marketing-mix decisions.

Each of the marketing-mix variables which, conventionally formulated, are summarized as product, promotion, distribution, and money price, can comprise utility. That is to say 5 each may affect ψ , the benefit stream. Of equal importance is the fact that each of the four marketing-mix variables can affect one or more of the demander's costs, P, T, and E.

The fact that any element of the marketing mix can affect either the demander's benefit stream or cost stream yields an important conclusion for the analysis of competition. The identification of "price" or "non-price" competition does not turn on the identity of the marketing-mix variable, but on whether its effect was on the demander's cost or benefit stream respectively.

Interpreting the Behavior of the Direct Money Price, P_{sd}

As in all questions of market and marketing behavior, it is useful to begin with the "null hypothesis" that the subject phenomenon is consistent with a competitive market. The hypothesis that the behavior of P_{sd} in part or whole has a competitive explanation of necessity enriches the theoretical framework of the examination of P_{sd}. Only with such a comprehensive theoretical framework can an empirical analysis validly test whether the observed degree of market responsiveness is consistent with the classical model.

To date, however, as noted above, the theory of pricing is so narrowly conceived that empirical analyses of the behavior of P_{sd} in relation to demand changes do not in fact test the hypothesis. Thus, to date, to have "proven" that P_{sd} has or has not responded to a change in demand is to have revealed <u>nothing necessarily</u> about the true market responsiveness.

The framework in which we wish to examine P_{sd}, the direct money expenditures (including the "prime price") by a demander to a supplier, assumes the supplier has <u>no</u> long-run monopoly power. Thus, the "null hypothesis" perspective is that the behavior of P_{sd} may be explained by phenomena other than long-run monopoly power. We return to this point in a subsequent section.

The analysis is set in the context of monopolistic competition — which is a just-sufficient differentiation of the product to provide the firm some choice as to the price. We assume the differentiation confers a degree of monopoly power no more than just sufficient for the firm to be a "price searcher" rather than a "price taker." The long-run equilibrium performance of such markets may closely approximate that of purely competitive markets.

The analysis of the behavior of P_{sd} in relation to a demand change is in three parts. The first is a brief consideration of a benefit-stream, ψ , response to a change in demand rather than a cost-stream, π , response. The second and third parts are the central arguments. The second part considers the situation in which π consists of only P_{sd}. The third part analyzes the cases in which π consists of more than P_{sd}.

With respect to a given change in demand, a less-than-proportionate response of P_{sd} or a lagged response of P_{sd} is the hallmark of "administered prices." We offer several substantive <u>alternative</u> ex planations for these responses. Let us note: None of our explanations necessarily implies any long-run monopoly power. Rather, all can be interpreted simply as wealth-maximizing behavior by a monopolistically competitive firm.

BENEFIT STREAM, ψ, RESPONSE

A complete discussion of the responsiveness of P_{sd} must include the case in which the firm responds to a change in demand totally in terms of the benefit stream, ψ. A monopolistically-competitive wealth-maximizing firm in response to a demand increase may find it optimal in the short-run to ration the scarce supply by reducing some of the utility of the product rather than by raising P_{sd} in relation to ψ. With a "product adjustment" response, the observed P_{sd} does not change. However of course, other things being equal, the $|\psi\text{-}\pi|$ relationship does change.(9)

We turn now to the interpretation of the behavior of P_{sd}.

DIRECT MONEY PRICE, P_{sd}, RESPONSES

Per equation 5 the effective price, π, of an end state consists potentially of seven demander-cost components:

$$\pi = P_{sd} + P_{so} + T_s + E_s + P_m + T_m + E_m$$

For the present let us assume that π consists only of P_{sd}. Thus, assume:

$$\pi = P_{sd}$$

(This, of course, is a strong assumption, for it implies that all acquisition-phase and use-phase expenditures of the demander consist only of direct money expenditures to the seller.)

1. Net P_{sd}. An obviously necessary but not sufficient task in identifying the true effective price of a product is to identify the net money-price portion. With respect only to P_{sd}, there are numerous (over 200 according to one estimate) direct and indirect ways it can be reduced. (See reference in Grether, Marketing and Public Policy, 1966, p. 57.) Thus, net P_{sd} means direct price net of all price shading and discounts, rebates and trade-in allowances, the inputed value of reciprocity gains for the demander, free warehousing, backhauls, and other such monetary benefits to the demander. That there are so many ways the actual net P_{sd} may differ substantially from the apparent net P_{sd} should be a humbling thought for any empirical researcher.

2. Long-run considerations dominate in an uncertain world. There is considerable evidence that wealth-maximizing firms in an uncertain

world, the real world, treat pricing as well as the other marketing-mix decisions as investments adjusted over time (Weston, 1972). In wealth-maximizing firms under uncertainty, it is not the short-run but the long-run demand and cost changes that are of primary relevance. The dynamic model of the wealth-maximizing firm under uncertainty is in sharp contrast to a static model that assumes both profit maximization in a world of certainty and the separateness of the pricing decision from other marketing-mix decisions. In short, the wealth-maximizing firm does not find each short-run demand or cost change to be necessarily of interest.

3. <u>Short-run inelastic demand</u>. The dominance of long-run considerations notwithstanding, suppose a firm considers responding to a short-run change in demand. First of all, the short-run elasticity of demand is typically less than the long-run elasticity, and in many cases is probably less than one. A firm with a reduced demand faces a lower (and possibly negative) marginal revenue compared to the marginal revenue it faces in making general (long-run) price policy. Thus, given the expected-profit and risk relationship, if the firm believes a money-price response in a recession is appropriate, the optimal policy may be to hold P_{sd} stable or to change it only in response to changes in long-run expectations (Weiss, 1977, p. 614).

4. <u>Reduction of profit variance</u>. The relationship between expected profits and risk may be such that (per equation 11) the firm maximizes its present value by responding fully to a change in demand, holding P_{sd} constant and allowing quantity to adjust to the full extent of the demand change. This strategy can minimize the variability of the profit stream. As Sherman states, "Maximization of the market value of a corporation's securities can provide a persuasive rationale for <u>not</u> reducing prices as demand falls, as long as profit risk can be reduced as a result." (1974, p. 150, emphasis in original) The attractiveness of a quantity adjustment to a short-run change in demand is directly related to the short-run inelasticity of demand.

Adjusting in part or in total by quantity rather than by P_{sd} is not an arbitrary decision. At times quantity adjustment, and at other times P_{sd} adjustment, is the optimal wealth-maximizing strategy. (Of course, when π consists of more than P_{sd}, the price adjustment may take more than one form.)

5. <u>Lagged responses of P_{sd}</u>.
    a. Uncertainty. Uncertainty is the most general explanation for lagged responses in P_{sd}. An uncertain world requires a firm to guess at demand which, given the opportunity costs always attendant with the changing of prices, means necessarily that price movements up or down are going to be in steps. Over time, the "true" price increases which would come about in an instantly reacting and perfect market, may look something like a straight line sloping upward. In an uncertain world, however, the true prices not to mention merely quoted money prices,

may "hang" from the line, such that there is a constant lag of price behind what supply and demand would indicate, except at the moment of catching up.

[I]f we fix our gaze only upon that final instant when the price rises, we can easily persuade ourselves that some "power" to raise prices freely is at work. (Adelman, 1958, p. 155)

b. Organization structure. Any tendency for a lag in price response may be accentuated if price decisions are made by committees or involve two or more administrative levels in the firm. Group decisions tend to be risk-averse, which means slower and more conservative decisions. In addition, if the data for price decisions pass through cost-oriented relay points, the lagged response may be all the more quantitatively unresponsive (Cyert and March, 1955). Due to the nature of the decision process, lags and risk-averseness in decision making are especially likely in functionally organized firms. To overcome slowness and excessive risk-averseness may explain why the vast majority of large firms in the U.S. economy have moved from a functional to a product-division organization – which reduces the span of control and simplifies other administrative complexities, and thereby reduces response time and encourages appropriate risk taking (Rumelt, 1974).

EFFECTIVE PRICE, π , CONSISTING OF MORE THAN P_{sd}

1. <u>Other components of P</u>. It would be unusual for P_{sd} to be the only money expenditures in both the acquisition and use phases. Typically, money expenditure P (per equation 5), consists of P_{sd}, P_{so}, and P_m. That is:

$$P = P_{sd} + P_{so} + P_m$$

Per equations 2. and 8. the sufficient condition for exchange may be written:

$$P + T + E \leq \pi * \qquad \qquad 12.$$

This implies per equation 10:

$$P \leq P*, \quad T \leq T*, \quad E \leq E* \qquad \qquad 13.$$

Thus, with respect to the case of $\pi = P$, a supplier must ensure that P is less than or equal to the demander's money constraint, $P*$. That is:

$$P_{sd} + P_{so} + P_m \leq P* \qquad \qquad 14.$$

A seller has the greatest potential control over P_{sd} and the least potential control over P_m. The critical parametric role of P_{so} and P_m

in the firm's decisions as to P_{sd} is clearly seen by rearranging and expressing as an equality:

$$P_{sd} = P* - (P_{so} + P_m)$$ 15.

Thus, the relationship $[P* - (P_{so} + P_m)]$ is one major constraint to the firm's ability to increase P_{sd}. Specifically, as $[P* - (P_{so} + P_m)] \to 0$, a seller's ability to increase $P_{sd} \to 0$.

2. P, T, and E as components of π . It is unusual for P to be the only component of π , for typically $T \neq 0$ and $E \neq 0$. Thus typically,

$$\pi = P + T + E$$

Therefore, per equation 12.:

$$P + T + E \leq \pi *$$

which, substituting further is:

$$P_{sd} + P_{so} + P_m + T + E \leq \pi *$$ 16.

Then, rearranging and expressing as an equality:

$$P_{sd} = \pi * - (T + E + P_{so} + P_m)$$ 17.

Thus, $[\pi * - (T + E + P_{so} + P_m)]$ is the second major relationship constraining the firm's ability to increase P_{sd}. Specifically, as $[\pi * - (T + E + P_{so} + P_m)] \to 0$, the seller's ability to increase $P_{sd} \to 0$.

3. Price competition by suppliers other than by direct changes in P_{sd}. Suppose a firm concludes there will be a long-run weakening of demand. The firm has many options for reducing π . There are numerous ways indirectly to reduce P_{sd}, as similarly there are numerous ways to reduce P_{so}, T_s, or E_s. The firm will choose the effective-price mix that has the largest long-run elasticity. Long-run elasticity is affected in part by the speed with which competitors may match the price reduction. Reductions in P_{sd}, P_{so}, T_s, or E_s that are not readily detected by competition or upon detection are difficult or require some time to match (such as changes in physical layout that reduce shopping time), will have large long-run elasticities. For that reason they are attractive strategies to a wealth-maximizing firm, and thus the firm may be expected often to conduct price competition in this form rather than by a direct change in P_{sd}.

4. "Perverse" movements of P_{sd}. The concept of effective price offers one explanation for money prices that move in a direction opposite to a change in general economic conditions. As general economic conditions improve (worsen), the opportunity cost of the time (and energy) of many demanders will increase (decrease).

Assume that some segment of demanders has a given reservation price, π^*, with respect to a given end state, Ψ. Assume the economy strengthens. And for simplicity, assume effective price consists only of money price and time price. That is,

$$\pi = P + T$$

and substituting per equation 2.

$$\pi = P + \frac{\overline{wt}_t}{(1+r)^t} \qquad\qquad 18.$$

Suppose that before the economic upturn $\pi = \pi^*$, which is the largest value of π that still satisfies the sufficient condition equation 8. It follows from equation 18 that as the opportunity cost of time, w, increases (other things being equal), $\pi > \pi^*$ and therefore no exchange will occur. To reestablish $\pi \leq \pi^*$, the firm must reduce P by an amount at least equal to

$$\frac{\Delta \, wt_t}{(1+r)^t}$$

Thus, the economic upturn induces a reduction of P (!), a completely explicable result vis-a-vis the sufficient condition of exchange, $\pi \leq \pi^*$.

CONCLUSIONS

What does one learn about the responsiveness of markets to demand and cost changes by observing money prices? Very little. Or more generally, what does one learn about demander and supplier behavior by observing money prices? The same answer.

Demanders are interested in the relationship of two comprehensive phenomena — total expected benefits and total expected costs. Money expenditures, direct and indirect, are seldom a demander's only expenditures and at times by no means his principal expenditures. His money expenditures may even be zero. Thus, if one focuses only on money prices — even net direct money prices — one may still be missing the major explanation of demander choice and hence supplier behavior.

The analytical focus must be on what demanders perceive as (1) the total benefits and (2) the effective price to them of those benefits. Completing the framework, the concepts of reservation price, π^*, and the component reservation prices, P^*, T^*, and E^*, establish the sufficient conditions for exchange.

It is the long-run behavior of the effective price, π, that is the sine qua non of the estimation of market responsiveness and monopoly power. With respect to a given end state, ψ , when P_{sd} increases, effective price, π , increases only if P_{so}, P_m, T, and E do not in total decrease by an equal or greater amount. A parallel statement holds for the relationship between a decrease in P_{sd} and a decrease in π . Thus, in the analysis of P_{sd}, one must control for the effects of the marketing mix on P_{so}, P_m, T, and E. Unless one controls for these other effects, changes in P_{sd} have no necessary implication whatsoever for any change in the effective price, π .

No one ever said that price analysis was supposed to be easy. But no one ever said that it was supposed to be misguided either. To treat money price as the indicator of market responsiveness is simply to abdicate one's analytical responsibility. Unless an investigation uses multivariate analysis in an inter-temporal framework capturing all marketing-mix effects on demanders' cost and benefit streams, one cannot do other than traffic in illusions about the actual price responsiveness of markets.

> "Tunnel vision" – inability to see anything but what is directly ahead – is usually cause for disqualification as a motorist. It should scarcely be a prerequisite for price analysis. (Adelman, 1958, p. 156)

NOTES

(1) The complexity of competition implicit in the framework of the present paper is in part similar to E.T. Grether's concept of "enterprise competition," in which money price is only one element (Marketing and Public Policy, 1966, pp. 57-58).

(2) The term demander is used to cover all buyers (intermediate and ultimate), lessees, or other clientele of the "product." This section of the paper draws on Narver (1978; and 1979).

(3) The critical role of the opportunity costs of non-monetary wealth in demander choice has been recognized and formally treated for some time in economics – for example, Becker (1965) – but explicit treatment in marketing has been only more recent and limited. (See references in Narver, 1978.)

(4) "Required" limits the definition to those outlays of money, time, and energy incurred for the purpose of attaining a given end state. (See Narver 1978).

(5) The functional form may be more complex than the simple additive form used in the present discussion.

(6-7) Assuming the convertibility of time and energy to money equivalents has expository advantages, for it permits a single rather than multiple budget constraints. But the central point is whether and to what extent time and energy have value.

(8) For an elaboration of the determinants of both $\pi *$ and its subsets, see Narver (1979).

(9) Each of the attributes comprising ψ is a continuous ray with utility systematically associated with the amount of the attribute. If there is less of an attribute than expected, the product's quality, and hence ψ, to that extent is lower. With a quality change there is at the minimum a shadow-price effect.

4 Research and Development Expenditures as a Competitive Strategy
David M. Grether

INTRODUCTION

Making a better mousetrap has been one of the standard methods of achieving competitive advantages in American industries. Of course, making an equally good mousetrap with lower costs can be just as effective. To the extent that businesses compete with each other through product and process improvements, then one would expect investment in these activities (research and development [R &D]) to be a primary competitive tool. It is natural to ask which types of firms tend to engage heavily in R & D. A clearly related question one might ask is which market structures are conducive to R & D activity and which are not. In addition, it is important to remember that market structure itself may be affected by firms' R & D activities – raising the question of R & D's impact on market structure (see the related paper by Preston in this volume). The most obvious situation in which market structure is affected by R & D activity is, of course, that of a monopoly position achieved and maintained by patents. This latter question – that is, essentially asking if market structure is really exogenous – is often not directly addressed in the literature.

The purpose of this paper is to survey one portion of the so-called market structure literature; viz., the empirical literature dealing with the relation between market structure and the level of research and development activity. Weiss (1969) has surveyed the empirical literature in the entire field of industrial organization, and Kamien and Schwartz (1975) more recently surveyed the literature concerning innovative activity in general. In order to allow for an intensive examination of one body of literature, the scope of this paper has been kept narrow. Readers interested in other issues – for example, the rate of adoption or imitation and the diffusion of technological information – are referred to these other studies.

There are two aspects of the literature which to a considerable extent dominate the discussion that follows. The first has to do with questions of causality. Thus, for example, in some papers a variable, such as expenditures on research and development, is treated as the dependent variable with quantities such as firm size, profitability, and so forth, as independent variables. Other writers, however, would consider the relationship the other way around; that is, profitability or sales growth might be the dependent variable with R & D among the independent variables. In rare instances, a writer might support both positions. Thus the literature clearly suggests that there is a simultaneous equations problem. The second feature noted was the seriousness of the problems of measurement. In many if not all fields of applications, one can find complaints about the quality of available data. Problems of aggregation, excessively long time periods between observations, insufficient degrees of freedom, and so forth are found in most areas, and industrial organization is no exception (Grabowski and Mueller, 1970). While those kinds of problems are serious, the market structure innovation literature has in addition several more fundamental difficulties. For instance, are patent statistics a measure of inputs into the innovative process or a measure of the output of the process (Comanor and Scherer, 1969)? Beyond questions as to the meaning of particular numbers, there are questions of how one could measure certain quantities, for example, the output of a firm's research department or the "size" of a technological breakthrough. Those who do research in the area are quite aware of the simultaneity problem as well as the difficulties of measurement. These problems are often discussed explicitly and even when not, they affect the research methodology adopted; for example, use of rank correlations as opposed to the usual correlation coefficients. Also, these problems are not all unique to the structure-innovation literature, but to a considerable extent are features of the entire field of industrial organization. Thus, prior to discussing the literature on research and development, it seems worthwhile to provide a brief overview of market structure analysis and the associated problems of measurement.

MARKET STRUCTURE ANALYSIS

The basic idea in this literature is that there are relationships running from market structure to firm behavior and therefore to the performance of the industry. As a practical matter, most of the literature is directed toward linking market structure and performance, performance being characterized by profit rates, price-cost margins, rate of technical progress, and so forth. One way of looking at the market structure literature is an attempt to determine a few (at least in principle) measurable variables which are sufficient for predicting the various aspects of industrial performance.

While the list of variables that describe market structure varies somewhat from one application to another, certain variables are generally considered important. These are: concentration, barriers to entry, product differentiation, price and income elasticity of demand, and the extent of economies of scale in production. For a discussion of the importance of these and other variables, see Bain (1959).

Concentration is generally measured by some feature of the size distribution of the firms in the industry in question. There is no general agreement on the appropriate definition of firm size; sales, assets, value added, and employment are all commonly used. However measured, the assumption is that if an industry is highly concentrated – i.e., is dominated by a small number of firms – price competition is less likely to prevail and nonprice competition and/or collusive-like behavior is likely to be more prevalent.

While a high level of concentration is itself thought to be significant, frequently one asks if this can be explained on purely technological grounds. One wants to know if policies designed to lower concentration (and thus, hopefully, increase competition) will incur offsetting costs in terms of losses of productive efficiency. Also, if economies of scale are such that only a few firms could be expected to survive, then this fact might be used as an argument for some sort of regulatory policy. Thus, the relation between the size of the overall market (measured in terms of output or sales) and the minimum efficient firm size (the smallest output at which average costs are at a minimum) is of considerable interest. The latter is estimated from analyzing cost and output data for the firms in the industries being studied. Note that if a firm must produce a substantial proportion of industry output in order to avoid a cost disadvantage, this may well discourage entry. Quite apart from the absolute size of the required investment, it is argued that the large relative size of the entering firm would lead to hostile reactions from the existing firms.

A rapid rate of growth in the output of an industry is considered to be a force tending to lower concentration and to promote competitive behavior. The idea is that new firms may enter and small firms grow without provoking the retaliation that would occur if the sales of the new or growing firms led to an absolute reduction in sales by the larger firms in the industry. Also, with new buyers coming into the market, the results of secret price cutting may be harder to detect. Historical rates of increases in output and estimates of income elasticity of demand are thus relevant to the description of market structure. Similarly, estimates of the own-price elasticity can be useful as indicative of the incentive to engage in price competition.

Product differentiation is important both as a possible deterrent to entry (heavy initial advertising outlays might discourage some potential entrants) and as an indicator of nonprice competition. While it is not clear how to measure the "degree" of product differentiation, the ratio of expenditures on advertising to sales is frequently used.

Finally, the conditions of entry are, as noted above, related to most of the other elements of market structure. In addition, other factors – for example, patents or the control of raw materials – could be important. Though entry conditions are often referred to as "barriers to entry" (the heights of which could presumably be measured), they are not usually quantified in any single index. However, frequently for cross-section studies, industries are divided into groups with "barriers" that are "high," "medium," "low," etc. (Bain, 1956).

There is a large empirical literature giving the results of attempts to verify the existence (or nonexistence) of relationships between measures of performance and market structure. These studies are summarized in the paper by Weiss (1969) referred to above. Note that the variables being used in testing various structure-performance hypotheses are for the most part endogenous. For example, Weiss (p. 384) suggests a simultaneous equation model for the joint determination of concentration and advertising intensity. It is posited that firms in highly concentrated industries tend to rely more on nonprice competition. This yields an equation in which advertising intensity is at least partially determined by concentration. On the other hand, consideration of entry conditions suggests that advertising together with the minimum efficient firm size and the overall size of the market determine concentration.

In some instances, the direction of causation is generally agreed upon. It is widely assumed, for instance, that increasing concentration makes collusion easier and leads to higher profit rates. The theories that have been put forward to explain the level of concentration and much of the relevant work have been reviewed recently by Ornstein, Weston, Intriligator, and Shrieves (1973). They explicitly pointed out the interdependencies among many of the variables frequently used and suggested some alternatives. Possibly as a result of this interdependence, the interpretation placed upon the related empirical work seems to be largely descriptive. For instance, several studies contain tests of the hypothesis that ceteris paribus, higher levels of concentration will be coincident with higher profit rates. Thus Weiss summarizes this literature as follows: "Almost all of the 32 concentration-profits studies except Stigler's have yielded significant positive relationships. . . . I think that practically all observers are now convinced that there is something to the traditional hypothesis. This is a considerable accomplishment" (1969, p. 371). When it comes to policy questions, however, it seems that the relationship is interpreted either as a reduced form equation (concentration exogenous) or as a relation from an appropriately recursive model. Kaysen and Turner (1959), for example, in their proposed revision of the antitrust laws specified that illegal market power "shall be conclusively presumed where, for five years or more, one company has accounted for 50 percent or more of annual sales in the market, or four or fewer companies have accounted for 80 percent of sales" (p. 267). The primary remedy under their proposal was division or divestiture of assets thus directly lowering concentration and thereby improving the performance of the industry.

One of the major questions examined in the market structure literature reviewed below is the following: What is the relationship between inventive activity and concentration? In other words, are there relevant systematic differences between firms in highly concentrated industries and firms in unconcentrated ones? If it is the case that concentration affects the level of inventive activity, the policy impor- tance of this question is self-evident. Will a vigorous antitrust policy – prevention of mergers among sizable firms and the breaking up of the giants such as General Motors – have a positive or negative effect on the rate of technological progress and, thus, on the rate of growth of the American economy? On the other hand, some – for example, Phillips (1966) – have argued that the nature of the underlying tech- nology and the results of research and development are what determine concentration.

Thus, it is not clear just how one should interpret a regression coefficient in a regression of, say, R & D expenditures on industry concentration ratios. To the extent that this is an equation from a simultaneous equations model such as that sketched above with regard to advertising, then ordinary least squares is not the appropriate method of estimation. Of course, without a more fully specified model, merely changing the estimation procedure cannot by itself be expected to lead to meaningful results.

MEASUREMENT

In order to test hypotheses about the relationships between inventive activity and market structure, one needs measures of both types of variables. For the former, the deficiencies of the measures used as well as problems involved in developing acceptable measures have been widely discussed (in particular, see Sanders, 1962; Kuznets, 1962; Comanor and Scherer, 1969; and Schmookler, 1954a, b, 1957, 1962). Most researchers have used either a measure of inputs into the research and development process (viz., the rate of expenditure or the level of employment) or patents. The primary disadvantage of patent statistics is the obvious one: the substantial differences in the economic and technical importance of patented inventions. On the other hand, patent statistics are widely available, and a patent does signify a new and potentially useful device.

Much of the difficulty with determining the input to or output from inventive activity is associated with trying to quantify these variables for a specific device or process. Thus, there may have been several independent unsuccessful (and unreported) attempts to invent the same thing. Also, it may not be entirely clear how much previous effort was devoted to distinct but related projects. Similar considerations can make it difficult to determine the economic magnitude of an invention, that is, it may lead to numerous related inventions (or improvements), the existence of which may have been dependent upon the original invention. These types of problems are avoided in most of the papers surveyed since in these studies the relevant variable is the overall level of such activities in a firm or industry rather than the amount associated with particular projects.

As Kuznets (1962) has pointed out, properly measuring inputs in terms of man-hours or dollar expenditures is not easy. Part of the difficulty is that published data generally do not allow one to distinguish between basic research, applied research, and development work. In addition, there is the usual problem of aggregating the efforts of individuals "endowed with different inventive capacities." Using wage payments instead of man-hours may not be a fully satisfactory solution to the latter problem: "Considering the difficulty of estimating the economic contribution of inventive activity ... the assumption of marginal productivity would surely strain one's credulity" (p. 33). Still, despite all these difficulties, it seems that it would be important if one could, using the market structure approach, explain the amount of resources devoted to industrial research and development.

As discussed in the preceding section, market structure includes more than just concentration. In practice, however, some measure of concentration is frequently the only market structure variable employed. Most studies measure concentration by the standard four-firm concentration ratio defined as the percentage of the total sales of the industry accounted for by the largest four firms. Often employment or assets are used instead of sales, and frequently researchers will use more than one measure to insure that the results obtained are not simply an artifact of the measure chosen. In fact, there are as many measures of concentration of this type as there are measures of firm size. As Shalit and Sankar (1977) note, no single measure of firm size is completely appropriate.

However one chooses to calculate the level of concentration, there are a number of quite serious practical problems in using such variables. For example, the presence of some vertically integrated firm in an industry may make shipments the relevant variable rather than sales, and may make concentration levels computed using assets or employment be quite different from those computed using shipments as firm size. The SIC industries may not be entirely suitable, so it may prove necessary to aggregate several concentration ratios (Kaysen and Turner, 1959). Kilpatrick (1976) has found that in practice there is little difference between averaging concentration ratios for several industries and computing directly the concentration ratio for the larger set of firms. The latter, of course, is a more appealing procedure (see Boyle, 1973). Also, concentration ratios are computed on the basis of national figures whereas in many industries the markets may be geographically segmented. For a discussion of these and other related problems, see Bain (1959) and Adelman (1951).

Quite apart from questions of implementation there are the questions of what "concentration" is; that is, what is it that one wants to measure, and how at least in principle ought it to be measured? In fact, it turns out that "concentration" means different things to different people and not surprisingly a number of ways have been suggested to measure it.

While concentration is expected to be related to the "level" of competition or the "degree" of competitiveness, it is not generally interpreted as an index of competition. Douglas (1969) provided a temporary exception to this rule. In his paper, Douglas argued that geographical dispersion, restrictive trade practices, contervailing power, "market division" (related to cross elasticities of supply among the several products produced by an industry), and problems associated with the census industry definitions all lead to differences between the measured or "apparent" levels of concentration and the "real" level by which he meant competitiveness. Douglas's work was attacked by Nightingale (1970a, b) on a variety of grounds, but most importantly on the interpretation of concentration. In his reply, Douglas stated that after thinking it over he had changed his definition. "Whereas previously intended as an index of competitiveness, 'real concentration' now refers simply to the degree of seller concentration at a more meaningful level of disaggregation. . . . From here it is plainly an additional step to an index of competitiveness, as the effect of restrictive practices, buyer concentration, further data problems, and possibly other factors as well, must be quantified and incorporated" (1970, p. 124). So concentration is a characteristic of the size distribution of the firms in an industry; however, it is not clear what characteristic is the appropriate one.

The four-firm concentration ratio is the measure most frequently used in practice; in part this is due to its availability. Concentration ratios based on the largest eight, twenty, and fifty firms are also available. Miller (1967) suggested using "marginal concentration ratios" to explain profit rate. The idea is that rather than looking only at the share of the top k firms, one also could use the share of the kth through mth largest firms. Given the various published concentration ratios it is possible to compute some of the marginal concentration ratios, for example:

$$MCR_{5,8} = CR_8 - CR_4$$

where CR_i is the share of the i largest firms and $MCR_{i,j}$ is the share of the ith to jth largest firms. Miller argued that rather than using CR_4 alone, as is usually done, it might often be better to use as much information as is available on the entire size distribution. Further, he advocated use of the marginal concentration ratios as a way around the problem of multicollinearity (CR_4 and $MCR_{5,8}$). Suppose one has a model in which the profit rate is determined by CR_4 and CR_8:

$$\pi_i = a + bCR_{4_i} + cCR_{8_i} + u_i$$
$$= a + (b + c)CR_{4_i} + c(CR_{8_i} - CR_{4_i}) + u_i$$
$$= a + (b + c)CR_{4_i} + cMCR_{5,8_i} + u_i.$$

Now if CR_4 and CR_8 are nearly collinear, then estimates of b and c may not pass standard significance tests. If the regression is estimated using $MCR_{5,8}$ instead of CR_8, the estimated coefficients of $MCR_{5,8}$

and CR_8 will be identical as will their standard errors (apart from roundoff errors). It could happen that the coefficient of CR_4 will become significant, but by the standard properties of least squares regression this is simply the sum of the estimated coefficients of CR_4 and CR_8, i.e., $\hat{b} + \hat{c}$. Thus, the two approaches are equivalent, and changing to MCR adds no new information.

Miller noted that in principle the entire size distribution is relevant and considered a model of the form

$$\pi_i = a + b_1 CR_{4_i} + b_2 MCR_{5,8i} + b_3 MCR_{9,20i} + b_4 MCR_{21,50i}$$
$$+ b_5 MCR_{51,\infty i} + u_i.$$

He correctly observed that there is an identification problem since the explanatory variables add to a constant (100). Eliminating the share of the smallest firms he estimated

$$\pi_i = a + 100b_5 + (b_1 - b_5)CR_{4_i} + (b_2 - b_5)MCR_{5,8i}$$
$$+ (b_3 - b_5)MCR_{9,20i} + (b_4 - b_5)MCR_{21,50i} + u_i.$$

Of course, it does not matter which variable is dropped, the results obtained will be equivalent. That is, if CR_4 is dropped, one will obtain estimates of $a + 100b_1$, $b_2 - b_1$, $b_3 - b_1$, $b_4 - b_1$, and $b_5 - b_1$, from which Miller's estimates could be deduced. Miller apparently did not recognize this and reported that equations "including $(100 - CR_{50})$ (but excluding each of the other marginal concentration ratios in turn) produced results without sensible economic interpretation" (1967, p. 267).

The usefulness of marginal concentration ratios has been disputed by Collins and Preston (1969). They noted that by definition $MCR_{5,8}$ cannot exceed CR_4, and that if CR_4 exceeds 50, then $MCR_{5,8}$ must be less than or equal to $100 - CR_4$. In order to eliminate the range restrictions, Weiss suggested using

$$V = \frac{MCR}{CR} \qquad\qquad CR \leq 50$$

$$= \frac{MCR}{1 - CR/100} \qquad\qquad CR > 50.$$

Weiss reported regressions estimated using the data of Collins and Preston with V replacing $MCR_{5,8}$. It turned out that the estimated coefficient of V had a positive sign, but was less than its standard error, leading Weiss to conclude that "MCR has little effect one way or another" (1969, p. 373).

Usually one interprets regression coefficients as being estimates of partial derivatives. That is, one is attempting to answer the question, "If x goes up by one, other things being equal, by how much will y change on average?" Now when the independent variables must sum to a constant, this question is meaningless; one must specify the changes in the other variables. As Collins and Preston in effect pointed out, omitting the share of the smallest firms from the estimated regression does not eliminate this problem. Neither, of course, can resorting to variables such as V. For example, Weiss regressed price-cost margins on CR_4, V, plus some other variables. Since the value of V is not constrained by the value of CR_4, one can ask about the effects of unit changes in CR_4 or V (ceteris paribus); however, the interpretation of these changes depends crucially on the value of CR_4. Notice that if CR_4 is larger than 50, V has a relatively straightforward interpretation, namely the level of concentration among the smaller firms in the industry.

There are a number of other measures of concentration in addition to marginal concentration ratios that use information about the entire size distribution of the firms in the industry. Three of these are related to entropy H.

$$H = -\sum_{i=1}^{n} s_i \log s_i$$

where n is the number of firms in the industry and s_i is the share of sales (employment, etc.) accounted for by the ith firm, and the logarithms are usually base 2. If s_i is taken as the probability that a dollar of sales goes to the ith firm, then H may be interpreted as the amount of information obtained in learning which firm made the sale (Theil, 1967; Khinchin, 1957). For a given n, H attains its maximum (log n) when all firms are of equal size suggesting the use of "relative entropy" defined as

$$G = \frac{H}{\log n}.$$

Another entropy related measure is F the "numbers equivalent" (Horowitz, 1971) defined by

$$H = \log F.$$

Suppose that for some particular industry, entropy is calculated to be H, then F is the number of equal-sized firms which would result in an entropy of H. Miller (1972) used G, F, and CR_4 to explain profit rates for 25 four-digit industries. In all of his regressions, G was significant with a positive coefficient and F insignificant. CR_4 appeared to be significant in regressions which also contained G, and was insignificant otherwise. Miller concluded that F, G, and CR_4 "reflected different aspects of market structure," but unfortunately, was not able to provide any clear interpretation for G, the one measure which consistently performed well in his regressions. The difficulty concerned comparing G's computed for industries with different numbers of firms.

Exactly the same difficulty arises in using the Gini coefficient. This coefficient, which is a measure of the inequality in a size distribution, is defined as the area between the Lorenz curve and the 45 degree line corresponding to cases in which all firms are of equal size. It can be shown (Kendall, 1943) that the Gini coefficient g is equal to:

$$g = \frac{1/2 \; \sum_i \sum_j |x_i - x_j|}{n^2 \bar{x}}$$

where x_i is the size of the ith firm and $\bar{x}$ is the average firm size. Hart and Prais (1956) suggested an interesting interpretation for the Gini coefficient. "Suppose the difference in the size of two firms provides a measure of the degree of 'dominance' that the one may exert over the other's price or output policy. . . . Then a measure of dominance for an industry as a whole may be found by taking the mean difference, irrespective of sign, between all possible pairs of firms. . . . The Gini coefficient can therefore be interpreted as a measure of average dominance in the group of firms considered" (1956, pp. 152-153). As Adelman (1959) has pointed out, the Gini coefficient by itself is not of much use for comparing industries with different numbers of firms as, for instance, it does not differentiate between an industry with two equal-sized firms and one with a thousand firms all of the same size.

There have been two rather similar attempts to obtain measures of concentration using an axiomatic approach (Hall and Tideman, 1967; Niehans 1958). Hall and Tideman posited six criteria that a measure of concentration should satisfy:

1. It should be a single number.
2. It should depend upon all the market shares.
3. It should increase whenever there is a shift from a smaller to a larger firm.
4. If each firm in an industry is divided into K equal ones, the measure should change by a factor of $1/K$.
5. It should be a decreasing function of N when an industry is divided into N equal firms.
6. It should range between 0 and 1.

Of the six properties it seems likely that most would find numbers 2, 3, and 5 unobjectionable in principle. Adelman (1951), however, argued that as a practical matter using the full size distribution is risky since this makes the measures sensitive to the often arbitrary industrial classifications of numerous small firms. Properties 4 and 6 are clearly ad hoc and serve primarily to narrow down the list of possible candidates. Hall and Tideman considered indices based upon

$$R = \sum_{i=1}^{n} i s_i$$

where s_i is the share of the firm with rank i, so that if s_i is the probability that a random dollar of sales goes to the firm with rank i, R is the expected rank. The index they suggested is:

$$TH = \frac{1}{2 \sum_{i=1}^{n} i s_i - 1}$$

Property 6 led them to consider functions of $1/R$, the exact form being chosen to satisfy property 4. Hall and Tideman noted that a large number of indices could satisfy their criteria and that one other popular index, the Herfindahl index HH (which will be discussed presently), does so. They reported that empirically both measures as well as CR_4 turn out to give essentially the same rankings of concentration. They concluded that if "HH or TH is the correct measure of concentration, then the concentration ratio is certainly a good proxy" (1967, p. 168).

Niehans (1958) was concerned with developing an index of average firm size rather than relative concentration, so he did not adopt property 6. He set down four criteria:

1. Same as 1 above.
2. If all firms in an industry are the same size, then the index should equal that size.
3. Same as 2 above.
4. If a large or "medium-sized" firm grows, other firms staying the same size, then the index should rise, and if a small firm grows, ceteris paribus it should fall.

The index proposed by Niehans is:

$$Y = \sum_{i=1}^{n} x_i s_i = \frac{\sigma^2}{\bar{x}} + \bar{x}$$

where x_i is the size of the ith firm and s_i its share of the industry's total sales or employment, $\bar{x}$ is the average firm size, and   is the variance of firm size (Hart 1961). Thus Niehans's index is larger than the average firm size unless all the firms are equal.

One other commonly used measure of concentration is the Herfindahl index:

$$HH = \sum_{i=1}^{n} s_i^2$$

where s_i is the share of the ith firm. Again if s_i is interpreted as the probability of the ith firm obtaining a given dollar of sales, then HH is the expected value of that probability. Stigler (1964) has argued that

HH is the appropriate measure of concentration in that it is related in a simple fashion to the ease with which firms can detect secret price cutting or cheating on a collusive agreement. In Stigler's theory, firms use classical hypothesis-testing rules and decide that secret price cutting is going on whenever actual sales fall below expected sales by a predetermined number of standard deviations. For example, suppose that in each period, n_n, new customers enter the market and "let the probability of attracting a customer be proportional to the firm's share of industry output, s. Then the variance of the firm's sales to new customers will be $n_n s(1 - s)$, and the aggregate for the industry will be

$$C = n_{n_i} \sum_{i-1}^{n} s(1 -s)$$

for n firms" (Stigler 1964, p. 55). Note that $C = n_n (1 - HH)$.

More recently, Dansby and Willig (1979) and Hause (1977) have presented theoretical justification for HH. Dansby and Willig derive HH and other indices from welfare maximizing criteria (maximizing consumer surplus). Hause argues that HH should be a lower bound for "reasonable" indices of concentration that range from zero for competition to one for monopoly. Hause, like other writers, assumes the cardinality of concentration without questioning it. As Schmalensee (1977) points out, generally one cannot compute HH as its computation requires the full size distribution. Schmalensee reports tests of a number of computible alternatives to HH. Unfortunately, which surrogate works best seems to depend upon the level of concentration as measured by HH. It does appear that the standard four-firm concentration ratio is superior (as an approximation to HH) to using one based upon the eight largest firms.

As with the entropy measures, the Herfindahl index can also be converted to a numbers equivalent. Thus, if an industry consists of n firms equal size,

$$HH = \sum_{i=1}^{n} (1/n)^2 = 1/n;$$

so the reciprocal of HH has an interpretation similar to F discussed previously.

As mentioned earlier, the concentration ratio CR_4 is the most commonly used measure. In part this is due to the fact that these figures are readily available, but an additional advantage is that it is more easily interpreted (at least understood) than the entropy measures or the other indices. In other words, to say that the top four firms in one industry produce x percent of the industry's output, whereas ten years earlier the top four produced y percent is a reasonably concrete statement whether or not its implications are entirely clear. Similar statements in terms of H, HH, TH, G, etc. are not so readily understood. These difficulties in interpretation provide much of the motivation behind the use of numbers equivalents (Horowitz, 1971; Adelman, 1959) as these measures are expressed in units that are on the surface at least more familiar.

In addition to their uses in comparing the levels of concentration among different industries, the various measures of concentration are also used in time series studies to determine if there are any discernible trends in concentration (Bain, 1970). The study of changing concentration over time has led to another entirely different class of measures based upon mobility (see, for example, Collins and Preston, 1969; Boyle and Sorenson, 1971). Suppose the firms in an industry are ranked according to some measure of size. The idea behind the mobility measures is roughly as follows: if there is intense rivalry within an industry, this should be reflected in changes in the rank orders as different firms gain and lose relative to the competition. Conversely, if there is little competition, one expects the rankings to be relatively stable. These considerations lead to measures of mobility such as rank correlations. The important thing to note here is that concentration or "competitiveness" measures based upon mobility could lead to orderings of industries that are quite different from those obtained using the other types of measures. The measures described previously either ignore rankings of the firms or weight them by firm size.

Each of the proposed measures of concentration is based upon some feature of the size distribution of a particular group of firms. Now in general one cannot expect to be able to summarize arbitrary frequency distributions with a single index. In fact, there have been a number of empirical and theoretical studies of firm size distributions (Adelman, 1951; Hart, 1957; Mansfield, 1962; Simon and Bonini, 1958 — see also Kalecki, 1945; and Champernowne, 1953). These studies generally deal with distributions that would arise if Gibrat's Law or the law of proportionate effect held, the key assumption being that the probability of a given percentage change in a firm's size is independent of the size of the firm. It has been well known for some time that this assumption will yield a skewed size distribution (the precise distribution depends upon the assumptions made about exit and entry). Clearly, if a parametric representation of firm size distributions (or the upper tail of these distributions) were known, it would have implications for measurement of concentration. Since concentration is simply a characteristic of the size distribution, it would be reasonable to use measures expressible in terms of the parameters of this distribution. Alternatively, representations of the parameters themselves might be used as explanatory variables. For example, Aitchison and Brown (1957) and Hart and Prais (1956) suggested using the standard deviation of the log normal distribution, and Simon and Bonini (1958) who derived a Yule distribution for firm size recommended the percentage of growth accounted for by new firms. For criticisms and defenses of these sorts of measures, see Adelman (1951, 1959), and Hart (1961).

In summary, there are a substantial number of ways that have been suggested to measure concentration (the preceding list is not a complete one). A few have some theoretical support, but most are simply empirically based. In addition to several quite different kinds of measures even within a given class of measures, there does not appear to be any consensus as to what form of the measure should be used – for example, entropy, relative entropy, or numbers equivalent (antilog of entropy). Studies comparing various measures do not seem to have produced a clear winner by any criteria. Fortunately, many of the measures tend to be highly correlated with each other, so possibly the exact choice does not really matter a great deal. See for example, Kilpatrick (1967) or Bailey and Boyle (1971). Nevertheless, the various measures are far from identical so that the quantitative results obtained from a statistical analysis will depend to some degree upon the measure chosen.

In general, it does not seem possible to make any very useful statement about the effects on estimated regression coefficients of the use of an "incorrect" index of concentration. For example, consider the following model:

$$y_i = \alpha + \beta x_i + \gamma z_i + u_i$$

where x_i and z_i are exogenous variables and u_i is the random error term. Suppose that data are available on y_i and x_i but z_i is unobserved. What is observed, however, is p_i – a proxy for z_i. For instance, z_i might be the output of a research department, firm size, or market power and p_i could be the number of patents applied for or new products introduced, the total of sales, assets or employment, or some measure of concentration. Clearly, using p instead of z will lead to estimates that do not have the usual least squares properties (unbiasedness, consistency, and so on).

McCallum (1972) and Wickens (1972) have considered the following question: When is the estimate of β obtained from a regression including p closer to β (in the sense of $\text{plim} |\hat{\beta} - \beta|$) than the estimate obtained using only data on y and x? What they showed is that if

$$p_i = z_i + v_i,$$

where v_i is uncorrelated with the other variables in the model, then use of the proxy variable will always give a "better" estimate of β. Since the result does not depend upon the relative variances of z and v, even a very poor proxy – that is, one with a low correlation with z – is better than none at all. To the extent that the discrepancy between p and z is due to sampling error, this result should be applicable. In the applications considered here, however, the differences between the desired variable and the various variables used to represent them can hardly be ascribed to sampling error. What happens, presumably, is that one picks a variable which is, hopefully, highly correlated with the correct one and introduces it into the regression equation in order to control for variations in the unobserved variable. Needless to say, this procedure could lead to either improved or worse estimates of β.

In the measurement error case, the correlations between the proxy variable and the other variables in the model are smaller in absolute value but have the same sign as the correlations between the correct variable and the other variables. Assuming without loss of generality that p and z are positively correlated, then if this same condition is satisfied, and the correlation between z and the proxy p is moderately large, that is, $corr(p,z) > corr(x,p) \cdot corr(x,z)$, where $corr(x,z) \neq 0$, then the estimate obtained using the proxy will be "closer" to β than that obtained without it. Thus, provided the proxy is sufficiently highly correlated with the true variable, behaves at least qualitatively like it, and does not make the multicollinearity problem worse, using the proxy will improve the estimate of β. While these kinds of assumptions may not seem unreasonable, they need not hold, as for instance, the relation, "is positively correlated with," is not generally transitive. Of course, even if these conditions are satisfied, the resulting estimates will not have the usual desirable properties. In summary, the substantial difficulties of measurement combined with the simultaneous equations problems mean that many results obtained by least squares regression methods should be interpreted with caution.

MARKET STRUCTURE AND R & D

The empirical papers discussed in this section deal with the relationships between various features of firms, market structure (concentration), and innovative activity. All these studies could have important consequences for policy (in particular, antitrust policy) though the papers do not necessarily directly discuss these policies. The first group of papers covered contains information of the role of product diversification in research and thus is primarily of interest with respect to the question of conglomerate bigness. The second group of results to be surveyed deals with the relation between firm size and the level of research activity. Considerable work has been devoted to determining if research intensity (R & D activity per unit of size) is an increasing function of firm size. Finally, the relation between concentration and research activity measured at the industry level is examined. Thus, it is hoped that these studies should provide some insight into the following kinds of questions: Who innovates? That is, what are the characteristics of the most innovative firms? To what extent are there economies of scale to R & D? Is market structure analysis a useful tool in studying innovative activity? Does it appear, for example, that certain types of market structures are relatively more conducive to the creation or adoption of new technologies?

Diversification

The relationship to be considered here is that between research activity and diversity. In his survey, Weiss (1969, pp. 393-94) said, "I judge that the issue is unsettled and a good candidate for more work, especially in view of its potential relevance to the conglomerate merger debate." There are three studies bearing on this issue: Grabowski (1968, diversification has a positive effect), Scherer (1965c, no systematic effect), and Comanor (1965, a negative effect). Weiss concluded that he "can reconcile Scherer with either Grabowski or Comanor but not with both."

Grabowski analyzed data on firms in the chemical, drug, and petroleum industry for the period 1959-1962. The basic model he estimated is the following:

$$\frac{R_{it}}{S_{it}} = a + bP_i + c\frac{I_{i,t-1}}{S_{it}} + dD_i + u_{it}$$

where

R_{it} = R & D expenditures in year t.

S_{it} = sales in year t.

P_i = number of patents received per scientist and engineer employed during the previous four years.

$I_{i,t-1}$ = after tax profits plus depreciation and depletion in year t-1.

D_i = the number of five-digit SIC products produced.

The equation was estimated by least squares separately for each industry. The specification is somewhat similar to Hamberg's (1966) in that the role of internal finance is explicitly allowed for. Note the direction of causation assumed here — research inputs depending upon the results of previous research and development activity. In all three regressions the estimates of d were positive and in two cases, chemicals (t-ratio 4.8) and drugs (t = 5.8) highly significant.

Scherer (1965a,b,c) used the same sort of index of diversity. The 447 SIC four-digit classification was reduced to 200 "technologically meaningful" industries, and diversification was measured by counting the number of these in which a firm operated. Scherer worked with data on 448 firms from the Fortune 500, and reported that the diversification variable was significant in regressions of R & D employment on sales, patents on R & D employment, and patents per billion dollars of sales on sales. However, when the sample was divided into two-digit SIC industries, "diversification played an uneven role." Generally, its coefficient was significant and positive in regressions explaining patents or

R & D employment only for the less technologically progressive industries. For the more research oriented industries, the coefficients were generally insignificant (even negative in regressions explaining patents).   Thus diversification does not appear to have a strong systematic effect on either R & D inputs or patents. Scherer explained these results as being at least to some extent an artifact of the measure of diversity chosen. Consider a firm operating primarily in a low research industry. The higher the measure of diversity, the greater the chance that the firm will have a division in a more research oriented industry.

Comanor (1965) had data on 57 drug firms (accounting for 80 percent of industry sales) and fit a rather elaborate model:

$$\frac{y_i}{S_i} = a + b\frac{RD_i}{S_i} + c\frac{(RD_i)^2}{S_i} + dS_i + eRD_i \cdot S_i + fD_i + u_i$$

where

y_i = sales during the first two years of all new chemical entities introduced during the period 1955-1960.

S_i = average sales over the period 1955-1960.

RD_i = number of professional persons employed in research (average of 1955 and 1960 figures).

D_i = index of diversity defined as follows:

Let D_{1t} = number of markets in which a firm operates that account for at least 2 percent of its sales in year t.
Let D_{2t} = proportion of sales outside of its "primary" market.

Then
$$D \equiv 1/6 \sum_{t=1955}^{1960} D_{1t}D_{2t}.$$

For the purpose of constructing these indices, 40 submarkets were identified.

Comanor also had data on the number of nonprofessional research and development workers and the model was re-estimated using total R & D employment.   Further, both specifications were rerun with y redefined as sales from all new products as opposed to just new chemical entities. In all four regressions, the coefficient of diversity was negative and significantly so in three of them.

Notice that the direction of causation assumed by Comanor is the opposite of that assumed by Grabowski. Even if Comanor's specification is the correct one, there still remains a simultaneous equations problem here due to the dating of the variables in the regression. In particular, consider the index of diversity. It is quite possible that a successful research program could lead to a reduction in diversity as defined by Comanor; and the greater the success, the greater the drop in diversity. This objection would not hold if diversity had been measured as of the beginning of the period rather than averaged over it.

Comanor also considered the possibility that the direction of causation may be opposite from what he had assumed. He argued that it could be that the successful introduction of new products generates funds used internally to expand research staffs, and thereby to diversify. He noted that if this latter specification is correct, then the timing can be reversed from that posited in his model. He did not formulate and estimate the alternative model, but instead he estimated his equations using alternative lag schemes. He found that regression equations of new product sales on future R & D inputs are inferior to equations using past R & D employment. In these latter regressions, new product sales (1958-1960) are explained by diversity based on 1955-1957, and as before the coefficients are negative and significant. Thus, for these regressions the objection about the dating does not hold. Note, however, that for some reason the same measure of firm size (average sales over the whole period) is also used in these regressions.

Size

There have been a number of studies which bear on the relationships between firm size and research activity. Generally, in these studies the level of R & D is measured by inputs, either employment or expenditures. Comanor's work mentioned above is an exception in that he did have an indicator of output.   Also, both Schmookler (1954a,b) and Scherer (1965a,b,c) have worked with patent statistics. While one tends to think of patents as an output of the research process, Comanor and Scherer (1969) concluded that at least for the pharmaceutical industry, patents may be a better measure of input. They reported the results of correlating series on patent applications and patents issued with both of the dependent variables used in Comanor's study as well as with both Comanor's measures of R & D inputs (professional and total employment in research).   Simple correlations were positive and statistically significant as were the partial correlations computed controlling for firm size. Generally, the correlations were higher between patents and employment than between patents and new product sales.

Each of the three papers discussed above with respect to diversity contains statistical evidence on the firm size/research question. Grabowski (1968) reports the results of regressing R & D expenditures on sales and sales squared for his samples of firms in the drug and chemical industries. In both cases the coefficients of the linear and quadratic terms are significant with the coefficients of sales being positive. The quadratic term is positive for the chemical industry and negative for drugs. Thus, research intensity (R & D expenditures per dollar of sales) increases with firm size in the chemical industry and rises at first and then falls as sales are increased for firms in the drug industry. Grabowski qualified his results noting that the measure of size is total sales rather than just sales in the product line associated with the research effort. This raises essentially the same point that Scherer made about the interpretation of his measure of diversity. Grabowski specifically pointed out that large drug firms do diversify into other areas. Indeed, the correlations between sales and the diversity index are positive for both industries (0.8 for chemicals and 0.2 for drugs).

Scherer (1965c) estimated various relations between patents issued in 1959 and sales and employment in R & D in 1955 for his sample of 448 large manufacturing firms. For the entire sample he found a significant positive effect of firm size (sales) on patents. There appeared to be significant differences in the propensity to patent between industries (splitting the sample into 14 two- and three-digit industries roughly doubled the explanatory power). Though the estimated magnitudes of the coefficients and their significance levels varied a good deal across industries, all the results with the exception of textiles indicated a positive association between sales and patents.

Scherer also estimated regressions of patents issued on sales, sales squared, and sales cubed (the coefficient estimates were positive, negative, and positive, respectively). He found diminishing returns to sales up $5.5 billion (which included all but three firms in his sample). The sample was divided into four subsamples (electrical, chemical, moderately progressive, and unprogressive) and the same regression run for each group with substantially similar results. In order to give less weight to the giant firms in the sample, cubic equations using the logarithms of sales were estimated. Diminishing returns were again apparent for the chemical and electrical groups, but less so for the others. Each industry grouping was further subdivided into size classes and separate regressions estimated for each. The results indicated increasing returns up to sales of $500 million for chemicals and electricals, slight decreasing returns generally for the moderately progressive group, and no discernible pattern for the unprogressives.

Comanor (1965) also included a measure of firm size in his regressions, though given the complexity of the estimated equation, its interpretation is difficult without access to the data. The coefficient of size is given by

$$a + dS_i + eRD \cdot S + fD_i ,$$

$$(+) (+,   (-)   (-)$$

(The signs of the estimated coefficients are shown in parentheses.)

and the coefficient of R & D input by

$$b + cRD + eS.$$

$$(-)   (+)   (-)$$

Comanor estimated the elasticity of new product sales with respect to R & D input for firms with sales of 1, 10, and 50 million dollars, the elasticity estimates being 1.4, 0.6, and 0.5, respectively.

Worley (1961) and Hamberg (1964, and 1966 Chapter 4) report in rather similar studies on the relation between firm size and R & D. Worley regressed the logarithm of the number of R & D personnel on the logarithm of firm size measured by total employment for a sample of 198 large firms in eight, two-digit industries. The data referred to 1955. In six out of eight cases (chemicals and allied products, petroleum and petroleum products, stone, clay, and glass products, nonelectrical machinery, electrical machinery, and transportation equipment) the estimated coefficient exceeded unity, being less than one only for food and kindred products and primary metals. The average of the estimates was slightly greater than one (1.08). The estimate was significantly greater than one at the 5 percent level only for petroleum and at the 10 percent level for electrical machinery, and none of the remaining estimates was significantly larger than unity at conventional levels. Of the two point estimates which were less than one, neither was significantly so. Worley came out against the hypothesis that size is a stimulus to research though he was appropriately cautious: "One cannot assert that the evidence offered here . . . nullifies the case for bigness" (Worley 1961, p. 186).

Hamberg computed correlation coefficients and rank correlations between R & D employment and firm size measured alternatively by total employment and book value of assets for 17 manufacturing industries in 1960. Of the 68 estimates, all but one were positive and nearly all the rest significantly so at a 5 percent level. To test the hypothesis that an increase in firm size is associated with a more than proportionate increase in R & D, Hamberg computed rank correlations between R & D intensity (percentage of employees in R & D) and both measures of firm size. The results of this experiment were more mixed (23 of 34 estimates were positive but most not significantly so). Hamberg also ran double logarithmic regressions between R & D intensity and firm size. Using employment as size, 12 of the 17 coefficients were greater than one with three passing at the .05 level (one estimate is significantly less than one). When firm size is measured by total assets, only ten are larger than one, though four others are larger than 0.98. In this case, while one coefficient (primary metals) is again less than one (.05) only two coefficients appear to be significantly greater. Hamberg concludes that "the case for bigness and fewness as a stimulus to industry appears, on the basis of fairly extensive evidence, to be quite weak" (1966, p. 68).

Scherer (1965b) commented on the work of Hamberg and Worley. He noted that if their elasticity estimates were mutually independent, then the evidence they presented, if anything, would support the case for corporate bigness. He also pointed out that many firms (especially small ones) do no R & D at all, but that Hamberg's sample did not include any such firms. Further, since both Hamberg and Worley used the logarithm of R & D input as the dependent variable in their regression equations, how to handle the zero observations is no small problem. He went on to demonstrate empirically that the estimates can be made greater or less than one by adopting various conventions for handling the zeros. For his sample (the same as used in Scherer 1965a), ignoring the zero observations gave estimates less than one, while replacing the zeros with a small positive number gave estimates greater than one. Regardless of the conventions adopted for handling the zeros, the measure of firm size used also affected the results. Measuring firm size by employment gave estimates that were the most favorable to bigness, while estimates based upon sales as the definition of firm size were less favorable, and those using total assets were the least favorable. Thus, Scherer showed that the statistical results obtained by Hamberg and Worley were quite sensitive to both the definitions of firm size and the treatment of firms which did not engage in R & D.

For his sample, Scherer estimated regressions with R & D employment explained by cubic equations in sales and the logarithm of sales. The results obtained were similar to those he obtained for patents. With the exception of the chemical industry and a small number of giant firms, his estimates indicated that R & D intensity was a decreasing function of firm size for firms with sales in excess of $500 million.

Hamberg (1966, Chapter 6) studied the effects of various characteristics of firms on the number of R & D personnel employed. His sample consisted of 405 large firms for the year 1960.

Hamberg argued that the size of the R & D effort should be related to the total sales of the firm. He felt that R & D should be positively related to sales, but that a negative relationship was possible as "a shrinkage of sales, or perhaps a retardation in their growth, could be a signal to increase R & D spending" (p. 117). Profits were also considered as a possibly important variable, and as with sales it was argued that the sign of the regression coefficient could plausibly be either positive or negative. To the extent that internal finance is important for R & D, Hamberg felt that depreciation expenses could be significant. He felt that the sign of this variable should be positive, but that a negative coefficient would not be unacceptable. The level of government R & D contracts held by the firm was also included as an explanatory variable. Hamberg argued that in general one would expect the sign of the regression coefficient for this variable to be positive. The coefficient could be negative, he argued, as a shortage of scientific personnel could lead a firm to reduce its own R & D effort as a result of increased government contracts. The level of gross investment in plant and equipment was included in the equation with the expectation of a negative sign (R & D expenditures compete with other investment projects for funds). Hamberg qualified this argument, however, noting that for tax purposes R & D expenditures could be treated as current expenses and might not be determined by the same budgetary processes as fixed investments. One other variable was included in the equation, namely the level of R & D employment lagged one year. Hamberg expected the sign of its coefficient to be positive.

According to econometric folklore, if one can argue for both positive and negative signs for a single regression coefficient, then one should worry about a possible simultaneous equations problem. Hamberg's study seems to be a case in point. Consider, for example, the case of profits. If profits provide a source of funds for R & D expenditures, then this suggests a positive coefficient and also is consistent with the direction of causation implicit in Hamberg's model. If falling profits are a signal to engage in more R & D, however, thus giving Hamberg's argument for a negative coefficient, then this position is consistent with profits being at least in part determined by R & D, though possibly with some time lag. In short, it seems that Hamberg is really arguing that a simultaneous equation model is appropriate, thereby casting considerable doubt on his results which were obtained by ordinary least squares.

Hamberg was concerned with heteroscedasticity and attempted to correct for this by deflating by firm size. All variables which are measured in money units were deflated by total assets lagged one year. R & D employment, however, was deflated by total employment unlagged. Hamberg remarked that using the same deflator for all variables would have been desirable, but that his procedure was more meaningful because of the different units of measurement. Note that the method of deflation used does affect the interpretation of the estimated regression coefficients.

The estimating equations were of the form (the firm subscripts have been omitted):

$$\frac{R_t}{E_t} = a + b\frac{P_t}{A_{t-1}} + c\frac{D_t}{A_{t-1}} + d\frac{G_t}{A_{t-1}} + e\frac{I_t}{A_{t-1}} + f\frac{R_{t-1}}{E_{t-1}} + u_t$$

where

R_t = employment in R & D

E_t = total employment

P_t = after-tax profits

D_t = depreciation expenses

G_t = government research contracts

I_t = gross investment

A_t = total assets

t = time.

Hamberg also estimated a number of variations on this model, varying the lag structure, using sales instead of profits, and deleting the government contracts variables.

Note that the use of different deflating variables makes the equation for R & D employment be the following:

$$R_t = aE_t + b \frac{E_t}{A_{t-1}} P_t + c \frac{E_t}{A_{t-1}} D_t + d \frac{E_t}{A_{t-1}} G_t + e \frac{E_t}{A_{t-1}} I_t + f \frac{E_t}{E_{t-1}} R_{t-1}.$$

If the ratios E_t/A_{t-1} and E_t/E_{t-1} are not constant across the firms in the sample, then the regression coefficients are made somewhat difficult to interpret. Even if these ratios are constant, the relationship between current and past levels of R & D needs to be reinterpreted and the constant terms in the regressions (which were not reported) become quite important. Suppose, for example, that E_t/E_{t-1} is equal to λ for each firm in the sample. Then

$$R_t = a\lambda E_{t-1} + \ldots + f\lambda R_{t-1} + u_t =$$

$$\lambda (a + f)R_{t-1} + \ldots + a\lambda \theta_{t-1} + u_t$$

where $E_t = R_t + \theta_t$. Thus, the coefficient should be the sum of the unreported constant term plus the estimated coefficient. For all these reasons Hamberg's results are difficult to interpret.

Hamberg estimated regressions using 1960 data for samples of firms in eight different industries. The results were mixed. Three variables generally entered with negative coefficients: profits (four of five), depreciation (six of eight), and gross investment (five of eight) with five coefficients being significant at .05 or higher levels of significance. The estimated coefficients for sales, government contracts, and lagged R & D personnel were generally positive with 13 of the 19 estimates being significant. The model was estimated without the government contract variable for 21 industries with similar results. Hamberg concluded that liquidity had little influence on R & D, and if gross investment has any effect, it is negative (of the 13 significant coefficients, 12 are negative).

Mansfield (1963b; 1968, chapter 2) estimated logarithmic regressions between R & D expenditures and firm size (sales) for samples of firms in the chemical, petroleum, drug, steel, and glass industries. The equation estimated was:

$$\ln R_{ti} = \text{year dummies} + (a + bt) \ln S_{ti} + e_{ti}).$$

In all cases the estimate of "a" was positive and significant. With the exception of the steel industry, all the estimates were significantly different from one, the estimate being greater than one for chemicals and less than one in the other industries. The estimates of "b" were not significantly different from zero, indicating that the elasticity of R & D expenditures with respect to firm size was constant over the period (1945-1959).

Loeb and Lin (1977) re-estimated the equations suggested by Scherer (1965b,c) Grabowski (1968) and Hamberg (1964). They used data on six unnamed but "representative" pharmaceutical firms. Their product is differentiated methodologically by their use of specification error tests developed by Ramsey (1969, 1970, 1974). Their general conclusion was that research intensity tends to diminish as size increases for that industry. Howe and McFetridge (1976) studied a sample of 81 Canadian firms in the electrical, chemical, and machinery industries over the period 1969-1971. The dependent variable in their study was expenditures on R & D, and the main independent variables were firm size (sales), profits, depreciation, the Herfindahl index of the three-digit industry, and government incentive grants. The equations were tested for homogeneity over time and heteroscedasticity was allowed for. Quite sensibly it was assumed that the scale of the disturbance variances varied with firm size. The effect of firm size was not generally significant, the estimated coefficients being a bit erratic. Also, the Herfindahl index was statistically insignificant. In the chemical and machinery industries the coefficient of government grants was not significantly different from zero. Thus, for these industries, one could not reject the hypothesis that the receipt of government incentive grants simply replaced R & D expenditures that the firms would have made. It should be pointed out that a condition for receiving the grants is that matching private funds are spent on the R & D projects being subsidized. Nevertheless, only for the electrical industry is there evidence that the grants actually caused increased private R & D expenditures.

Shrieves (1978) studied a sample of 411 firms. The criteria for being chosen was that they could be assigned to a three-digit industry and were included in COMPUSTAT and the 1965 edition of Industrial Research Laboratories of the United States. The dependent variable was R & D employment and the main independent variables were the percentage of 1965 R & D financed by the federal government, firm size (again sales), and the four-firm concentration ratio. The coefficient of the governmental subsidy variable was negative and significant, which is consistent with the Canadian results discussed in the preceding paragraph. The results on size and concentration tend to indicate that, ceteris paribus, small firms in concentrated industries do more R & D than others. The results are flawed by the inclusion of a number of more or less uninterpretable variables based on applying factor analysis to sets of characteristics of the product market and the technology. Factor analysis was used to reduce the dimensions of the explanatory variables. In this sense it was successful, but not surprisingly the results are hard to interpret. It is unclear why this is a preferable state to "confounding," that is, multicollinearity among known variables.

Shrieves' findings on size and concentration were also obtained by Rosenberg (1976) using a sample of 100 of the Fortune 500. A firm was entered in the sample only if its primary area of production was classified as high or low technology. For this study, R & D was measured by the percentage of employment and firm size by market share.

Fisher and Temin (1973) have argued that most studies of the relation between firm size and the level of R & D activity are inappropriate. They argued that these studies are attempting to test the so-called Schumpeterian hypothesis (Schumpeter, 1942) that "there are increasing returns in R & D both to the size of the R & D establishment and to firm size," as follows:

Let   R   =   number of workers in R & D.
      S   =   total number of workers in a firm.
      N   =   S - R.
  F(R,N)   =   the average labor productivity of R & D.

Hypothesis:

$$\frac{\partial F}{\partial R} > 0$$

$$\frac{\partial F}{\partial N} > 0$$

The empirical literature has mainly been concerned with whether

$$\eta = \frac{S}{R}\frac{dR}{dS} > 1$$

Yet the question of the impact of antitrust policy really involves the relation between the <u>output</u> of R & D and firm size. That is, whether

$$\varepsilon = \frac{S}{R \cdot F} \frac{d(R \cdot F)}{dS} = \eta + \frac{S}{F}\frac{dF}{dS} > 1.$$

Fisher and Temin argue that η being greater than one is neither necessary nor sufficient for ε greater than 1 or for the truth of Schumpeter's hypothesis. Thus they conclude that the empirical work is "of very little interest."

The general point made by Fisher and Temin seems sensible, namely, that many of the interesting questions involve the behavior or the output of the innovative process while, in general, all that is measured are the inputs. Further, though the studying of the relationship between firm size and R & D effort may be interesting, it does not bear directly on the question of increasing returns, either to firm size or research effort.

In summary, the evidence suggests that firm size is positively related to R & D effort. Research intensity in general does not seem to be an increasing function of firm size at least when attention is restricted to the largest firms. The major exception seems to be the chemical industry; in most others there is evidence that research intensity decreases with firm size. As Scherer noted, many small firms do no R & D and thus studies that deal only with large firms may bias the results against bigness. In particular, if there is some threshold size required for a firm to have a research program, these studies could not detect it. Weiss has stated that this latter problem is most likely of little concern from the policy point of view as antitrust policy generally involves only the largest firms in an industry.

Concentration

Hamberg (1966, chapter 4) correlated total industry, company-financed R & D expenditures with an "average concentration indicator" using 1958 data on two-digit SIC industries. The measure of concentration used was a weighted average of the concentration ratios for the relevant five-digit industries. The correlation was positive (0.50) and significant. A similar result was obtained when industry R & D intensity was correlated with concentration ($r = 0.54$). Hamberg also calculated rank correlations of 0.46 (significant) and 0.36 (insignificant), respectively. Hamberg stated that he considers the rank correlations more accurate. He concluded that there is "too much variance in industry R & D spending left unexplained by industrial concentration to attach much importance to the latter variable as a determinant of R & D" (1966, p. 64).

Horowitz (1962) computed rank correlations between several measures of research and four-firm concentration ratios, average employment, and average value added for two sets of data relating to two- and three-digit industries. He used the Niehans index in calculating average firm sizes. The measures of research used were: the percentage of firms that responded to the survey and had research organizations, research intensity, the percent of research laboratories in the largest 20 percent of the firms, and the percentage of firms with R & D expenditures but without their own research laboratories. Concentration was correlated significantly with all four variables, the signs being plus, plus, minus, minus, respectively. Correlations calculated using the firm size variables were quite similar. Horowitz noted that firms in highly concentrated industries are more likely to engage in research and tend to spend a higher percentage of their sales than firms in less concentrated industries. He concluded that the evidence is consistent with the hypothesis that bigness is conducive to research effort. But he also stated that "it is not clear, however, whether the large firm in the concentrated industry has created the research laboratory, or whether the research laboratory has brought about the emergence of the large firm and increased concentration" (p. 300).

Scherer (1967) analyzed data on the number of scientists and engineers employed in 56 industries in 1960. He regressed the logarithm of the number of technical personnel on the logarithms of concentration (CR_4) and total employment in the industry. The concentration variable entered with a positive sign and was "highly significant." The coefficient was still positive and significant (nearly four times its standard error) when dummies for certain industry groups (electrical, chemical, traditional, regional, durable goods, and consumer goods) were added. When the ratio of technical personnel to total employment was regressed on concentration, the results were similar though somewhat less favorable to the Schumpeterian hypothesis. In this linear form of the model, however, the addition of the industry dummies resulted in a substantial drop in the significance of concentration. While in all cases the results suggested that increasing concentration was associated with larger research effort (controlling for industry size), whether or not the result was statistically significant depended on the choice of functional form.

Comanor (1967) studied the relationship between R & D personnel (both total and professional) and concentration, barriers to entry, and firm size. He gives the results of log-log regressions of R & D input on firm size (employment) for 21 industries, and in the majority of cases the coefficients were less than one. These estimates were then regressed against average firm size and CR_8 with the results that both variables were positively related to the estimates, but only firm size was significant. These regressions taken together suggest that Comanor was working with the following random coefficient model:

$$\ln R_{ij} = a_j + b_j \ln S_{ij} + \varepsilon_{ij}$$

$$b_j = c + dC_j + e\bar{S}_j + u_j,$$

where

R_{ij} = R & D inputs for the ith firm in the jth industry.

S_{ij} = size of the ith firm in the jth industry.

C_j = eight-firm concentration ratio for the jth industry.

$\bar{S}_j$ = average firm size for industry j.

Combining these relations gives:

$$\ln R_{ij} = a_j + c\ln S_{ij} + dC_j\ln S_{ij} + e\bar{S}_j\ln S_{ij} + u_j\ln S_{ij} + \varepsilon_{ij}.$$

Comanor's two-step procedure while inefficient does yield unbiased estimates of the parameters a_j, c, d, and e. However, there is a heteroscedasticity problem at the second step so that statements as to which variables are statistically significant are suspect.

Comanor also estimated the following regression:

$$R = a + b \cdot C + cD + dC \cdot D + eE_1 + fE_2 \text{ and } u,$$

where

R	= average number of research personnel (adjusted for firm size).
C	= 1 if CR_8 exceeds 70.
D	= 1 for consumer nondurables and material inputs.
E_1	= 1 if technical entry barriers are "moderate."
E_2	= 1 if technical entry barriers are "high."

Comaner found that research levels tended to be higher in the industries classified as having moderate entry barriers and, ceteris paribus, in consumer durables and investment goods. He interpreted this as the effects of higher degrees of product differentiation. It appeared that research staffs were larger in the highly concentrated industries though the effects were small for consumer durables and investment goods. The dependent variable for this regression was obtained from the double logarithmic regressions mentioned above, evaluated at "typical" firm sizes.

Williamson (1965) used data from Mansfield (1963b; 1968, chapter 5) to examine the relationship between the proportion of important innovations introduced by the four largest firms and concentration in the steel, petroleum, and coal industries. He fit logarithmic and linear regressions between the P/C and C where P is the percent of innovations introduced by the four largest firms, and C is the percent of industry capacity held by the largest four firms. The results indicated that the largest four firms would contribute more than proportionately to innovation only at relatively low levels of concentration. Williamson split the data into two subperiods (1919-1938 and 1939-1958) to test the stability of the regression equations and concluded that the relations had not shifted over time. The entire sample consisted of six observations (thus the last mentioned regressions had one degree of freedom each), and Williamson was appropriately cautious in his interpretation.

Leonard (1971) argued the case that R & D expenditures influence the subsequent growth of an industry. He reported correlations between R & D intensity (1957-1959) and subsequent rates of growth of sales for 16 industry groups and found high positive correlations between R & D and growth during the following five years. He also found quite low correlations between company financed R & D as a proportion of sales and previous sales growth. Using the proportion of company financed research personnel in total employment as a measure gave similar results. Leonard presented a good deal of other evidence to support his hypothesis, but collinearity generally made it difficult to distinguish between the variables. For example, R & D intensity was highly correlated with growth of capital stock.

Tilton (1973) claimed that the causation went the other way. To support his claim, Tilton correlated earlier sales growth with Leonard's measures of R & D input using total inputs rather than just company financed R & D. In reply, Leonard claimed that Tilton's data were suspect, and redid the calculations using data that he considered to be better. The results are correlations intermediate between Tilton's and Leonard's original calculations (though significant at the .05 level).

Wilson (1977) studied a sample of 350 manufacturing firms which reported both royalty payments and R & D spending in 1971. Wilson finds both R & D intensity and royalties as a fraction of sales decrease with concentration (four-firm concentration ratio) and increase with profits as a fraction of sales. Wilson's results are suspect, however, as included among the explanatory variables is a possibly ordinal variable constructed by the author to measure the "'multidimensionality' of the industries' product." For a discussion of the difficulties that use of non interval-level data in simple regressions present, see D.M. Grether (1974, 1976).

Overall, it appears that concentration is positively related to R & D, though the evidence on this is not overwhelming. Further, there does not seem to be general agreement as to the proper interpretation of any such relationship. In other words, even if one believes that the association between concentration and research intensity is established, one cannot conclude that concentration caused the increase in R & D. Minasian (1962) concluded that R & D expenditures explain productivity increases as well as the level and rate of growth of profitability. He considered the alternative hypothesis that profitability determines R & D, but for his data (a sample of 19 chemical firms) he rejected this hypothesis. Also, Comanor (1965), Hamberg (1966), and Leonard (1973) assume that R & D influences growth of firms and industries while Grabowski (1968), Hamberg (1966), and Tilton (1973) assume that growth and profitability at least partially determine R & D. In fact, both Tilton and Leonard seem to agree that there could be mutual interdependence.

In conclusion, it seems that there are good reasons for arguing that simultaneous equations models are more appropriate than the single equation approach that has generally been used. It should be apparent from the preceding discussion, however, that research workers are well aware of the problems of interdependence. In other words, the problem is not simply one of choosing the correct statistical procedure. One needs both more fully developed theoretical models (Montgomery and Quirk, 1974) and better data (Grabowski and Mueller, 1970). One hopes that much future research in this area will be based upon explicit models of firm behavior. At the least, this should allow for a clear distinction between endogenous and exogenous or predetermined variables. Thus, hopefully one can avoid studies of the "effects" of diversification, debt-equity structures, or other endogenous variables on the "productivity" of R & D expenditures.

It should be noted, however, that some of the best and most interesting work in this area has been largely descriptive – for example,

Scherer's work (1965c) on patent statistics – and there is still room for a good deal of exploratory empirical work. We may not need more studies of, say, R & D expenditures of two-digit industry groups, but relatively little is known about the breakdown of these efforts between development and various types of research activities at any level of aggregation. Also, even at the firm level, aggregation problems may obscure the interpretations of seemingly straightforward relations. For instance, as Scherer (1965c) and Grabowski (1968) have pointed out, the tendency for large firms to be diversified makes it difficult to interpret the correlation (or lack of it) between firm size and R & D. In addition, if hypotheses concerning more detailed aspects of market structure or organizational structure of firms are to be examined, studies of specific firms, industries or innovations could be important: for instance, comparisons of two industries with similar market structures (reputations for technical progress), but different records of productivity gains (market structure).

5 The Experience Curve Effect on Costs and Prices: Implications for Public Policy

Donald N. Thompson

BACKGROUND

Part of the work and analysis reported here was carried out in 1977 and 1978 as background to the Report of the Royal Commission on Corporate Concentration, of which the author was Director of Research. The commission recognized the conflict between realization of benefits from mergers through economies of size or scale, and resultant high levels of concentration with possibly less competitive market behavior, and wished to identify those characteristics of merging enterprises most likely to produce economies of scale. The goal was to produce guidelines such that a competitive practices tribunal might estimate when detriments from a merger might (to quote one report to the government), "with reasonable probability, be on balance offset by real-cost economies." (Skeoch, 1976, p. 125).

As the work of the commission progressed, a great deal of our attention was directed to the experience curve phenomenon, which had previously little emphasis in competition policy analysis in Canada. We quickly concluded that while the experience curve might have only limited long-term implications for merger policy, it offered direct and short-term insights into a range of issues in competition policy, including the relation between profitability and degree of industry concentration, the advantages of size or conglomerate status in subsidizing cash flow requirements for new products, the need for adequate financial resources and long-term planning horizons for small and medium sized businesses in fast-growth sectors, and the need to

*Contributions of a number of research personnel at the Royal Commission on Corporate Concentration and elsewhere who were involved in these studies are acknowledged with thanks. The conclusions expressed are of course the sole responsibility of the author.

Some of the materials in this paper were earlier included in "Mergers and Acquisitions: Motives and Effect," the 1978 Canada House Lecture, at Canada House, London, March 9, 1978.

promote, rather than restrict, dominant companies in some sectors. The experience curve also had direct implications for industrial strategy, which reflect back indirectly on things such as the vigor with which competition policies dealing with industrial structure are pursued.

Ultimately, the merger conclusions in the commission's report (Report, 1978) were based on factors other than the experience curve and related analyses. Much of our work in this area is reported for the first time here.

Two caveats must be stated. The first is that the analysis was carried out against the background of a rather unique set of Canadian economic problems; indeed, the title might well read "Implications for Canadian Economic Policy." The Canadian economy is made up of small markets dispersed over a wide geographic area. Canada has a domestic market of only 23 million, and is one of the few developed economies whose industries do not have access to a large free trade area. Dispersed markets often prevent Canadian producers from realizing economies of scale, or the productivity enjoyed by firms in more populous and geographically concentrated markets. Canada is a high-wage country, facing increasing international competition both from low-wage countries and from developed countries whose industries can realize economies of scale in production and in research and development through access to large markets. Some of the public policy implications in applying experience curve analysis to such an economy will also hold true in a larger market such as the United States; some quite obviously will not.

The second caveat is that a great deal of the literature and research on the experience curve has come from one source, The Boston Consulting Group (BCG), and particularly from one publication entitled Perspectives on Experience (Boston Consulting Group, 1968). The BCG is a private, profit-making organization, and most of its work is proprietary. Some of the BCG results have been replicated in the United Kingdom, West Germany, Japan, and Canada, but the majority of the material is best described as persuasive, although neither well nor completely documented. There is some theoretical literature, most of it based on the Alchian-Hirshleifer modern cost theory (Alchian, 1959; Hirshleifer, 1962), and support from the PIMS project at Harvard (discussed below), William Shepherd's work from FTC data, and at least two rigorous econometric studies – Rapping on World War II Liberty ships, and Kenneth Arrow on the Horndal iron works in Sweden.

THE EXPERIENCE CURVE PHENOMENON

History

There is general agreement that three broad classes of economies of size or scale exist in the industrial sector: those that are product-specific, those related to plant size, and those related to firm size.(1) Product-specific economies of scale come about because increasing the volume of production of a specific product or of closely related products tends to decrease the average total cost per unit produced. Product-specific economies have been recognized as having great potential in producing real-terms reductions in unit costs, but the reasons for this have not always been well understood.

Disentangling the contributory factors is difficult because increasing volumes of production of closely related products are often accompanied by technological advances, may be embodied in newer, larger plants, or may involve an observable process of managers and operators learning from experience how to operate particular technologies and facilities more efficiently.

Learning effects have been isolated from scale and technology effects in a number of studies, beginning with the U.S. aircraft industry where it was noted in 1936 that reductions in unit costs were related to cumulative output of particular aircraft (Wright, 1936). The Stanford Research Institute and the Rand Corporation carried out further studies of these learning effects in the late 1940s, concluding that doubling cumulative airframe output was accompanied by a reduction in average labor requirements of about 20 percent. Later, it was determined that the learning effect was about twice as large in assembly (26 percent) as in machining (14 percent), the difference being attributed to similarity of most machining, whereas assembly work involved greater complexity and uniqueness (Hirsch, 1956). This result was later generalized to conclude that learning is related to the proportion of manual to mechanical effort in a given operation (Nadler and Smith, 1963).

The General Principle

In 1968, the Boston Consulting Group, which had documented combined scale, technological, and learning effects for many industries, proposed a general observation based on its consulting work, that the characteristic decline in the unit cost of value added was consistently 20 to 30 percent each time accumulated production doubled, and that the rate of decline was consistent from industry to industry (BCG, 1968).(2) They further hypothesized that this decline in costs (in constant dollars) would go on without limit with every doubling of accumulated experience, and would exist independently of the rate of growth of experience. Calculations over the past decade, from about 190 studies of 40 to 45 industries, suggest that subject to some definitional and measurement problems, there is no evidence so far to reject these hypotheses. (They do not apply, however, if major elements of cost or price are determined by patent or natural monopolies, or by government regulation).

In a generalized form, the concept can be stated as follows:

The Experience Curve Concept: <u>Those costs related to value added appear to decline at a fairly constant rate, every time total production experience doubles.</u>

Thus, when costs are plotted against cumulative volume on a linear scale, the resulting graph will take the form of a characteristic hyperbolic cost function.

If the relationship is shown on double logarithmic scale (which has the property of showing percentage change as a constant distance along either axis), the plotting of observed cost data will show a characteristic straight line, reflecting the consistent relationship between experience and costs.(3) Figs. 5.1 through 5.4 indicate examples from the production of heavy oil from the Alberta Tar Sands; hydroelectric power generation; life insurance operating expenses; and production of float glass.

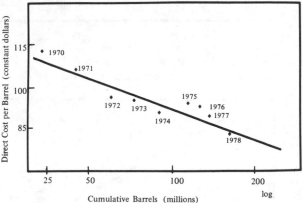

Source: Research Program, Royal Commission on Corporate Concentration, Government of Canada; updated through 1978 by author. Data compiled by Information Centre, Department of Energy, Mines, and Resources, Government of Canada.

Fig. 5.1. Direct costs per barrel, heavy oil production, Alberta Tar Sands.

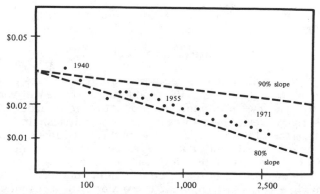

Source: Research Program, Royal Commission on Corporate Concentration, Government of Canada. Data compiled by Information Centre, Department of Energy, Mines and Resources, Government of Canada.

Fig. 5.2. Hydroelectric power generation Canadian accumulated billion kwhrs.

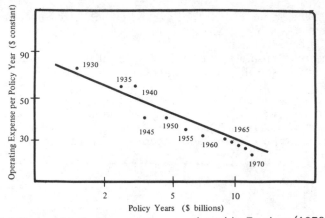

Source: Institute of Life Insurance, reproduced in Review (1978), p. 92
Fig. 5.3. U.S. Life Insurance Industry operating expense per policy year
1930-1970.

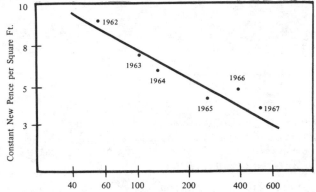

Source: United Kingdom Monopolies Commission, reproduced in <u>Review</u>
(1978), p. 92.
Fig. 5.4. Pilkington Brothers Float Glass cumulative million square feet,
United Kingdom.

Rate of Cost Decline

In the 190 studies of which the author is aware, the rate of decline in
value added with a doubling of production experience varied from
industry to industry; in automobile production it is about 12 percent
(with this figure verified in three separate countries); for color television sets, about 15 percent; for steel and related industries, about 20
percent; for semiconductors and integrated circuits, as high as 40-50
percent (and the result of that high rate can be seen in operation with
the recent steep declines in the price of calculators and digital watches
from firms like Texas Instruments). The majority of industries measured
in BCG studies fall between 20 percent and 30 percent; those studied in

Canada, West Germany, Japan, and the United Kingdom have for the most part fallen between 15 percent and 25 percent.

The reason for the steady decline in real unit costs with greater production experience is not completely understood, even though widely observed. Certainly it is partly due to "learning by doing" for workers and management, more time spent by management on cost-cutting measures, automation of more processes, increased line-balancing so that idle machine time is decreased, greater use of standardized parts, decreased inventory carrying costs, and lower finance and procurement expenses as the "law of large numbers" comes into play.

A dramatic example is found with the case of International Business Machines' computer production. From 1972, when IBM's System/370 replaced System/360, to 1979, when the 4300 series replaced System/370, IBM's accumulated computer production "experience" almost tripled. Ulric Weil, chief computer analyst for Morgan Stanley, estimates that 4300 equipment cost only about one-fifth as much to make in 1979 in real dollars, as System/370 gear originally did. Logic chips for the 4300 series can hold over 700 circuits each, and are cheaper to make in devalued dollars than the chips for the most advanced 370 generation mainframe, which had a capacity of only 44 circuits.

Because of this advance and improvement in methods of mounting the chips on printed circuit boards, a 4331 central processor is built with only four and one-half boards. The comparable System/370 model required 15 boards.

Rather than leave the reader with the feeling that cost declines are dependent on striking technological advances, a second, less dramatic example might be presented. The number of parts in one North American-produced automobile door lock mechanism declined from 17 to 4 between 1954 and 1974, with the cost of the mechanism falling almost 75 percent in real dollars over that period. The improvement was credited to as many as 20 individual advances, including improvements in metallurgy and casting techniques.

Each cost element (including overhead, sales expense, advertising, and research and development) will have a different history of past experience. Cost elements obtained on the open market will decline in cost as a function of the total usage of the relevant market, not the usage of the producer. Some internal value-added elements will accumulate experience from multiple products or applications, while others accumulate experience from a single unique application. Thus, a change in volume of one product can change the rate of cost decline of an otherwise completely independent product if they share a common cost element. The cost of any product can be viewed as the total of a set of experience curves for the different materials and assemblies making up the final product. If one discrete element dominates this total, or if the component curves reflect the same experience rate, the curve should be unbroken and characteristic.

Conditions for Validity

The two important conditions of validity for the experience curve analysis seem to be that the product whose cost pattern is being observed be stable throughout the period of observation, and that value-added rather than total cost be measured (although this is less important if value-added is a large component of the unit cost). Predictably then, experience analyses are most clear cut for heavy industrial goods, chemicals, synthetics, and more generally in capital-intensive industries. Nevertheless, experience analyses appear to be helpful in understanding the competitive dynamics of an industry, and the strategic options for public policy, even in situations which do not satisfy these two conditions.

It is obvious that for validity, when performing experience curve analyses one must correct for inflation by deflating the raw data and if necessary, reflating the forecast. Use of the gross national product deflator proves most satisfactory, because use of a sector deflator has the effect of minimizing evidence of the effect being measured.

It has never been assumed that these observed or inferred reductions in cost with volume increases are automatic. They depend on a management under competitive pressure to force costs down as volume increases. It is competition that produces survivors who achieve the full potential reductions, and who use the optimal combination of cost elements compared to competitors' combinations. This proviso may be most important in explaining the observation that many of the largest, most experienced firms clearly do not have either the lowest costs or the highest margins.

The significant variables in computing cost reduction with experience are thus prior accumulated experience, shared experience, value added, component growth rate, and relative competitive volume. Growth rate in product experience is the most important of these variables: if production rate is not growing, then the rate of cost decline per year slows down and approaches zero.

Cost-Price Relationships

The actual decline in costs may be obscured because prices do not decline at the same rate as costs. If there is no competition, and the company is well managed, the differential should show up as a steadily increasing profit margin. Where there is competition, the differential will rarely be fully converted into profit. Some will take the form of promotion and other nonprofit inducements.

If costs decline at a predictable rate, it is possible to examine related price curves for correlation. The analysis usually used plots industry unit price (or weighted average unit price for different sizes or grades, if appropriate) against total historical industry units. Average industry costs are weighted by the unit production of each competitor.

Fig. 5.5 shows a stable price pattern, where price follows cost and the margin between them remains fairly constant over time as experience accumulates. This sort of stable price pattern is rare in North American marketing practice. My colleague Don Daly has concluded that virtually the only stable price patterns found are those in Japanese industry, and that this provides partial explanation for phenomena such as the great stability of market share in many Japanese industries over time and over various stages of the product life cycle.

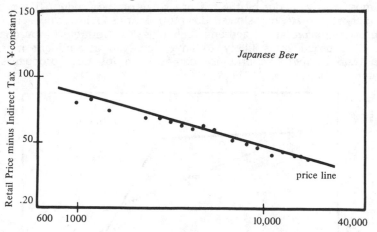

Industry Total Accumulated Volume (million tons)

Source: Sallenave (1976), p. 22.

Fig. 5.5. A stable pattern

Fig. 5.6 shows a stable-unstable-stable pattern, by far the most common among North American industries studied. Price charged by the leading firm at the introductory life-cycle stage are initially below average industry costs. The rate of cost reduction exceeds the rate of price reduction for a period of time, creating a market-leader supported price umbrella which typically exists over the rapid growth period of the product life cycle. However this phase is highly unstable, because characteristically during the period new competitors are attracted, existing firms are expanding production, and the dominant firm is losing market share.

At a point usually corresponding to the beginning of what is called the "competitive turbulence" stage of the product life cycle (Wasson, 1978), a shakeout period begins. At some point either the leading producer, or a secondary producer which has been gaining market share under the price umbrella, decides to buy a larger market share by reducing either actual or effective price. It seems accepted in the literature that such breaks in price are more likely the faster the growth of the product, the larger the number of producers, and the greater the difference between price and cost for the lowest cost-producer.

At some point the price war ends, very often with price again below average industry cost, although perhaps not below cost for the leading producer. Marginal producers are either eliminated, or have differentiated their product and sought protection in serving smaller, specialized sub-markets. Survivors recognize that they have more to gain from coexistence than from overt price competition, and evolve at least temporarily to a more conventional shared-oligopoly position (Rutenberg, 1978; Robinson and Lackhani, 1975). The end of the unstable phase will almost always occur by the mature stage of the product life cycle, when market growth has slowed down.(4) At this point, when product characteristics have stabilized and technology is available by purchase, the leading producer is likely to have achieved a dominant market position and competitive pressure comes from low-cost producers in other countries.

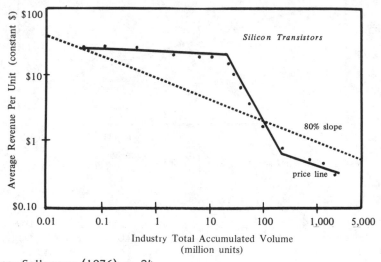

Source: Sallanave (1976), p. 24
Fig. 5.6. A stable-unstable-stable pattern

However, dramatic short-term cost improvements may lead to creation of a new price umbrella, and renewed price cutting. This was the case with the IBM example referred to earlier. The IBM 4331 performs about as well as the old System/370 model 138, but costs as little as $65,000, compared with an original list price of $350,000 for the 138. The 4341, a much larger machine, starts at $245,000, compared with about $1,750,000 for its equivalent in the 370 line. More dramatically, one megabyte of memory (about eight million bits of information) cost $70,000 in Series/370 at the beginning of 1978. The price for 4300 memory at the beginning of 1979 was $15,000 per megabyte.

Cross Sectional Experience Curves

It is commonly observed that at a point in time, cost differentials between competitors are far less than relative experience levels might indicate. A competitor with twice the experience (and perhaps twice the market share), typically has only a 5 percent to 10 percent cost advantage, rather than the 25 percent to 30 percent predicted by the experience curve. This differential is the "cross sectional" experience curve at a point in time.

The explanation for relatively modest cross-sectional cost differentials is argued by proponents of the experience curve concept to be found in differing histories of competitors. Specifically, the points made are that:

● competitors who enter late should be able to start at lower costs than the pioneer through purchase of state-of-the art technology,
● competitors who enter late will almost always grow relatively faster than established companies, if only to approach competitive scale,
● some late entries from related fields bring with them cost advantages through prior experience in common components,
● materials and services common to competitors' decline in real cost over time on their own cost curves, without much regard for the relative growth or experience of specific customers who also may be competitors of each other. (Cross Section Experience Curve, n.d., 1-2)

Fig. 5.7 shows a cross-sectional experience curve for Allis Chalmers (AC), Westinghouse (W), and General Electric (GE), for the manufacture of steam turbine electricity generators. General Electric, with the greatest accumulated experience at any point in time, had the lowest unit costs. Relative cost levels and market shares remained stable as all three competitors moved in step over time down a common experience curve. During this period, General Electric consistently earned more profit from this area than did Westinghouse, which in turn was more profitable than Allis Chalmers. The slope of the experience curve relating the three companies' direct costs to each other is close to 90 percent, rather than the 75 percent curve found for General Electric alone. Cross-sectional experience curves for the cellophane industry in the United Kingdom show the same slope and profitability-market share relationships (Hedly, 1976, pp. 8-9).

Experience, Concentration, and Profitability

If the experience leader or dominant producer has a real cost advantage over other producers, this could be expected to show up generally in higher profitability, as in the previous example. Since prices in many industries tend to reflect unit costs of smaller-scale manufacturers, it would be expected that profits in concentrated industries as a whole would be higher than in fragmented industries, because concentrated industries contain some very large companies with substantial accumulated experience, and significantly lower costs. A positive association between profitability and degree of industry concentration has been noted by a number of researchers (Goldschmid, 1974, pp. 162-245).

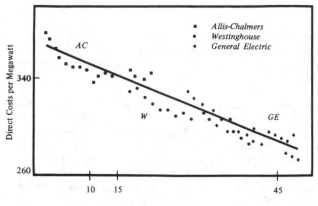

Cumulative Volume (million megawatt)

Source: Boston Consulting Group, in Hedley (1976). Confidential information from General Electric, Westinghouse, and Allis Chalmers was made available as a result of antitrust legislation.

Fig. 5.7. Direct costs per megawatt steam turbine generators 1946-1963.

Evidence on the association between profitability and individual companies' market shares (and thus accumulated experience), is found in results of the Profit Impact of Market Strategy (PIMS) program of the Marketing Science Institute at Harvard University, (recently taken over by the Strategic Planning Institute in Cambridge, Mass.). PIMS involved a cross-section analysis of data from 600 businesses, with "business" defined as divisions, products, and other profit centers, involving a distinct set of products and/or services. As indicated in table 5.1., the PIMS analysis found a strong positive correlation between market share and profit margins (Schoeffler, 1974; Buzzell, 1974). The data is reported to have been replicated for 80 businesses in the United Kingdom, with similar results (Review, 1978, p. 84).

As indicated in table 5.1, there is a strong positive correlation between market share and profit margins. Groups 1 and 4 charged similar prices and offered products of comparable quality, so that the progressively higher returns of Groups 2, 3, and 4 seem to reflect cost advantages relative to smaller competitors in the same markets. Group 5 companies are harder to compare, because they claimed higher quality of product and charged higher prices.

Table 5.1. Relationships between Market Share
and Unit Cost Advantage.

	Group 1	Group 2	Group 3	Group 4	Group 5
1. Number of businesses investigated	156	179	105	67	87
2. Market share	Less than 10%	10-20%	20-30%	30-40%	Over 40%
Costs and Margins					
3. Pretax profits/sales	-0.2%	3.4%	4.8%	7.6%	13.2%
4. Pretax profits/sales adjusted for effects of price premia charged by each group*	-0.2%	3.3%	4.1%	7.0%	9.6%
5. Implied unit cost advantage relative to businesses with less than 10% market share	---	3.5%	4.3%	7.2%	9.8%
6. Quality index**	15	20	20	20	43

*The average price charged by each group, relative to its competitors, is provided in the PIMS analysis on a 5-point scale. These results are interpolated and used to adjust profit margins in relation to those of the Group 1 businesses.

**This index is based on each business' estimate of relative superiority/inferiority of its own product.

Source: The data are found in Buzzell (1974). The analysis in this form is reproduced from Review (1978), p. 90.

There is some other evidence that superior profitability in concentrated industries reflects efficiency rather than the exploitation of market power. In a study by the Department of Industry in Great Britain for 1970, 1975, and 1976, industrial concentration was found to be highly correlated with industry foreign trade performance in terms of generating a positive trade flow. This is consistent with higher profitability of concentrated industries reflecting superior efficiency. If higher profitability derived from the exploitation of market power in the domestic market, but hid deficiencies in productivity and innovation, one might expect to find an inverse relationship between concentration and international competitiveness (Review, 1978, p. 85).

A large number of companies have based strategy on the experience/market share findings of BCG and PIMS, among the better known ones being General Electric, Texas Instruments, B.F. Goodrich, and American Standard. However, there are also examples of low-market share companies which consistently show a higher rate of return than do larger rivals with greater accumulated experience. In a 1978 article, R.G. Hamermesh and his associates cite the steel industry, where Kaiser, Armco, and Inland, with a small share of national market, consistently outperform the much larger firms of U.S. Steel and Bethlehem on return on investment criteria. Other outstanding performers identified by Hamermesh were Crown Cork and Seal in metal containers, Burroughs in computers, and Union Camp in paper products (Hamermesh, 1978). The researchers identify and analyze four characteristics that seem to explain this success: the firms compete only in areas where their particular strengths are most highly valued, make efficient use of limited R & D budgets, take a cautious approach to possible growth, and have leaders who are willing to question conventional wisdom.

MANAGERIAL IMPLICATIONS

There are a number of important management and managerial strategy implications of experience curve analysis, which are extensively described in the literature (for example, Hedley, 1976; Delombre and Bruzelius, 1977; Boston Consulting Group, 1968).

Some examples are given here for illustrative purposes, and because the points are relevant to the discussion of competition policy and industrial strategy which follows:

- If costs are inversely proportional to market share, then high market share has a calculable value
- Cost declines are predictable, and can be used as a basis for both cost control and management evaluation
- Price reduction is predictable in some situations. If prices are not paralleling costs, then price instability is predictable
- The relative growth of companies in an industry is more important than absolute growth in a dynamic environment. A company with a structural cost disadvantage can compensate for it by a dynamic cost advantage, by accumulating experience faster than the competitor who enjoys a structural advantage. How much faster one must grow to overcome a given structural disadvantage is calculable

- A technological gap between competitors may turn out to be an experience gap
- Costs will decline proportionately faster when cost elements can be shared among more than one product
- The effect of product line extension can be evaluated through interaction of experience and the volume of combined cost elements
- A "make or buy" decision can be evaluated in terms of the relative experience between the buyer and the potential supplier
- A choice of design element alternatives can be made on the basis of whether initial experience is high or low compared to future expected volume
- Relative debt-carrying capacity increases if market share, and thus relative experience, increases
- Knowledge of cost-volume and experience/profit relationships for competitors is suggestive of a proper strategic response in a number of situations, for example, when competitors have unequal financial resources, when competitors have different time horizons, when competitors begin business at different times
- Knowledge of position of the firm and its competitors on the experience curve is a basis for analysis of and planning for a product portfolio

In summary, it may be said that experience curves have extensive managerial application as a planning tool and as a learning tool. They have application as a forecasting tool in those cases where assumptions of steady-state (or predictable) growth, standard products, and fixed operating leverage, are realistic.

While the implications of the experience curve for business strategy are far-ranging and widely recognized, the implications for competition policy and other areas of public policy are much less widely discussed or recognized. The remainder of this paper discusses some of the implications of cost-experience relationships for public policy issues, and for the interaction between business economics and public policy.

Competition Policy

If experience curve analysis is valid – and even if treated skeptically, with awareness of limitations – it raises questions about a number of commonly held assumptions in competition policy and regulatory economics. For example:

- An underlying assumption of competition policy is that efficiency or cost is not necessarily a function of size or experience. Experience curve analysis suggests that it is.
- Competition policy assumes that there can be many competitors with similar cost, efficiency, and profit configurations. Experience curve analysis suggests that the basic competitive relationships in a growth industry are inherently unstable until such time as one competitor has a recognizable cost advantage over competitors.

- Traditional economic analysis of highly concentrated industrial sectors suggests that firms in these sectors can and do exploit consumers through various forms of consciously parallel, "follow the leader" behavior, including higher price levels than would exist in a more competitive structure. Experience curve analysis suggests that concentration is the natural outcome of a process which confers on the leading producer a real cost advantage, and it is this advantage which produces superior profitability rather than exploitative behavior or restraints on competition.
- Competition policy assumes that even short-term pricing below cost may constitute predatory behavior, and should be prevented or constrained.   Experience curve analysis suggests that short- or medium-term pricing below cost may be rational behavior — for example, by a latecomer to a product area who has access to large financial resources compared to existing producers. In the turbulent growth period of a new product, it makes sense for the competitor with the greatest financial resources to lead in price cutting to insure a high continuing market share. Even when price is reduced below short-run cost, to the point where competitors with limited financial resources cannot survive, this is not necessarily irrational. Under normal circumstances, the price cut need never be revoked. Moving down the experience curve should lower costs sufficiently to provide normal margins within a reasonable time span. Because of price elasticity, a very deep price cut may even increase the market enough to shorten the payback period to less than what it was before the cut.

Dominant firms

Experience curve analysis provides some empirical support for the idea that competitive relationships are inherently unstable until a dominant producer has emerged.   There is an implication that the dominant producer should be allowed to emerge, and that competition policy should focus on the conduct of dominant firms in mature industries, rather than on evolving structure in a rapidly growing industry.

The consumer may be better off if public policy permits or even encourages the dominant producer to emerge, even in the absence of import or other competition. This is particularly true if physical volume of a product is growing rapidly, and thus each year's volume is a high percentage of total previous experience. In a steady-state situation, an annual growth in physical production of 5 percent per year will double past experience in about 15 years; a growth of 10 percent in about seven years, of 15 percent in about five years, and of 25 percent in just under three years.

One implication of a high rate of growth is the great increase in capital investment required to maintain (or to increase) a share in a growth market.   To try to maintain or increase share in a growing market is to be committed to a rapidly escalating series of investments during the growth phase. A good current example is the microprocessor industry, where rapid growth and evolving technology have left only four or five firms in the world able to sustain the capital investment and research and development expenditure necessary today, for market leadership tomorrow. Another is General Motors' investment of $3.2 billion per year from 1975 to 1979 in developing fuel-efficient, down-sized "X-cars" (Chevrolet Citation, Buick Skylark, Oldsmobile Omega, and Pontiac Phoenix), which its domestic competitors were unable to match. GM's share of domestic auto sales rose from 49 percent to 60 percent over the period.

Failure to maintain investment at the necessary rate, either because of unwillingness to do so, or inability to raise additional debt or equity capital, will cause a firm to drop off the experience curve, and to fall into a market position which becomes less tenable as initial market share (or expected share) erodes. This type of financial limitation has been cited as one disadvantage facing the European aerospace industry in selling the Panavia Tornado fighter aircraft, and the various models of the Airbus (Nuts and Bolts, 1978). It is a particular problem in Canada, where planning horizons measured by payback periods tend to be shorter, and financial institutions more conservative in the provision of capital (RCCC, 1978, chs. 10 and 11).

In terms of strategic product portfolio analysis, a firm with products in the "star" position of high cash requirements because of high growth rate, but high cash generation potential because of high market share, might in the absence of adequate capital investment see such products deteriorate to become "question marks" or "dogs," where cash genera-tion ability is low because of low market share. It is very difficult to break out of a "question mark" or "dog" position with a mature product. The firm which fails to achieve dominant status either faces years of continuous cash investment with little return, or the need to divest.

In a market where rapid growth is taking place and firms are moving down the experience curve, a change in market share is worth a great deal, and can sometimes be accomplished in a short time by a firm with a long planning horizon (and long pay-back horizon), and with adequate financial resources. The cost of prohibiting or inhibiting a company from seeking growth and dominance in such a market, whether through competition policies, limiting financial assistance, or other means, may be to see dominance fall to a foreign firm.

Mergers

Although much of the Royal Commission's work on the experience curve phenomenon was directed at formulating merger policy, the implica-tions for merger analysis remain uncertain. Accumulation of experience and the achievement of cost reductions are assumed to occur within a company, although for several reasons, industry statistics are often used in graphical presentations. Experience analysis also applies essen-tially to specific products, not to companies. Is it then valid to assume that combined accumulated experience achieved through horizontal merger can be pooled and translated into lower costs for the merged firm?

Experience curve analysis does suggest that the opportunity for experience transfer would be greatest during the rapid growth phase in the product life cycle. As a minimum, this may argue in favor of permitting the usual "failing firm" horizontal mergers.

Allowing a small firm in a growth-stage industry to undertake a merger with any acquirer willing to take it over, may still doom the benefit side of the merger from the start. Merger with a partner unable to finance the needs of accelerating growth will in time still force the company into a marginal position which may become untenable as initial market share erodes. If shortages of term finance, venture capital, or new equity exist for small- and medium-sized firms in Canada, as is generally accepted, then to maximize benefits, mergers under growth-industry conditions should only be undertaken by large, financially secure firms – which may themselves be dominant in other areas. Such firms may have the greatest (or in some cases the only) likelihood of competing successfully against foreign producers who are also accumulating production experience at a rapid rate.

The problem of transferring scale advantage through merger would also be less important in the rapid growth phase, where continual investment might rationalize the increased size and experience of the merged firm. Existing scale advantage (or disadvantage) is less important in high-growth industries, where future investments undertaken by combined companies are relatively more important than those already in place.

It follows also that problems of achieving experience transfer would be greatest at the mature, slow-growth stage of the product life cycle. At the maturity stage, the pooled experience of marketing and distribution scale can be readily shared, but the problems of rationalizing plants and management styles may take a long time to work out. There is some evidence for Canadian mergers in mature industries that economic benefit does not appear for a considerable number of years (although this may be due in part to pre-merger guarantees to government of "no disruption" of merging firms, and similar factors) (D.N. Thompson, 1979).

Even in the presence of a dominant firm, oligopoly, and a mature product life cycle stage, the experience curve suggests that something might be gained by encouraging the growth of small- and medium-sized competing firms by merger. The reason is that if product-specific benefits from experience pooling occur (even in the long run), prices could be expected to decline parallel with declines in the cost experienced by these (still) high-cost producers. Any increase in the high-cost firm's production profit margin creates a huge inducement for it to invest in greater market share. This is an unstable situation for a dominant firm and will likely lead to its dropping prices in parallel with the costs of the next highest cost producer (but not its own costs).

Experience curve analysis also provides some understanding of the lack of success of so many conglomerate firms. In general, performance in terms of average return to the stockholder, earnings before interest and taxes as a percentage of total assets, and growth in earnings per share, are inversely related to the degree of corporate diversification (Gort and Hogarty, 1970; Mason and Goudzwaard, 1976; Lecraw and Thompson, 1978). While diversified firms may accomplish some cash-flow subsidization and other synergies, in general a conglomerate which attempts to have non-dominant positions in a great many areas is unlikely to be successful.

Experience curve analysis would imply that it would not be in the public interest to break up a dominant firm in a high-growth industry. But what about breaking up a dominant firm in a slow-growth, mature industry? Here the answer is not clear cut, and will depend on many factors including the capital intensity and scale effects in the industry involved.

One available case history involves the forced breakup of the aluminum industry in the late 1940s. One might predict that the breakup of a dominant firm in a moderate-growth, scale intensive industry would result in an upward shift of experience curves to a position of stability at a higher slope. As indicated in fig. 5.8, this is what appears to have happened in the aluminum industry.

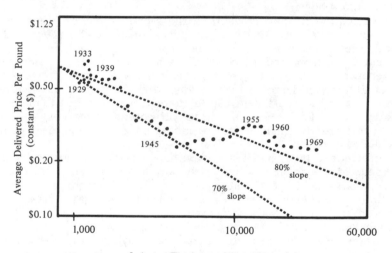

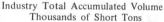

Source: BCG (1968), p. 86.

Fig. 5.8. Primary aluminum-U.S. production.

In practice, using experience curve criteria in evaluating proposed mergers would require a considerably more sophisticated evaluation process than has existed to date, at least in Canada. Even market analysts are not normally privy to the necessary data (if they exist at all) on market size, growth rates, and competitive shares. Also, problems of defining and segmenting a product's market parameters are difficult enough for insiders, but may be impossible for outsiders intent on competition policy considerations.

Trade Barriers and Foreign Ownership

An obvious implication of the experience curve is that free trade can produce great cost reduction for individual firms by allowing them to expand volume, and move down their experience curve more quickly.

Countries in a free or open trade area can each accomplish lowered costs of production. On the basis of an average 80 percent experience curve for an economy, two countries of equal size with completely free trade could each achieve potential savings of about 20 percent on value added. Four economies of equal size would have potential savings of about 40 percent. Canadian entry to a free trade arrangement with the United States would offer a potential saving of 40 to 50 percent on value added for surviving Canadian industries, and U.S. firms would have a potential of about 5 percent reduction because of increased size of the combined market. The benefit for Canada would be proportionately greater in this analysis, although the cost, both in terms of short-term dislocation and in giving up self-sufficiency in many sectors, would be much higher.

The situation for new products in the growth phase of life cycle is even more clear cut. The first producer of a new product has a potential cost advantage which can be of sufficient magnitude to offset differentials in labor and materials costs in other countries. However, maintenance of this cost advantage is dependent upon access to a market at least as large as that of any potential competitor (and, of course, on access to sufficient capital to expand production to maintain market share). Each time the size of potential market vis-a-vis competitors is cut in half, costs are increased 20 to 30 percent of net value added or more.

The effect of tariff barriers, and perhaps more important, of foreign ownership of Canadian industry with parent-imposed export restrictions, puts Canadian firms at a considerable disadvantage vis-a-vis firms in large domestic economies such as the United States, Japan, and the European Common Market countries.

On balance, experience curve analysis supports what advocates of freer trade have been saying for many years. By restricting productive scale, trade barriers and economic nationalism impose some cost penalties on very large economies, but the impact is minor. The most severe impact of trade restriction falls on smaller economies which would otherwise tend to become specialist, low-cost producers of some goods, and importers of most others.

National Industrial Strategy

One implication of experience curve analysis pertains to the relation of taxation and financial structure to firm growth and innovation. Any political, taxation, or financial structure which leads to short pay-back or planning periods will cause prices to be maintained even though costs go down. A competitor whose time horizon includes near-term profit, but does not fully evaluate long-term consequences, is under a major strategic handicap when product volume is growing rapidly. Under these circumstances, competitors with longer time horizons who forego a price umbrella and sacrifice current profit to acquire increased market share, should be more likely to succeed in the long run.   And as indicated earlier, Canadian planning horizons as measured by pay-back periods tend to be shorter than is true in the United States. This is usually attributed to a combination of influences from the Canadian tax system, the high degree of foreign ownership, and the conservatism of the banking sector.

Another implication of the cost-volume relationship pertains to industrial strategy for mature, slow-growth industries. In most such industries, the rate of technological change also slows. State-of-the-art technology is often available by purchase or license, enabling competitors in new locations to enter the business.

A new entrant will always start from a lower position on the experience curve, if only for scale, capacity utilization, and organizational reasons. An entrant who can enjoy more rapid growth than existing firms can close this gap somewhat, but this is difficult to do in a mature market where "buying" market share is extremely expensive.

However, an entrant who can enjoy much more rapid growth than existing firms, either through exploiting a previously closed market or by successful market segmentation, may be able to overtake the dominant producer in cost reduction. Often, lower labor and materials costs accelerate this process.

The most effective use of experience curve-based industrial strategy – for both growth- and mature-stage products – is seen in the case of Japan. Exploitation of product-specific economies, combined with a willingness to sell initially at a very low margin while growth in production experience is taking place, plus a protected home market, has enabled the Japanese to achieve worldwide comparative advantage in shipbuilding, steel, cameras, consumer electronics, and to bid for it currently in microwave ovens, printing machinery, computers, and duplicating machines (Abegglen, 1971).

A case example illustrates the point. In the mature-stage automobile industry from 1970 to 1976, Canadian industry increased its production experience at a compound annual rate of about 4.2 percent, and accumulated experience thus would double about every 15 years. The average annual decline in real costs would be about 0.75 percent. The U.S. automobile industry increased its production experience over the same period at a compound annual rate of 3.7 percent, thus accumulated experience would double every 18 years, with a decline in real costs of about 0.6 percent annually.

The Japanese automobile industry increased production experience at an estimated annual rate of 28 percent, which means accumulated experience would double in under three years, and real costs would drop about 7 percent per year. In three of the six years, this was below the Japanese inflation rate.   The figures contribute to an understanding of the value component that has allowed Toyota, Datsun, and more recently Honda to take a steadily increasing share of the world's automobile markets.

NOTES

(1) There are several possible definitions of economies of scale for any one industry, and the methodology for using data in measuring economies is dependent on which definition is being used. Also, the implications of findings on economies of scale are often unclear; such findings are certainly country-specific, and may be industry specific. A brief outline of the analytics and measurement problems is given in Report (1978), pp. 46-67.

(2) In general, learning is highly significant in labor-intensive operations, and scale is most important in capital-intensive industries' experience curve. However, the interrelationships are apparently more complex than this. There is evidence for the plastic resin manufacturing industry that the rate of decline in unit cost of value added with a doubling of experience, increased with larger scale (and more capital-intensive operation).

(3) Growth in accumulated physical volume, rather than dollar volume, seems most relevant here. If prices decline with costs, physical volume will over time increase at a rate approximately twice the rate of dollar volume.

(4) It is important to recognize that figs. 5.1 to 5.6 are plots against total units produced, and not against time. Although experience increases with time, the relation may be quite irregular.

6 Predatory Marketing
Lee E. Preston

The line between aggressive competition and competition-destroying market behavior has never been easy to draw. Blatantly tortious practices (e.g., false advertising) aside, the social desirability or undesirability of a particular course of market conduct depends heavily upon the entire industrial context within which it takes place. In an essentially atomistic industry functioning on the basis of an easily interruptible flow of current transactions, the general rule is that any legitimate business practice is an acceptable mode of competition; indeed, minor excesses are unlikely to alter the competitive process sufficiently to affect the general pattern of market outcomes, and probably will be corrected by the competitive process itself. By contrast, in situations of tight oligopoly the danger is that competition will not be aggressive enough, that the range of strategies and strength of competitive effort will not generate sufficient pressure for cost and price reduction, nor an adequate range of market alternatives.

*The material presented in this paper was developed in the course of my own involvement as an expert witness in computer industry litigation over the past several years. All of the material specifically referred to here is a matter of public record, and I have attempted to distinguish as sharply as possible between factual statements and my own interpretation of events. Even so, other analysts with different perspectives and backgrounds would undoubtedly select other or additional points for emphasis, and reach different conclusions. In developing my own understanding of these matters, I have benefited greatly from contact with Professors Alan K. McAdams, Leonard W. Weiss, Jesse W. Markham, H.S. Houthakker, and Mark I. Weinstein, as well as with numerous attorneys who would probably prefer to remain anonymous. None of these individuals, and certainly none of the litigants involved, is in any way responsible for the contents of this paper.

The difficult cases of competition versus predation arise in neither of these contexts, but rather in market environments containing established "dominant firms".(1) The essential question is this: Setting aside entirely the issue of how and why a particular firm may have come to occupy a "dominant" market position, but given that such a position exists and has persisted over some period of time, should public policy place any limits on the acts and practices of such a firm that are not equally applicable to other firms in the economy and, in particular, to competitive challengers within the dominant firm's own sphere of economic activity?

A minority view holds that the answer to this question is a simple negative (Bork, 1978). Particular forms of market conduct are either approved or disapproved on the basis of their general acceptability and without regard to specific context, initiating agent, or ultimate effect. Since price competition is generally desirable, all price competition is desirable, and giving away one's product perhaps the most desirable practice of all! An apparent majority, on the other hand, would agree with Grether that "Both persons and business enterprises can be expected to show restraint in the exercise of abilities and capacities" (E.T. Grether, 1966, p. 106). Thus, although the mere existence of a certain degree of market power, which Grether refers to as "the ability to act," may not be itself objectionable, "ability" plus "willingness" — particularly when both are demonstrated by actual behavior — may serve to identify socially undesirable market situations.

The example of giving one's product away is instructive in this connection. An atomistic firm may readily give away all its output — and eventually all its capital — with only temporary impact on its competitors. When it is finished with its philanthropic behavior, and therefore no longer in business, they may continue in operation as viable economic entities. Contrast the position of the dominant firm, which might conceivably give away a sufficient amount of products and services — particularly in one out of many product lines, in one out of many market areas — that selected individual competitors could, in fact, be driven from the market while the apparent philanthropist itself survives with its position of market dominance strengthened. Disregarding any price discrimination issues that might be raised, this is, of course, the extreme form of the "predatory pricing" problem. A considerable literature has grown up suggesting that such tactics are unlikely to be profitable even for the dominant survivor and, thus, that such behavior is unlikely to be commonly observed.(2) But the issue here is not whether or not such behavior is either profitable or likely; the question is whether such behavior, which both requires an initial base of market power (i.e., "ability to act") and results in an enlargement of that base by the demise of a particular targeted competitor, is an acceptable mode of market conduct.

An apparent majority view — including that of most significant antitrust cases in which the issue has been clearly raised — holds that there are patterns of conduct open to moderate-sized competitors but precluded for firms with significant market power.(3) The classic example in the antitrust record is, of course, Alcoa,(4) in which the acquisition of bauxite deposits and power sites in advance of demand – practices certainly appropriate and socially desirable under competitive conditions – were condemned as part of a course of conduct aimed at preserving monopoly power and raising entry barriers.   This general principle was followed by Judge Wyzanski in the United Shoe Machinery case, when he stated that the law does not allow an enterprise to maintain control of a market through practices that are, in themselves, entirely legal but not "economically inevitable."(5)

With particular reference to price and product actions, Wyzanski summarized a series of specific events in the following conclusion:

> These nine representative instances conclusively show that in the face of competition, and with the purpose of meeting or defeating that competition, and retaining or expanding its own share of the market, United follows the policy of reducing its own rates . . . or introducing new models at lower rates than comparable older models . . . or maintaining rates on a particular machine type despite a policy of increasing rates on other machine types to meet increased material and labor costs . . . or even of introducing a new model so designed and priced that it will reach only that area of the shoe manufacturing industry which is being assailed by a competitor. . . . (6)

Although Wyzanski noted that in no case was there any indication that United expected it would fail to earn "its out of pocket expenses for manufacture and service" on these products, nevertheless he concluded: "United has fixed its prices in order to minimize competition."(7)

But how are responsible executives, courts, and outside analysts to distinguish between product, price, promotion, and distribution policies that involve merely the exercise of "skill, foresight and industry," even on the part of dominant firms, from those courses of market conduct that are proscribed by public policy? The only clear consensus seems to be that there is no precise list of acts or practices that, even under specified conditions, can be identified as a priori objectionable. On the contrary, thoughtful analysts stress the need to consider an entire course of conduct – not individual acts – in assessing both the intent and the impact of the market leader's response to competitive challenges. Acknowledging the difficulty of the task, Sullivan writes:

> Predatory conduct will usually display two identifying characteristics. First, there will be something odd, something jarring or unnatural seeming about it. It will not strike the informed observer as normal business conduct, as honestly industrial. Second, it will be aimed at a target, at an identifiable competitor or potential competitor, or an identifiable group of them. . . . Perhaps the characteristic feature of a non-tortious predatory thrust is that the predator is acting in a way which will not maximize present or foreseeable future profits unless it

drives or keeps others out or forces them to tread softly. (Sullivan, 1977, p. 108-113)

The past decade of litigation in the computer industry provides a rich environment within which to investigate these issues.(8) The industry is important, both in absolute size and in the widespread impact of its technology and products throughout our society. From its origins almost three decades ago, the industry has grown at an explosive rate, and no end to that growth is yet in sight. Furthermore, during this entire period of astonishing growth and technological change, a single firm — IBM — has unquestionably occupied a position of market leadership. This position has been challenged by active rivals, which have included some of the leading industrial firms in the economy (GE and RCA) as well as many smaller and highly specialized companies. In spite of the rapid growth of the industry, some major entrants have abandoned their efforts and other appear to have settled into stable, but limited, market positions. Over the past decade, antitrust litigation has been a substantial activity of firms in the industry (indeed, computer industry litigation has become almost a separate, and not insubstantial, sub-industry in itself), with the result that an enormous volume of business records and sworn testimony by industry participants has become a matter of public record. Out of this mass of material, the present paper selects illustrative examples of the conduct of IBM in response to a variety of market developments involving the manufacturers of plug compatible peripheral equipment (PCM's) and third-party leasing companies.(9) The emphasis throughout is on a reconsideration of this experience from a marketing perspective in order to identify appropriate guidelines for public policy. Neither a comprehensive industry study nor a detailed consideration of legal issues is intended.

MARKET POSITION: MEASUREMENT AND POWER

In the preceding section, the term "dominant firm" was used without either a precise definition or any indication of its specific applicability to IBM. A dominant firm is generally identified as one having more than 50 percent occupancy of a market, and no close rivals. (Scherer, 1910, pp. 164, 213-38) A dominant firm in this purely structural sense may or may not exercise market leadership in technological or other ways, and may or may not possess sufficient power (i.e., "ability to act") to obtain monopoly profits or to guide the direction of market evolution to its own advantage. Although these latter properties are commonly assumed to be associated with structural dominance — and, indeed, the term "dominant firm" certainly suggests that something other than mere market occupancy is involved — careful assessment of a firm's market position requires attention to both issues: (1) the measurement of its market occupancy, within appropriately defined and relevant markets; and (2) the assessment of its "ability to act." After a review of some relevant evidence concerning the computer industry, Professor Leonard

W. Weiss concluded "that IBM is a dominant firm, that it is protected by high barriers to entry, and that it has earned exceptionally high profits." He also argued that the Department of Justice monopoly case should have rested on these points alone, without any detailed investigation of IBM's conduct.(10) The latter issue would, however, remain relevant for private litigants claiming damages.

Market Definition

It is a curious fact that an analysis of the nature and impact of IBM's conduct with respect to the PCM companies, and to a lesser extent the leasing companies as well, hinges on the matter of market definition. The issue is not one of measurement, although that problem is troublesome enough, as we shall see below, but rather concerns the concept of the market itself — the network of supply and demand relationships — within which the behavior under analysis is understood to take place.

At the outset, it is necessary to distinguish between the computer industry, or even more broadly the electronic data processing industry, and any of the several specific markets within which suppliers and demanders may interact and in which the strength of competitive forces may be assessed. Although construction of one-of-a-kind computers began in the late 1940s, and Univac was responsible for the first commercial installation at the U.S. Census Bureau in 1951, the computer systems market may be said to have originated with the introduction of the IBM 650 in 1954. The computer systems marketed were collections of hardware, software, and associated services, offered together at a single "bundled" price, and initially available only on a lease basis.

IBM was required to depart from its traditional lease-only policy under the terms of the 1956 consent decree with the U.S. Department of Justice; however, leasing has continued to be the major mode of computer system placement up to the present time. Other firms entering the computer systems market during its first decade tended to follow the pattern established by IBM and Univac, and attempted to develop and market complete computer systems and place them with users primarily under a lease arrangement. As noted above, some of these firms succeeded in establishing a viable base of systems customers; others were unable to do so for a variety of reasons. None of them succeeded in undermining IBM's position as the dominant firm.

By about 1970, the computer systems market had stabilized into something very close to its present configuration, depicted by the pie-chart in fig. 6.1. IBM accounted for well over half of all market activity (however measured); among the small group of other participants, none accounted for as much as 10 percent. An important factor in this stabilization process — particularly in arresting the growth of Honeywell and in convincing GE executives that they would never be able to catch up with the market leader — was the introduction of IBM's System 360 in 1964. Much controversy has surrounded the 360 an nouncement, which took place long before actual product development had been completed and violated a number of IBM's own procedural guidelines. But whether or not the announcement itself constituted a subtle form of "misleading advertising," the eventual success of System 360 marked a highly significant step in the evolution of the computer systems market. The key concept was that of a <u>family</u> of systems, spanning the middle range of computer processing capacities, relying on a single software and operating system base and, most importantly, relying heavily on a common set of peripheral devices.

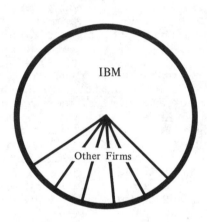

Fig. 6.1. Suppliers in the computer system market, circa 1970.

The success of System 360 served not only to preserve IBM's position of market leadership – in concept and performance, as well as in placements – in the <u>systems</u> market, but also created the possibility of a new set of markets, in which peripheral equipment compatible with the 360 series could be produced and sold by others. Similarly, the pricing of the 360 series created attractive opportunities for third-party leasing. A favorable ratio between lease and purchase prices encouraged independent firms to purchase IBM equipment, usually already in place on lease from the manufacturer itself, and then re-lease it to users on more favorable terms. The third-party leasing companies thus took advantage of IBM's own pricing strategy, which was at that time designed to encourage purchase, and permitted the traditional pattern of user-leasing to be continued, only at lower prices.

A rough analogy with the creation of markets for, say, tires and gasoline as a result of the growth of the automobile industry is not inappropriate. The difference, of course, is that IBM itself had been entirely responsible for both peripherals production and systems leasing until such time as these economic activities became large and attractive enough to attract other market participants.

In any event, as the number and value of IBM 360 installations grew rapidly during the late 1960s, a varied group of smaller firms began offering tape drives, disk drives, supplementary memory units, printers, and other peripheral devices suitable for use in an IBM-system environment. These companies – which included Telex, Memorex, Calcomp, Storage Technology, etc., – were engaged in manufacturing, marketing, leasing, and servicing equipment directly to final users, and at lower cost, and sometimes higher performance levels, than IBM itself. As a result, the IBM segment of the system market took on a new configuration, schematically indicated by the pie-chart in fig. 6.2.

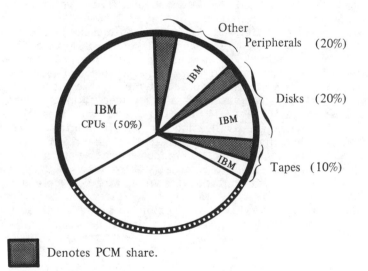

Fig. 6.2. Suppliers of IBM systems and peripherals, circa 1970 (approximate percent of total systems value in parentheses).

Two points should be carefully noted about the PCM development. One is that IBM continued to account for the great majority of installations in each category of equipment (i.e., disks, tapes, etc.) on IBM systems. Second, the PCM development occurred only in connection with IBM installations; it did not involve the installed systems of other manufacturers to any significant extent. PCM activity was limited to IBM installations not primarily for technological reasons, but because the size of the market presented by other installations was simply insufficient to justify other companies adapting themselves to the unique marketing and service requirements of each manufacturer's systems environment. Some of the PCM companies produced equipment to order for other systems manufacturers (referred to as "OEM" operations), but this activity did not require the marketing and maintenance capability, nor the responsibility for leasing arrangements, necessary in the final user market. Control Data, the only firm that operated in all three markets (systems, IBM-PCM, and OEM), maintained separate marketing and service organizations for each of the three phases of its operations, and for one period of time also owned COMMA, an independent organization providing maintenance and service on IBM systems.

If the trends of the late 1960s had continued unabated, there is at least the hypothetical possibility that the computer systems market might have contracted significantly, and that a group of interrelated "boxes and services" markets might have evolved, something along the lines suggested by fig. 6.3. The evolution of such markets would have been stimulated not only by the growth of the PCM companies but also by the independent third-party leasing companies, some of which were assuming increasing initiative in the assembly and placement of "hybrid" computer systems, composed of pieces of equipment produced by several different manufacturers and serviced by independent organizations specializing in that function. There was thus at least some possibility that aggressive leasing companies and other types of market intermediaries might become the critical actors in determining the configuration and placement of computer systems, with a corresponding reduction in the extent of market control exercised by the systems manufacturers. Whether this development was ever more than a remote possibility, and how it might have affected computer systems companies other than IBM, is impossible to say, since these trends were abruptly arrested by changes in IBM's market behavior.

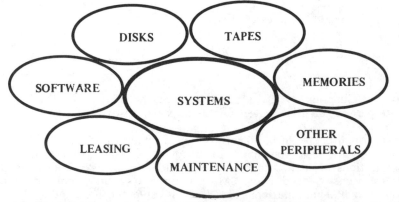

Fig. 6.3. Hypothetical cluster of "boxes and services" markets in the computer industry.

Market Measurement

Turning to the issue of market measurement, the surprising fact is that very little accurate data is publicly available concerning the sales, shipments, products, and services of the computer industry.(11) IBM does not belong to the major industry association, and has routinely refused to cooperate with any sort of industry-wide data gathering activity not required by law or the courts. Most of the basic data to be used in measuring any of the several computer industry markets come therefore from private commercial sources, which depend on the voluntary cooperation of reporting parties and utilize a variety of definition criteria and estimating procedures.

In addition to problems of data availability and inconsistency, there has been considerable debate as to the appropriate means of measuring market occupancy − current shipments, the conventional measure in most industries, or installed base. The latter has been the primary measure with respect to computer systems since the 1950s, and is the basis for IBM's own internal market information system, COMSTAT. Use of the installed base as the conventional measure of market occupancy appears to have developed quite naturally because of this historic emphasis on lease placements rather than purchase. Relative shares of the installed base correspond roughly to shares of lease revenues, and convert both lease and purchase placements to a common denominator. However, the installed base measure has much more to recommend it than convenience, since the installed base is in a sense the "ultimate scarce resource" − analogous to an advantageous geographic location or rare mineral deposit − and thus constitutes the foundation of a firm's position in the computer systems market.(12) The installed base of each systems supplier provides the environment for its successive product enhancements and, in the course of time, for entire system replacements. The great importance of software, personnel, and user procedures and practices in effective computer utilization creates very substantial barriers against the easy shift from one systems supplier to another, and the rate of repeat-customers among all systems suppliers has been in the 90 percent range for many years. The installed base measure thus both reflects past market activity and is an important determinant of future activity as well.

In addition, the relative stability of the installed base strengthens its value as an indicator of long-term market position. The computer industry has been characterized by a series of technological cycles (the successive "generations" frequently mentioned in the industry literature), and different firms have participated in these at different times, resulting in sharply divergent patterns of short-term activity (peak shipments of new equipment from one firm coinciding with either early development or late-period stability in another) that have little to do with long-run patterns. Finally, the installed base measure is by definition "net"; new shipments directly matched by returns do not show up as any net change in the firm's market occupancy. Changes in the installed base over time are, of course, directly analogous to current net shipments figures, and shares in this total should in principle reflect short-run market developments. Unfortunately, the data gathering and estimation procedures of the various private parties generating installed base statistics do not produce very reliable estimates or period-to-period net changes and shares therein.

In any event, inspection and cross-comparison of the various available collections of data concerning market occupancy within the computer industry yield, unsurprisingly, a uniform impression of IBM's continuing dominant position. IBM's share of the value of all installed commercial computer systems has been in the 70 percent range since around 1960, according to most sources, including IBM's own internal data. IBM's share of the net additions to the installed base over the period 1964-75 was approximately 69 percent.   PCM equipment amounted to about 10 percent of IBM systems value by the mid-1970s; and thus IBM's own sales or lease responsibiity for systems placements was slightly over 60 percent in recent years.

Somewhat lower estimates of IBM's position are obtained from an analysis of U.S. Census data for SIC Industry 3573-Electronic Computing Equipment.   The universe involved here is larger than the computer system market alone, but assuming that IBM is the largest firm in the census industry, a "maximum IBM share" of census-industry activity may be estimated on two different bases. The results show an estimated 53 percent maximum share in 1967, declining to 42 percent in 1972, when the calculation is made on an "industry value added" basis; and 61 percent in 1967, declining to 53 percent in 1972, when calculated on a "product shipments" basis. Neither the actual data reported to the census by IBM, nor the basis for its internal preparation, have ever been publicly revealed.

IBM shares of the number or value of specific types of peripheral equipment in use on IBM systems are subject to considerable estimating errors; moreover, PCM shares wil necessarily be higher in terms of numbers of units than in terms of value, since PCM equipment is cheaper per unit. The best available estimates indicate that IBM's share of tape sub-systems attached to IBM systems declined (from an initial 100 percent) to about 90 percent by value by 1971 and to about 75 percent by 1977; tape units account for less than 10 percent of total systems value. With respect to disk sub-systems, which account for nearly 20 percent of total systems value, IBM's share declined to about 85 percent by 1971 and 80 percent by 1977.(13) As noted above, the total value of non-IBM devices attached to IBM systems has amounted to about 10 percent of total systems value in recent years. In short, IBM has continued to account for the great majority of all equipment installations and revenues arising from the use of IBM systems throughout the period.

Power and Profit

Given IBM's measured market occupancy, its universal popular recognition and the ubiquity of its products, the presence of some degree of market power may be almost too readily assumed. However, the special character of IBM's market position is clearly reflected in its long-term record of profitability.   Unusually high profits may, of course, be earned by market innovators for short periods, and by firms peculiarly well-situated with respect to production technology, scarce resources, or even efficient management over the long-term. However, persistent high profits and high market share, particularly in a rapidly growing market, strongly suggest that the firm enjoys a significant and enduring advantage over its rivals, hence an insulation from competitive pressures, and, in short, market power.

The record of IBM in this respect is, like the record of market occupancy, overwhelmingly clear. No other firm of its size – either in the economy or in the context of a relevant industry or market – presents a comparable record of profitabiity over two decades. Table 6.1 compares the long-term profit record of IBM with that of all manufacturing corporations as reported by the Federal Trade Commission. IBM's rate of return on equity is from 50 percent to 100 percent higher than the national average in almost every year and in any significant period of years grouped together. The rate of return on sales is between two and three times the average for all manufacturing companies, and the computer industry is not highly capital-intensive. Table 6.2 compares IBM's profit experience with that of other major computer systems companies and three selected groups of other companies for the five-year period of greatest interest in connection with the challenged acts to be discussed below. (COMPUSTAT groups 3570 and 3573 contain the principal computer and office equipment companies.) Once again, IBM's record of profitability is substantially higher than any standard of comparison suggested by these data.

It has sometimes been suggested that IBM's extraordinary profit record might be due to some combination of natural advantage (e.g., long-term market participation, as reflected in the installed base) and genuine economies of scale, rather than to "monopoly power" in the strict sense (i.e., ability to raise price above marginal cost). Certainly the installed base is an advantage, although its "naturalness" is a matter of debate, and IBM may possess other genuine advantages in personnel and management as well. In addition, there are undoubtedly various sources of scale economies scattered throughout the complex of computer production and marketing activities. However, there is no substantial evidence that any of the surviving systems companies is not large enough to achieve the greater part of any such economies that may be available. Furthermore, some of the existing sources of economies arise from the systems concept itself and the unique association of each system's characteristics with a single manufacturer. If greater standardization of hardware and functional characteristics took place, so that greater flexibility in both product substitution and service-marketing activity were possible (as in the automobile industry, for example), then even lower costs might be achieved throughout the industry without the necessity of efficient minimum scale levels in company-specialized operations. In any event, IBM's system prices have typically been from 10 to 30 percent above those of other systems manufacturers for comparable equipment, and this fact combined with the profit results strongly suggests that the effects of market power – rather than natural advantage and scale economies – are being observed.(14)

Table 6.1. Profitability Ratios, IBM and All U.S.
Manufacturing Corporations – 1956-77

	Profit After Tax % Revenues		Profit After Tax % Equity	
Year	All Mfg. Corp. (a)	IBM(b)	All Mfg. Corp. (a)	IBM(b)
1956	5.3	9.8	12.3	20.7
1957	4.8	9.2	10.9	14.3
1958	4.2	10.7	8.6	17.5
1959	4.8	10.8	10.4	17.3
1960	4.4	11.2	9.2	17.3
1961	4.3	11.5	8.9	17.5
1962	4.5	11.7	9.8	17.5
1963	4.7	12.6	10.3	18.2
1964	5.2	13.3	11.6	19.1
1965	5.6	13.3	13.0	18.5
1966	5.6	12.4	13.4	15.8
1967	5.0	12.2	11.7	17.0
1968	5.1	12.7	12.1	19.1
1969	4.8	13.0	11.5	17.7
1970	4.0	13.6	9.3	17.1
1971	4.1	13.0	9.7	16.2
1972	4.3	13.4	10.6	16.9
1973	4.7	14.3	12.8	17.9
1974	5.5	14.5	14.9	18.2
1975	4.6	13.8	11.6	17.4
1976	5.4	14.7	13.9	18.8
1977	5.3	15.0	14.2	21.5

Source: (a) Economic Report of President, 1979 (Table B-83, p. 280); New Series, 1974-77.

(b) IBM Annual Reports & 10-K's: 1956-63 domestic only; 1964-73 worldwide.

Table 6.2. Selected Profitability Ratios (1969-1973)

	Pre-Tax Return on Revenue (%)	Pre-Tax Return on Equity (%)	After Tax Return on Equity (%)
IBM	25.72	33.34	17.19
-- Other Major Computer Systems Manufacturing Companies:			
Burroughs	14.91	21.53	11.69
Control Data	6.30	6.21	5.61
Digital Equipment	14.85	19.94	11.87
Honeywell	7.08	19.27	9.85
NCR	2.32	5.87	2.92
Sperry Rand	7.75	18.99	9.99
Above 6 Companies	7.43	14.93	8.34
-- All Companies in COMPUSTAT Groups 3570 and 3573, Excluding IBM (60)*	9.43	19.54	9.73
-- All Manufacturing Companies with Net Sales of $1 Billion or More (175)*	10.51	22.79	12.12
-- All Manufacturing Companies (1851)*	9.78	21.88	11.70

Source: Standard & Poor's Compustat Services, Inc.

*Number of companies in each category, 1973.

93

An indication of market power fully as significant as profitability but ordinarily very difficult to document is the ability of a firm to direct the pattern of development within its industry to further its own best interests. Such exercises of market leadership are ordinarily conducted through product innovation and sales promotion. There are other dimensions of market leadership however, as the following example concerning the development of formal technological standards indicates.

Throughout the history of the computer industry the issue of technological standardization — languages, data encryption, equipment interface, even basic terminology — has been a source of controversy. On one hand, it has been argued that formal standardization by industry and/or government action is undesirable because it limits creativity, and unnecessary because each major innovation becomes a de facto standard in any event. On the other hand, standards advocates contend that adoption of basic guidelines provides a basis for innovative adaptation and development and, in particular, that competitive opportunities are opened up by any uniform standard system that widens the range of product substitution. A 1978 report of the General Accounting Office contains a detailed account of federal government efforts to establish standards in the computer industry. Carrying the subtitle "Many Potential Benefits, Little Progress and Many Problems," the report cites some deficiencies in standards development and enforcement on the part of federal agencies, but places primary emphasis on the lack of cooperation, and even direct opposition, of some computer manufacturers. Particularly cited is the fact that "From 1967 to the early 1970s, some of the computer manufacturers were influential in frustrating and eventually ending an effort to develop an interface standard being considered internationally."(15) An appendix documenting this experience in detail quotes from an IBM internal memo, but with the company name deleted, the following summary of its "philosophy":

--   It is to a users advantage to have an I/O interface standard of some sort.

--   It is to [IBM's] advantage to have an internal standard I/O interface.

--   It is not to [IBM's] advantage to have an external I/O interface standard.(16)

The "IBM Confidential" document from which this quotation was extracted contained highlights from an "I/O Interface Standardization Briefing Meeting" held in Paris, October 28-30, 1969, and attended by an international group of IBM executives. The document itself continues:

[I]t can be concluded that IBM should not be in the position of encouraging any external I/O interface standardization. Our first and overriding objective is to see that no external standard is adopted.(17)

The first federal standards in this area were adopted over industry opposition in February, 1979.(18)

THE CHALLENGED ACTS

We come now to the heart of our story, the group of market actions that have been challenged by impacted parties, public agencies, and outside analysts as constituting "predatory" market behavior, "monopolization," and/or "attempts to monopolize." Again, it should be emphasized that our concern is not with the validity of these charges as matters of law, but rather with their substance as matters of market analysis. Our interest is to determine whether these acts constitute socially desirable or undesirable market behavior, and therefore to establish norms for public policy, which may or may not conform to current statutes and their interpretation.

The acts themselves, of course, must be seen not only in the context of the dominant market position described in the previous section, but in the context of each other. A sequence of acts, taken together, may constitute a course of conduct that has both meaning and impact far beyond their individual importance. This point, at least, has been explicitly affirmed as a matter of law:

> [T]he Court of Appeals approached Continental's claims as if they were five completely separate and unrelated lawsuits. We think this was improper. In cases such as this, plaintiffs should be given the full benefit of their proof without tightly compartmentalizing the various factual components and wiping the slate clean after scrutiny of each. . . . [I]n a case like the one before us, the duty of the jury was to look at the whole picture and not merely to be individual figures in it.(19)

The challenged acts were principally of two types: product modifications and price changes. The product modifications generally involved price changes as well, and indeed were means of effecting selective price changes without disturbing regular prices for established products. Two price changes unrelated to product modifications are also of importance: (1) The Fixed Term Plan (FTP) announced in May, 1971; (2) The change in lease/purchase price ratios begun in 1968 and carried through in the introduction of the 370 Series in 1970 and thereafter. The exclusionary impact of FTP and subsequent long-term lease plans has also been emphasized by some litigants.

The unity of the peripheral equipment pricing and product actions as a single course of conduct can best be observed in a brief chronological summary (see table 6.3). Internal IBM memoranda reveal that the potential problem posed by the appearance of PCM competitors was recognized as early as 1967. Technological superiority of some of the PCM devices was noted, as well as their price advantages; a periodic series of "Satisfaction Surveys" subsequently revealed that users generally considered PCM equipment equal or superior to that of IBM. A series of product improvement options were presented to top management during 1968, but none of these were adopted. The steady increase in PCM placements was carefully monitored, and in late 1969 the PCM development was officially designated a "Key Corporate Strategic Issue" (KCSI), with the objective of identifying actions that would inhibit sales of PCM equipment and damage "competitor's marketing/financial position."

Table 6.3. Chronology of IBM's Challenged Acts
Involving PCM Competition

Date	Product Actions	Pricing Actions
1970		
September	2319A (Mallard) disk subsystem	Price reduction up to one-half compared to comparable equipment
November	3420 (Aspen) and Mandan tape Subsystems	Price reductions up to one-third compared to comparable equipment
December	2319B/A2 disk subsystem	(1) Price reductions same as 2319A; (2) Eliminate additional use charge on all disks
1971		
May		Fixed Term Plan
1972		
August	SMASH Announcement	

Perhaps the earliest formal reaction was a change in IBM policy with respect to the disclosure of interface information on new products. The traditional policy had been to disclose such information at the time of product announcement, or shortly thereafter. In 1970, a decision was made to provide such disclosures only at the time of first customer shipment, which might be from a few months to a year after the announcement date. The availability of this information was, of course, critical to the PCM companies, since their products necessarily required modification to take account of changes in the IBM-systems environment.

A task force formed to study the PCM issue and make specific recommendations initiated a number of activities that proved to have long-term consequences. A series of intensive studies of several PCM companies, particularly Memorex and Telex, were undertaken. These studies stressed financial requirements, cash flow, and price-cost relationships rather than technological matters. The notion of product modifications (with or without price changes) designed to inhibit the attachment of non-IBM equipment to IBM systems surfaced in various forms in the task force's deliberations. The task force also considered the possibility of a long-term lease plan including price discounts. The 1956 Consent Decree had restricted introduction of long-term leases for a ten-year period, and periodic consideration since 1966 had always led to the conclusion that such schemes would be too costly in terms of foregone revenue. The task force affirmed this conclusion, and apparently believed that such a scheme could not be limited to peripheral equipment only.

A number of specific disk and tape drive modifications and selective price reductions, to be discussed in detail below, grew out of the work of the task force. However, it was apparent that these actions alone would not eliminate the PCMs, and a subsequent "Blue Ribbon Task Force" was appointed in early 1971. After much internal wrangling, this group presented the eventual proposal for the Fixed Term Plan, which became effective June 1, 1971.

FTP, subsequently followed by the "Extended Term Plan (ETP) and other long-term leasing schemes that have now become standard IBM marketing procedures, marked the culmination of the entire series of IBM actions with respect to pricing. Similarly, the "SMASH announcement" of August 1972, which set forth a "new attachment strategy" such that most peripheral devices would be directly attached to the central processing unit (CPU) in a manner designed to impede their replacement by equipment from other sources, marked the culmination of the product-modification aspect of the entire course of conduct. We now turn to a brief description of each of these acts.

Product and Pricing Actions: Disk Drives

On the System 360 and the early models of System 370, peripheral devices were attached to the CPU through an intermediate device called a "control unit." Prior to the designation of peripherals competition as a "KCSI," a plan had already evolved to integrate the control unit function directly into the forthcoming intermediate-sized 370 CPU models, the 370/145 and 370/135.

The configuration eventually adopted — code-named "Mallard" — involved the separation of the control unit into two segments, one of which would be placed under the covers of the CPU itself, the other in a drive box along with three drives. With this configuration, PCM control units could not be attached to the CPU; and, as one internal memorandum stated, "IBM will at least be assured of the first three drives." The Mallard strategy – formerly designated as the 2319A – for System 370/145 was announced in September, 1970, with both systems and drives intended to become available in 1971.

Although the 2319A configuration was officially designated as "optional" on the new systems models, it was priced so as to become the standard arrangement. Monthly rental was $1555 per month, as compared to $2875 per month for a comparable 2314-type installation with three drives. The effective price-per-drive for the 2319A (setting aside the value of the control unit function) was $333 per month, as compared to $535 per month for the 2314-type device in the one-spindle configuration, $460 in the two-spindle box, and $436 in the four-spindle unit. Since this price sequence would suggest a price somewhere between $436 and $460 per spindle for a three-spindle configuration, or an overall revision of the entire price sequence if basic cost changes are involved, the departure from the established pricing pattern is striking. All users not migrating to 370/145 systems continued to pay the established rates on their 2314-type devices; thus, given the functional identity of the drives themselves – an element of overt price discrimination was clearly involved.(20) (It has been estimated that an across-the-board reduction of the same magnitude would have cost IBM $5 million per month in revenues.)

In December, 1970, the 2319A price reductions were extended by the announcement of additional variations, including the 2319B subsystem which consisted of a separate control unit (essentially the old 2314 control unit, with some interface changes but no change in price) and a three-drive box with appropriately modified electronics and interface and a $333 per spindle price. The 2319B subsystem was attachable to all 360 and 370 systems, and thus could effectively replace both the existing inventory of IBM's own 2314-type devices as well as compete with similar products of the PCM companies. The December, 1970, announcement also contained a significant price reduction unrelated to product modifications. IBM equipment leases conventionally levied an additional charge for usage in excess of 176 hours per month.

Revenues from such charges amounted, on the average, to an additional 12 percent over the monthly rental price. In this announce-ment, all such additional charges were eliminated on the 2319A and 2319B subsystems, and on the old 2314-type inventory and newly-announced 3330 disk drives as well. All of these price changes became effective immediately, but the modified products were not themselves available. Thus, users encountered both delays (during which they continued to pay the old 2314 prices) and the cost and inconvenience of removing 2314 subsystems and returning them for replacement. Never-theless, the PCM companies had to respond immediately, since the newly-announced prices became the effective reference figures for user decision-making.

Extensive debate and voluminous documentation has been generated over the question of whether or not the 2319A/B price reductions were in any sense "below cost." Although in my own view the competitive impact of these product/price changes does not depend in any significant way on their relationships to costs, the analytical problems raised by this question are not without interest.(21) The costs involved are, of course, IBM's own costs of production and marketing for the entire 2319A/B product line, and these cannot be reduced to a unit-cost basis in any meaningful way. The relevant comparison thus involves <u>program</u> costs and revenues – i.e., the aggregate cost and revenue associated with the entire product group, over its economic life – and, since ex ante decision-making is involved, both costs and revenues must be considered in anticipated, rather than actual, terms.

In addition to the problems inherent in any such forecasting task – and in the appraisal of forecasts ex post and by outside parties – two critical cost issues arise: one is the appropriate treatment of indirect costs; the other the analytical relevance of inter-product production and profit relationships. IBM conventionally allocates most indirect costs among its products by the "revenue apportionment" method. According to this procedure, the aggregate of all indirect costs is allocated among products in the same proportion that each product's revenue bears to total revenue. Following this method of allocation, if a product's price is reduced and total physical production and sales volume remain unchanged, total revenue will fall by the same percent as the price reduction, and allocated indirect costs will also be reduced by the same percent, even though actual cost-generating activities are in no way altered. Such a method of cost allocation is, of course, absurd from an economic perspective; and it is in fact still in use by only a declining minority of firms. Therefore, in some of the analyses of IBM's pricing undertaken in the course of litigation, plaintiff experts have adjusted IBM's reported cost data to reflect the same levels of allocated cost per unit of output that would have prevailed if no price change had occurred – that is, to estimate long-run marginal and average cost on the assumption that the initial indirect cost allocation was in some sense "correct."

The second cost consideration reflects the effect of cross-elasticity of demand among related products, and is referred to in the IBM Financial Procedure Manual as "Impact." Product and price changes generating additional sales of other products and services (i.e., complementarity) would be said to have positive impact; substitution effects, of course, result in negative impact. Conventional IBM financial analysis includes an estimate of the cost, revenue and profit results of a particular decision both before and after impact. From an economic perspective, of course, impact is a relevant consideration (cost or profit) for decision-making purposes. Nevertheless, the introduction of impact adds yet another estimation factor into the "below cost pricing" analysis.(22)

IBM's overall planned price-cost structure can be roughly described as follows:

Revenue	100%
Direct Costs	30
Indirect costs (revenue-apportioned)	40
Profit margin	30

Within this structure, and adhering to the revenue-apportionment method of cost allocation and disregarding impact, a price reduction of more than 50 percent is required to generate a "below cost" result (as compared to a 30 percent reduction if indirect costs held constant in dollar terms). With this much room to play in, it was inevitable that none of IBM's selective price reductions would be shown to be "below cost" according to its calculations. By contrast, when indirect costs are held at pre-price reduction levels and IBM's own impact analyses are taken into account, the Mallard program shows a projected loss of 27 percent of anticipated revenue, and the 2319B program a loss of 5 percent.(23) Neither of these estimates takes account of the elimination of the additional use charge.

Product and Pricing Actions: Tape Drives

IBM's actions with respect to disk drives were closely paralleled by product and price changes with respect to tape drives, although the technology involved was somewhat newer. The original System 360 tape drive, the 2401, had been the initial target of PCM competition in the mid-60s, and in 1968 IBM introduced an improved drive, the 2420. Although originally intended for use on both System 360 and 370, the 2420 also encountered rapid competition from the PCMs, and plans for a modified version were developed. The result was code-named "Aspen" (formally the 3420) and involved a genuine improvement of the tape control unit so that individual drives attached radially rather than serially. Interface changes were, however, also made so that existing 2401 and 2420-type drives, whether IBM or PCM, could not be attached. Monthly rental for a seven-track subsystem was reduced from $1020 for the 2420 to $670 for Aspen, or about one-third. An additional price-cut for 2401-type tape drives used on smaller systems was made possible by actual re-use of returned equipment in a product code-named "Mandan," which was modified to reduce performance flexibility. Once again, neither of these products appears to have been priced below short-run direct cost, but when both pre-price reduction indirect cost allocations and impact are taken into account, Aspen shows a projected overall loss of 5.8 percent, and Mandan of 16.7 percent, of anticipated revenue.

The Aspen analysis also provides direct evidence of the trade-off between profitability and market share made by IBM executives in the course of these decisions. Just prior to announcement, a number of high-profit strategies for Aspen were rejected outright, and the final choice made among the following:

Aspen Price	Aspen Overall/Program Profit	Estimated PCM Percent Installed Tapes
High	$805 million	30%
Medium	778 million	21
Low	753 million	18

The "Medium" alternative was chosen, for a net reduction of $27 million in overall program profit, but a gain of 9 percent in market share.

Pricing Actions: FTP

As noted above, the possibility that a long-term leasing plan might be adopted had been considered by IBM management off and on ever since the expiration of the ten-year prohibition on such policies established by the 1956 Consent Decree. Long-term lease proposals were repeatedly put forward within IBM as a possible strategic response to both PCM competition and the growth of leasing companies, but were repeatedly rejected as costly (in terms of lost revenues), discouraging to user migration to more powerful and expensive systems, and possibly illegal. The PCM companies, by contrast, offered fixed-term leases from the beginning, and some of them did not place equipment at all for periods less than one year, although all such arrangements were, in fact, cancellable without penalty. Third-party leasing companies also offered term leases under various price arrangements. Neither PCM companies nor third-party leasors levied an additional use charge on their customers, a fact that increased the true IBM-PCM price differential to 20-25 percent.

Once it appeared that the selective price reductions and product modifications described above would not in themselves halt PCM activity, across-the-board pricing actions began to receive intensive consideration. Although it was strongly argued by some executives that long-term lease plans could not legitimately be limited to peripheral products, and certainly not to selected peripheral products on which continued PCM competition was anticipated, the eventual FTP announcement of May 27, 1971, offered lower monthly rental prices only for tape drives, disk drives, and printers, and there were some exceptions even within these product groups. Regular monthly list prices were discounted by 8 percent for a one-year lease and 16 percent for two years, with severe penalties for cancellation. Additional use charges were eliminated for all products leased under FTP, and maintenance charges on new installations of these products were also reduced. At the same time, purchase price reductions of 15 percent were announced for all of these products. Salesmen's compensation for FTP placements continued, however, to be based on standard monthly rental charges.

It is a curious fact that the specific discount terms offered — 8 and 16 percent — never seem to have been made the subject of detailed financial analysis within IBM; at least, no record of such an analysis has come to light after a decade of document discovery. The final result appears to have been reached as a negotiated compromise between marketing executives, who favored a larger discount, and the legal department, which apparently favored a smaller discount, or none at all. In any event, FTP with 8 to 16 percent price reductions, and the elimination of traditional additional use charges, was announced effective June 1, 1971.

Customer response to FTP was greater than anticipated, with strongly favorable results in terms of market share, but powerful effects upon profits. The product forecasts and financial analysis used to justify the FTP decision assumed that PCM's would obtain up to 100 percent market shares of the relevant peripheral devices by 1975. This assumption was preposterous on a number of grounds, including the fact that it would have required PCM manufacturers to more than double their levels of annual output each year throughout the period covered by the forecast. Nevertheless, as compared to the forecasted revenue for the five-year period (declining as the PCM's gained larger market shares), the FTP proposal was projected to result in a revenue increase of $714 million. By contrast, a subsequent analysis showed that FTP had reduced profit by $102 million in 1972, and projected a total profit reduction of $671 million through 1976, as compared to previous long-run operating plans prepared without regard to any consideration of FTP. After the seriousness of these revenue reductions begin to sink in, IBM announced increases in the prices of CPUs and memories of 4 and 8 percent, with some maintenance charges increased up to 25 percent. Implementation of these increases was delayed by the August 15, 1971 nationwide price-freeze, but they were eventually permitted to go into effect in January, 1972. An internal document estimated that the overall result of the price increases and decreases would be "a wash" as far as total systems revenues were concerned. IBM cost analysts emphasized that these increases could not be justified on the basis of increases in product costs, since no such increases had in fact occurred. The eventual justification to the Price Commission referred to "increased cost of doing business." Why such costs, if they existed, would be peculiarly associated with CPUs and memories, and not with the peripheral devices on which prices had just been reduced, has never been explained.

Although extremely costly, FTP was highly successful in accomplishing its primary objective — halting the erosion of the peripheral lease-base by the PCMs. FTP was never expected to result in any actual increase in IBM's market share over time. Its purpose was simply to stabilize the situation until new products then in the development stage would become available. In order to lock-in customers for these new products in the same fashion made possible by FTP, a new scheme known as the extended term plan (ETP) was announced in 1972. No initial one-year leases were permitted under ETP, and no apparent price discounts were involved; the lease/purchase ratios for new products under ETP were substantially the same as those that had prevailed before the FTP announcement. Customers preferring the earlier type of 30-day leases were required to pay a 17.5 percentage rental premium.

Pricing Actions: Lease/Purchase Ratios

Third-party leasing companies began to appear in the computer industry shortly after IBM was required to offer equipment for purchase as well as lease, and on comparable terms, by the 1956 Consent Decree. Their growth was encouraged by the fact that IBM offered customers an annual "technological discount" on the purchase of already installed equipment, up to a maximum of 70 percent of the original price. In October, 1965, following the introduction of System 360, this discount structure was eliminated, and a maximum discount of 12 percent from the original price, available after one year of lease, was allowed. However, just one year later, in September, 1966, the need for increased cash flow to finance the rapid expansion of 360 production stimulated IBM to alter the lease/purchase ratio in favor of purchase. This change, together with the rapid growth of 360 placements and their anticipated long economic life, greatly stimulated leasing company activity, and by 1967 these firms accounted for more than 10 percent of the total value of IBM systems in use.

Up to this point, third-party lessors had apparently been viewed by IBM management as rather inconsequential, and essentially benign, participants in the computer industry, and as customers rather than competitors. However, concern over the growth and increasing influence of these organizations lead to their careful consideration at an IBM management conference in Bermuda in September, 1967. The conclusion was reached that leasing companies should be considered competitors and threats to IBM's control over its own installed base; their continued growth was therefore to be discouraged.

A number of internal policies, including some changes in salesmen's compensation and responsibilities when installations were transferred to leasing company ownership, were considered and some of these were actually adopted. However, the key to leasing company operations was the ratio between purchase and lease prices in relation to the useful life of IBM equipment. The ratio of the monthly lease charge to the purchase price (referred to as the "multiplier") determines the "break-even" life of an installation. If, in fact, the installation will remain in use for a longer period, then it will pay users to purchase their own equipment or, alternatively, third-parties to purchase equipment and lease it to users on more favorable terms than those offered by IBM. IBM's pricing of System 360 encouraged leasing companies to expand rapidly; however, it was obvious from the beginning that any increase in the lease/purchase "multiplier" would seriously impact leasing company operations.

Lease/purchase multipliers on the System 360 were in the low 40s after the 1966 pricing action.(24) After the Bermuda conference, two new System 360 models – the 360/25 and 360/85 – were announced with multipliers above 50, and multipliers around 50 were substantially announced for System 370 units.

These changes, and their obvious implication that IBM did not intend to permit the continued growth of third-party leasors, drastically impacted both the current operations and the capital access and long-term prospects of these companies. Many of them went bankrupt; three brought legal actions against IBM (one settled with financial concessions, one is awaiting re-trial after a directed verdict in favor of IBM was overturned, and one is pending); and third-party leasing activity as it had existed during the 1960s was essentially terminated. In its place, a new leasing industry – based on long-term and/or full pay-out leases, and financed primarily by large financial institutions (Bank of America) and the financial arms of major corporations (GE Credit) – has come into being. Third-party leasing in this latter form remains an important function in the computer industry and, in fact, accounts for about 25 percent total installed value, the highest level in history. However, the possibility that third-party leasors might constitute an independent competitive force – actually competing with the manufacturer in the financing and remarketing of systems, and potentially in the assembly of system elements from diverse sources so as to constitute a kind of wholesaling or market-making intermediary – has apparently disappeared.(25)

The SMASH Announcement

Just as the announcement of FTP was the grand finale of the wave of pricing actions, so the SMASH announcement of August, 1972 marked the general adoption of the product modification strategies initiated with Mallard and Aspen. SMASH included a number of different product actions, all with the effect of limiting the ability of customers to use PCM products and specifically focused on replacement memory products for which independent competition only began in earnest in 1971. Two new, large CPUs were announced, the 370/158 and 370/168, with substantial memory units price-bundled to the CPU and therefore protected from competitive exposure. By comparison with previous systems, CPU prices were increased and memory prices reduced in those announcements. These and other product modifications affecting the 370 Systems also had significant effect on systems already purchased and in place by third-party leasing companies. In addition, the so-called "New Attachment Strategy" involved an extension of the original Mallard concept to the newer 3330 and subsequent disk drives. As with Mallard, a portion of the disk control unit was moved to a location under the covers of the CPU, the interface was altered to make attachment of non-IBM products more difficult, and price adjustments were made which encouraged customer choice of the new configuration.

APPRAISAL AND CONCLUSION

Now that the course of conduct of IBM with respect to the PCMs and the leasing companies has been summarized, a final appraisal must be made. Did this course of conduct constitute "predatory marketing," an "attempt to monopolize," and, to the extent it was successful, "monopolization," as critics have claimed, or simply aggressive competition as IBM has insisted? The answer depends both on the fundamental position of IBM in its markets and on the kind of competitive challenge presented by the smaller firms.

With respect to the third-party leasing companies, the answer seems to be that they were brought into being entirely by IBM's own pricing policies, and their continued existence and profitability was necessarily dependent upon those policies. Their role in the marketing system of the industry might be best described as suppliers of a resource (risk-lease capital) used in connection with IBM products by final users. Although they might have evolved to perform independent marketing functions, they had not in fact done so to any significant extent before the fundamental economics of their operations was altered by IBM actions. In fact, because of their basic dependence on IBM as a source of supply for the systems to be placed under lease, they were never in a position to generate independent competitive pressures, although they certainly deprived IBM of lease revenues (at the same time generating purchase revenues) for those installations that they took over. The conclusion is that the third-party leasing companies were customers and marketing intermediaries for IBM, not substantial competitors, and that their elimination from the market did not alter the character of competition within it in any significant way.

The significance of the leasing company acts is their indication of IBM's basic strategic policy of customer control, and its willingness to vary pricing policies without regard either to cost factors or legal requirements in order to achieve strategic goals. Recalling the "reasonableness" requirement of the 1956 Consent Decree with respect to lease purchase price relationships, one cannot help but wonder in what sense all the different lease/purchase multipliers adopted in the course of these actions would pass a "reasonableness" test. Indeed, if multipliers varying over nearly 20 months (from the low 40s to the high 50s) on the same types of equipment within a relatively short time period are all "reasonable," then it appears that lease/purchase price relationships are in no way constrained by the "reasonableness" requirement.

The situation with respect to the PCM companies is fundamentally different. They appeared in the market because of the large and growing demand for equipment to be used in conjunction with IBM systems, and their relationship to IBM was essentially that of the tire companies to General Motors.(26) Unlike the leasing companies, the PCM's were in no way customers for IBM products. They offered direct competition to IBM with respect to their own products, and potential competition through the development of additional products and even entire systems. They also threatened the basic systems-orientation of the industry, although an evolution away from systems and toward separate box-and-services markets would have come slowly, if at all.

IBM internal documents exhibit an extraordinary schizophrenia with respect to the PCM "threat." On one hand, it was difficult to believe that these insignificant-size firms could constitute a serious challenge to mighty IBM which had, after all, so intimidated a powerful firm like GE that it abandoned a multi-million dollar investment and a multi-billion dollar revenue growth potential in the computer industry. Asked in 1978 whether or not he believed in 1970-71 that the PCMs repre-sented a serious threat to IBM's growth, Thomas J. Watson, Jr., then chief executive officer of the company, replied:

> No, is the answer. They were one of many things that we were thinking about . . . A matter of concern . . . along with many other matters of concern . . . I never thought that there was any vague possibility that this segment of the competitive world could possibly bring IBM's growth to a standstill.(27)

On the other hand, the plain fact was that the PCMs were growing rapidly, that their products were superior to IBM's in certain respects, and that their mere presence constituted evidence both that IBM's prices were extraordinarily high – else how could these companies not merely exist but thrive at prices substantially lower than IBM for virtually identical products? – and, furthermore, that the "systems concept" around which the entire computer industry had become organized and which had provided the basis for IBM's long-term market position was not the only, and perhaps not the most desirable, way in which this sphere of economic activity could be organized.

All of these latter considerations suggest that the PCMs were perhaps somewhat more significant than their limited sizes and market positions indicate.   Nevertheless, given the vastly different initial position of IBM and the continuing growth in the market – including other dynamic developments, such as the minicomputer explosion, in which none of these firms (including IBM) was at that time a significant participant – it seems hard to believe that any one of these firms would ever have become of any greater importance in the entire industry than say, Digital Equipment is today. Certainly, the notion that these organizations constituted some sort of ultimate strategic threat to IBM's long-term growth and profitability is, as Mr. Watson perceived, absurd.

Under these circumstances, how is IBM's strategic response in the form of sharply-targeted product and pricing actions to be assessed? A certain amount of organizational paranoia was clearly involved. Perusal of the minutes of the Management Review Committee – IBM's top decision-making body at the time – during 1969, 1970, and 1971 suggests an organization approaching a state of hysteria. At times the meetings occurred almost daily, and it is apparent that subordinates were being pressed into 24-hour duty to prepare the reports, analyses, and proposals required for consideration at each successive session. A weekly status report on PCM activity was initiated; and the detail with which specific price and product decisions were considered by the top management group would astonish analysts who imagine such bodies to be concerned with "long-range policy making" alone. One is tempted to observe that it might have been better for all concerned — IBM, its competitors, and its customers — if there had been less top management involvement in the entire process, since it appears that lower levels of the organization would have responded sooner, more flexibly, and probably less drastically if allowed to do so. In particular, top management resisted the price reductions so long that, when they came, they took on the character of a blitzkrieg.

Nevertheless, the fact remains that top management did assume responsibility for the entire set of strategic decisions, and that their overall pattern constituted a course of conduct that has become the focus of considerable public policy debate. What evaluation shall we make of it all? Does this set of product and pricing actions, undertaken by a firm with a long-established position of market dominance and with the clear intention of curtailing the growth, and perhaps even the existence, of new and relatively small market entrants, constitute a socially-undesirable pattern of behavior deserving to be characterized as "predatory marketing," or is it merely an example of aggressive competition, perhaps unfortunate in its impact on certain fledgling organizations but ultimately at least tolerable, if not actually desirable, from the viewpoint of society at large?

Surprisingly enough, IBM itself has provided a very clear answer to these questions. A few years after the 1956 Consent Decree, IBM issued a set of "Antitrust Guidelines" for the instruction of its executives, and these have been periodically updated, with varying titles, up to the present time. The 1968 version, which was current at the time of most of the challenged acts, contains a foreword by Burke Marshall, then IBM General Counsel; an introductory statement by Watson; and reproduces the 1956 Consent Decree and subsequent Final Order as an appendix. This document was supposed to be required annual reading by IBM executives.

In his introductory statement (actually the text of an address presented to top management in 1961), Watson suggests the following test with respect to practices which, although not necessarily illegal in themselves, "would add fuel to the antitrust fires":

> Turn the situation around. Suppose that you were a competitor — small, precariously financed, without a large support organization, and without a big reputation in the field — but with a good product. How would you feel if the big IBM Company took the actions . . . ? Would you consider that the IBM Company was using a sales tactic which IBM possessed solely because of its size and reputation, and which therefore, was unavailable to you? . . . We cannot simply shoulder people around, or give the appearance of doing so.(28)

Further into the text of the document, a more specific example is offered:

In order to prove that a company has monopolized, it must be shown that it (a) possesses the power in a particular market to set prices or foreclose entry to competitors, and (b) has achieved or retained that power by illegal or exclusionary practices.

EXAMPLE: Company X has 80% of the electronic widget market. Its prices are double those of the competition and are unresponsive to normal market forces. Recently two new companies almost succeeded in establishing themselves in the market, but X drove them out by selective price-cutting, unhooking their orders and disparaging the quality of their products.

In the example, a court would hold that X possessed the power to set prices and to exclude competition, and had retained this power by illegal and exclusionary practices.(29)

IBM's position and practices also appear to conflict with the standards of its own chief economic consultant on antitrust matters, Professor Franklin M. Fisher.(30) Rejecting a simple "market share" test for monopoly, he writes: "The right question to ask is whether that large share would survive an attempt to charge high prices and earn monopoly profits." Unfortunately, he believes that "judgments about profits as an index of monopoly power are very difficult, if not impossible to make" (I should say "difficult but not impossible"), and so turns to entry barriers ("the single most misunderstood topic in the analysis of competition and monopoly"), and finally to issues of market conduct and predation. In this latter connection he offers the following dicta:

1. "Conduct, to be suspect, ought at least to be more restrictive than necessary." Referring to Alcoa and United Shoe, he observes: "In both cases, one can say that the conduct involved restrictions on competition which basically had no other purpose. The market could have functioned and the firms been profitable with less restrictive action."
2. "Conduct should not be condemned if it is precisely the conduct which competition would lead us to expect."

Of course, judgments as to what is "necessary" and/or "expected" are highly subjective, but nowhere in the vast public record now available can I discover any claim that the peripheral product modifications described above were in any sense "necessary," nor am I aware of any argument that selective, rather than across-the-board, price reductions and deliberate sacrifices of millions of dollars of anticipated profits are "expected" under normal competitive conditions.

Thus it would appear that IBM's challenged acts conflict both with its own proclaimed standards and with independent appraisal criteria. Although each of the individual acts in and of itself is subject to extenuating explanation or the Scots verdict of "not proven" because of inadequate data or debatable assumptions, neither the purpose nor the effect of the overall course of conduct can be dismissed on these bases. It seems apparent that IBM set out to destroy both the third-party leasing companies and its major PCM competitors, and that it substantially succeeded. Furthermore, the tactics utilized to achieve these results were neither major product improvements nor price changes that have any apparent justification unless they contain or eliminate the market activity of competitors. Under the circumstances, the conclusion seems inescapable that IBM engaged in "predatory marketing" for the purpose of protecting and strengthening its dominant position within the computer industry and preventing the evolution of that industry in directions that would reduce its ability to retain a dominant market position over time.

NOTES

(1) It is possible that dominant firm-type problems will arise in the form of coordinated behavior among tight oligopolists, as was alleged with respect to the Big Three tobacco companies during the 1930s. Such situations are, however, readily detected and proscribed because of their collusive character; the coordinated behavior itself need not be evaluated.

(2) From a review of this literature, Telser argues that predatory behavior is not quite as unlikely as some simplistic analyses would suggest. (Telser, L.G. "Cutthroat Competition and the Long Purse," Journal of Law and Economics, 9 (1966), pp. 259-277.)

(3) Posner, Richard A. Antitrust Law: An Economic Perspective. (Chicago, Ill.: University of Chicago Press) 1976, ch. 8, pp. 171-211. Fisher, Franklin. "Diagnosing Monopoly", Quarterly Review of Economics and Business, Vol. 19, No. 2, Summer 1979, pp. 7-33.

(4) United States v. Alcoa, 148 F.2d 416 (2d Cir. 1945).

(5) United States v. United Shoe Machinery Corp., 110 F. Supp. 295 (D. Mass 1953), at 345.

(6) 110 F. Supp. at 329.

(7) 110 F. Supp. at 325.

(8) The principal economic study of this industry is: Brock, Gerald W. The U.S. Computer Industry. (Cambridge, Mass.: Ballinger Publishing Company), 1975.

(9) The third-party leasing companies referred to here are those purchasing IBM equipment and making it available to users on a risk-lease basis. Leasing companies specializing in PCM equipment were essentially part of the PCM marketing activity, and are not considered separately here.

(10) Weiss, Leonard W. "The Structure-Conduct-Performance Paradigm & Antitrust," University of Pennsylvania Law Review, Vol. 127, No. 4, April 1979, see especially pp. 1124 and 1138.

(11) An interesting reflection of this situation is the fact that Patrick J. McGovern has been able to move into the class of "new millionaires," with a reported net worth in excess of $50 million according to Fortune (February 12, 1979), by creating the International Data Corporation, which has as its sole product information concerning the computer industry. Other organizations, particularly Auerbach, Datamation, and Arthur D. Little, have also embraced this information void as an attractive business opportunity.

(12) When the Univac-RCA and Honeywell-GE combinations took place circa 1970 the principal benefits acquired, particularly in the first instance, were the installed base customers of the departing firms.

(13) Computed from International Data Corporation data.

(14) These price differentials have been repeatedly testified to as matters of corporate strategy by executives of other systems companies in the course of U.S. v. IBM. Their presence has been demonstrated statistically by the studies of Ford and Ratchford, although the precise amount of the price differential has been questioned by Brock and Michaels. Differences among the results obtained by these analysts depend primarily on the specific systems and time periods selected for study, performance characteristics analyzed, and econometric techniques used. Without trying to unravel all these threads, it seems sufficient to note that both customers and suppliers for computer systems appear to be generally agreed that IBM systems typically have carried a price premium, and that the existence of such a premium has been confirmed to varying degrees in several independent academic investigations. See: (1) Ratchford, Brian T. and Gary T. Ford. "A Study of Prices and Market Shares in the Computer Mainframe Industry," Journal of Business, Vol. 49, April 1976, pp. 194-218. (2) Brock, Gerald W. "A Study of Prices and Market Shares in the Computer Mainframe Industry: Comment," Journal of Business, Vol. 52, January 1979, pp. 119-124. (3) Ratchford, Brian T. and Gary T. Ford. "A Study of Prices and Market Shares in the Computer Mainframe Industry: Reply," Journal of Business, Vol. 52, January 1979, pp. 125-134. (4) Michaels, Robert. "Hedonic Prices and the Structure of the Digital Computer Industry," Journal of Industrial Economics, Vol. 27, No. 3, March 1979, pp. 263-275.

(15) U.S. General Accounting Office, Report to the Congress, The Federal Information Processing Standards Program, April 19, 1978, p. 18.

(16) Report, p. 44.

(17) GX 3592, dated December 11, 1969, pp. 003-004.

(18) It should be noted that other computer systems companies have opposed various standards proposals for various reasons; however, this evidence of formal opposition by the industry leader seems to have been particularly critical to the entire standards experience.

(19) Continental Ore Co. v. Union Carbide & Carbon Corp., 370 U.S. 690 (1962), at 698-99.

(20) Final legal department approval of the Mallard strategy apparently hinged on its being given a numerical identification outside the existing 2314-type numerical sequence, and made an optional feature rather than bolted onto the CPU as initially proposed.

(21) The "below cost" test identifies some price reductions as clearly abnormal; it does not, however, identify all price changes that may have significant anti-competitive impact. The full range of analytical issues associated with the concept of predatory pricing is discussed by Professor Almarin Phillips in another paper included in this volume. The view that the distinction between predatory and other price cuts "turns not on form but on intent" (to which I would only add ". . . and effect") is most strongly presented by B.S. Yamey, "Predatory Pricing: Notes and Comments," Journal of Law and Economics, Vol. 15, (April 1972), pp. 129-142. A definitive legal critique of the well-known Areeda-Turner criteria for predatory pricing is presented in Judge Robert H. Schnacke's opinion in Transamerica Computer Co. v. IBM, C73-1832, Northern District of California, October 18, 1979.

(22) "Impact" was ruled out for this purpose, although permitted to be introduced as evidence of intent, by Judge Robert H. Schnacke in Transamerica Computer Corporation v. IBM.

(23) These estimates and those in the following section were made by Arthur Andersen & Co., and assume the same economic life of products that was assumed by IBM in its own analyses at time of announcement. These results were not permitted to be introduced into the trial record in precisely this form.

(24) There are a number of technical features of the multiplier calculation, depending upon the treatment of monthly maintenance charges and other factors, but these data are sufficiently accurate for purposes of these comparisons.

(25) Itel, one of the 1960's leasing companies, now confines its independent leasing activity primarily to non-computer areas.

(26) General Motors could certainly engage in the production of tires if it chose to do so. And it could conceivably modify its wheel assemblies and/or price its tires so that only GM tires were economical and safe on GM cars. Would this be an appropriate mode of competition in the tire market?

(27) Deposition, July 24-28, 1978.

(28) IBM Business Conduct Guidelines, 1968, p. 5.

(29) IBM Business Conduct Guidelines, 1968, pp. 8-9.

(30) Fisher, F.M. "Diagnosing Monopoly," Quarterly Review of Economics and Business, Summer 1979, Vol. 19, No. 2, pp. 7-33.

7 Predation and Antitrust Rules: The Complications When Quality is Considered
Almarin Phillips

INTRODUCTION

A heated argument concerning predatory behavior has developed in recent years. At one extreme, a view exists that largely dismisses the relevance of any concept of predation. With a strong implicit assumption that, regardless of firm size and conduct, markets always afford opportunities for potential competitors, John McGee argues that no rationally operated, profit-maximizing firm would engage in any form of behavior that might be thought of as predatory. Short-term losses from predation would always exceed the present value of future gains, and merging with rivals would be superior to forcing them out (McGee, 1958). Further, this view holds generally that firms do not become large and hold or gain market power because of conduct that might be regarded as monopolizing. Firms become large because they are in some sense more efficient and produce more net social value than do their rivals.(1)

There appear to be none at the opposite extreme who contend seriously that anything done by a large firm that has adverse effects on actual or potential competitors is per se harmful. Nonetheless, the suspicion that bigness is achieved and maintained by hardly more than nonpassive responses to changing market and technological conditions is a strong one in some quarters. It finds expression in Judge Hand's dictum that there can be "no more effective exclusion than progressively to embrace each new opportunity as it opened."(2) This position becomes especially vexing if the embracing of opportunities involves the introduction of new products or new cost-reducing production methods without evidence of either intent or strategic timing aimed at foreclosing the opportunities of specific rivals.

Most of the economic literature falls somewhere between the extremes. Richard Posner stresses that the offense of predation should be restricted to practices that may exclude an equally or more efficient competitor.(3) Posner holds that, "If the forbidden activity is defined as pricing intended to weaken or destroy a competitor, too much is forbidden."(4) Intent is difficult to prove but, even where shown, Posner contends that it should be permissible to exclude less efficient firms. On the other hand, "if predatory pricing is defined as pricing below cost . . . we may forbid too much or too little, depending on how we define cost. . . . "(5) To be predatory, Posner feels that it needs to be shown that a firm sells below short-run marginal cost or sells below long-run marginal cost with an intent to exclude. An ostensibly clear "rule" is proposed.

Phillip Areeda and Donald Turner (1975) have argued that, excepting the case where "clear direct evidence of disciplinary intent" exists, the second Posner criterion is inappropriate.(6) Utilizing familiar "welfare triangle" propositions, Areeda and Turner maintain that reducing price to short-run marginal costs adds more to social benefits (total revenue plus consumer surplus) than it does to social costs (total production costs) and, hence, should be permitted. "[M]arginal cost pricing leads to a proper resource allocation and is consistent with competition on the merits." (1975, p. 712) Without pressing any analytic details, they conclude that the same rule is applicable to cases involving promotional spending and product variations.

The Areeda-Turner "rule" has not gone unchallenged. Plaintiffs, without using welfare analysis, have said that, "The sole benefit of the below cost approach is that it insures that the defendant will always win." Prior to the appearance of Areeda-Turner, but following Posner, B.S. Yamey had rejected a simple cost-based rule. Yamey concluded that predation "is independent . . . of whether the deliberate price cutting . . . takes the price below cost . . . [A]ll that is necessary is that price is taken to a level lower than which would otherwise prevail. . . . " (Yamey, 1972) In context, however, Yamey would find predation only where price cutting was used strategically, temporarily, perhaps repeatedly, and intentionally to injure an actual or potential rival. Indeed, Yamey cautions that "to describe an established firm as a predator simply on the basis of a record that it had reduced the price of its product and then raised it when a rival withdrew . . . would make it virtually impossible for an established firm with a large share of the market to compete effectively with smaller firms or new entrants." (Yamey, 1972, p. 135) While Yamey suggests indicia helpful in distinguishing predation from competitive responses, no simple rule or rules were proposed.

In response to Areeda-Turner, F.M. Scherer also rejected a rule based on costs alone.(7) Noting that price equal to short-run marginal costs is not always consistent with welfare maximization, Scherer insists that a number of factual circumstances must be analyzed in each case. "Courts that attempt to substitute simple cost rules for such analyses of effect and intent . . . are likely to reach economically unsound decisions."(8) Distinctions between offensive, strategic behavior and ordinary defensive responses are implied in Scherer, but they are not stressed.

Oliver Williamson (1977) entered the debate with primary attention to a per se test that would deal with strategic responses by dominant firms. He points out that under the Areeda-Turner rule, dominant firms could utilize an MC = MR monopoly price in the pre-entry threat situation, and strategically drop price to P $\geq$ MC when an entry threat appears. Their output would rise in the threat situation to the point that entry would become unprofitable. Williamson argues that the rule should be expressed in terms of output rates, with predation indicated if the dominant firm increases its output when entry occurs or becomes probable. Pre-entry welfare gains would result from such a rule. The dominant firm, that is, would be required to keep price low throughout the pre-entry period since the strategic P $\geq$ MC response on the occasion of threat would be deemed predatory. With considerable adumbration, Williamson proposes a rule that avoids inquiries about intent, is easier to apply than is a cost rule, and is shown to be welfare-superior to the Areeda-Turner rule.

More recently, William Baumol has proposed a "quasi-permanence price reduction" rule. The established firm would be "left free to adopt prices that protected its interests without being permitted to readjust those prices in response to further moves by the entrant or after the entrant's demise."(9) Thus, the established firm may respond to entry threats, but only with prices such that the anticipated long-term changes in revenues from the price change equal or exceed the changes in costs. Subsequent price changes would be allowed only when basic market conditions changed. Baumol recognizes that it would be preferable from a welfare point of view if there were means to assure that consumers had the advantages of stationary limit prices prior to threats of entry, but fails to arrive at a Williamson-type rule to achieve this. He also notes that a multiproduct firm might still "cross-subsidize" products where entry is likely by high prices on others. A standby rule for an investigation of costs in such circumstances is somewhat cautiously advanced.

THE INTERDEPENDENCE OF DEMAND AND COSTS WITH QUALITY: STRATEGIC ASPECTS

The demand and cost functions considered in the analyses summarized above are of the traditional two-dimensional variety. The demand function gives the relationship between price and output rate; the cost function, the relationships between costs and output. Reductions in price increase the quantity demanded from the focal firm and reduce (with Cournot-type assumptions) the residual demand schedule for other firms by an equal amount. With constant marginal costs (an analytic convenience), the gain in welfare is the integral under the demand curve between the output at the higher price and that at the lower price, minus marginal cost times the difference in outputs. Welfare rises until this "triangle" disappears, or until price equals marginal cost.

The demand and cost functions are conceptually different when quality changes are introduced. The quantity demanded becomes a function of price and quality, with the conventionally depicted demand function shifting to the right as quality increases. The latter condition is, indeed, definitional of "quality increase." The condition holds whether the quality changes come in discrete increments (e.g., number of flights per day by an airline on a given city pair) or as a continuous variable (e.g., percent butterfat in milk). Thus, the inverse demand function becomes:

$$p = D(x,q); \quad D_x < 0, \quad D_q > 0, \quad\quad\quad 1.$$

where p is price, x is the output rate, and q is a measure of quality.

Costs are also a function of quality, but here the functional form of the relationship depends on the type of quality change involved. Designate as Type A quality change that which entails a simple upward shift in short-run marginal costs, with no change in fixed costs. Changes in the butterfat content of milk, changes in the amount of fresh fruit per frozen pie, and other changes in the quality or relative quantity of inputs per unit of output are examples. An illustrative cost function for Type A quality change could be depicted as:

$$c = C(x) + \beta qx; \quad C' > 0, \quad \beta > 0, \quad\quad\quad 2.$$

where c is total costs and β is a (constant) "marginal cost per unit of quality." Thus, the marginal cost of output depends on the output rate and the quality of the product, varying directly with the latter by β per unit of quality. Other more complicated functional relationships can easily be envisioned, but these are unnecessary for the present arguments.

Type A quality changes require no new facilities, no new technology, little lead time planning, little or no change in the modes of use by customers, and they are inherently reversible (though not necessarily profitably). In Baumol's terminology, they have no intrinsic "quasi-permanence." These attributes enhance the possibility of product quality being used strategically by a dominant firm, especially where quality is a continuous variable. Various combinations of price changes and quality changes could be used to affect the residual demand available to potential entrants. Moreover, since price as well as quality can be increased or decreased strategically, they can be used to create uncertainty for the potential entrant. The residual demand can, in effect, be shifted at will by an existing, dominant firm.(10)

Type B quality changes are defined as those that have a demand effect but do not influence the cost function. Within ranges, the cost function remains simply $c = C(x)$ since $\beta = 0$. The demand function remains $p = D(x,q)$. Such quality changes may be less common than Type A, but they do exist. An air carrier, for example, may increase flight frequencies on one or more of the city pairs it serves. The output of available seat miles rises, but there may be no change in the marginal cost per seat mile.(11) To the extent that this can be accomplished by increasing the utilization rate of aircraft and other facilities, average cost will fall. The greater frequency increases demand, nonetheless. It has the effect of reducing the real price to travellers by lowering the waiting time between flights.

Type B quality changes, like Type A, have few inherent limitations on their strategic use by dominant suppliers. They lack intrinsic "quasi-permanence," also. Type B quality increases can be used even without a price reduction – indeed, even with price increases – to reduce the residual demand of entrants or rivals. Where more than one product is supplied by a given firm using common facilities (e.g., an airline serving a network of city pairs), the strategic use of "quality change discrimi-nation" may be possible. Thus, flight frequency could be increased on one city pair by using equipment released through lowering the fre-quency of flights on another city pair. The marginal cost per seat mile could stay the same on each. Again, the potential entrant may be faced with uncertainty if the dominant carrier varies flight frequency for that purpose.

Type C quality changes originate in a form of demand comple-mentarity or, more generally, in the demand for features ancillary to the principal product. The demand function (ignoring quality changes in x) is:

$$p = D(x,y,q_y); \quad D_x < 0, \quad D_y > 0, \quad D_{qy} > 0, \qquad 3.$$

where y is the output of the complementary or ancillary product (or service) and q_y is the measure of its quality. Costs, illustratively, become:

$$c = C(x) + K(y) + \Gamma q_y y; \quad C' > 0, \quad K' > 0, \quad \Gamma > 0, \qquad 4.$$

where the latter two terms are, for y, analogous to the cost expression for x in equation 2. Γ is the marginal cost of a unit quality for y. Other forms for 4. are, of course, possible to construct.

As an example, consider that x is some make of automobile and that y is the availability of repair and maintenance. Then the y and q_y terms in equation 3. say that demand for the automobile will vary directly with the availability and the quality of the service. The K(y) term in equation 4. indicates that costs rise as service availability (e.g., number of repair stations) increases. The $\Gamma q_y y$ term indicates that the cost per unit of service availability will be positively related (at marginal cost Γ) to the quality of the service made available. Notice that the K(y) term and, under reasonable circumstances, the Γ coefficient have fixed cost (i.e., fixed with respect to x) elements in them.(12) No technological change is involved, however.

Type C quality changes are less easy to use in a short-term strategic manner than are Types A and B. Whether customers come to the service facilities or service is taken to customer location, facilities with some permanence are necessary. These may be quite specialized facilities, requiring trained personnel. There are set-up of "front end" costs, as well as operating costs in the K(y) term. While the level and quality of the ancillary good may be increased or decreased in relatively short time periods, there may be a close identification of the primary product, x, with the ancillary product or service, y. That is, the functional attributes of x may depend critically on y so that the demand for x is very sensitive to variations in y and q_y. In many circumstances, the strategic use of y to prevent entry threats or to retaliate against rival actions may be impossible. The use of y and q as a longer term, profit-maximizing device — with consideration given to contingent probabilities of others' behavior — including the probability of entry into either x or y — may at the same time be essential; that is, Type C quality variations may be used as a stationary limiting device, with employment prior to obvious entry threats.

Type D quality changes are those that originate in R&D activities or from some other form of advanced resource application. The C(x) expression changes. The changes involve variations in either or both the cost and performance of a product or service. The demand function can still be taken as that in equation 1, but care is necessary in its interpretation. In particular, x is no longer easily viewed as a given product. Its characteristics change with q, resulting in the familiar "apples and oranges" difficulty. Moreover, the changes in q are likely to be discrete rather than continuous (e.g., a typewriter either does or does not have a ball-type head). For Type D changes, some quality choices are made across inflexible attributes, rather than in a continuum. In these circumstances, an illustrative cost function would be:

$$c = C(x) + \beta qx + S_q; \quad C' > 0, \quad \beta \gtrless 0, \quad S_q > 0, \qquad 5.$$

where q is a vector of attributes and β is a corresponding vector of production cost differences associated with the various attributes. S_q denotes the search costs (or R&D costs) required in anticipation of producing x with the various q attributes. Since there is a choice of some q from among alternative q's, the S_q costs involve investigation of the unused q's, as well as of costs of the variant actually chosen.

It is not impossible to use Type D changes strategically. If there are ongoing S_q expenditures, the actual timing of q choices might be made when entry threats or rivals' actions require them. Even in these circumstances, however, the S_q expenditures derive from long-term contingency planning and cannot themselves ordinarily be effectively turned on and off for short-term strategic purposes. Further, unlike Types A, B, and C, the new cost expression relevant after a quality change may have lower total and marginal costs than does the old one. At the same time, $D_q > 0$ is in the demand equation.

Because $D_q > 0$ and/or because C' is lower, there is no reason to conclude that Type D changes occur only for strategic reasons. Even the profit-maximizing pure monopoly could make S_q expenditures, realizing a positive rate of return on them because of the $D_q > 0$ and cost effects over time. Moreover, the Type D changes could reflect an ongoing, dynamic limit policy on the part of the existing firm, with continuous attention to the contingency of entry threats based on new technology even when no actual threat is apparent.

PROFIT MAXIMIZATION AND WELFARE WITH QUALITY CHANGE

The courts have given considerable attention to the Posner and Areeda-Turner rules.(13) In addition to the question of whether prices are below average or marginal costs, some courts have suggested that unlawful predation could occur with "pricing above marginal or average variable costs but below the short-run profit-maximizing price where barriers to entry are high."(14) The application of these tests is difficult even in the absence of quality changes; it is more difficult and often irrelevant with such changes.

With continuously variable Type A quality changes, short-run profit maximization occurs where the marginal cost of output (given quality) in equation 2 is equal to the marginal revenue from output (given quality) in equation 1 and, simultaneously, the marginal cost of quality (given quantity) in equation 2 is equal to the marginal revenue from quality (given quantity) in equation 1. If continuous change is not possible, maximization implies the selection of a set of inequalities consistent with the greatest profits.

Maximization with Type B changes is essentially the same as that for Type A, varying only in that the marginal cost of output does not vary with quality. For Type C changes, the price of x, the quantity of x, the price of y, the quantity of y, and the quality of y require simultaneous determination.   Partial derivatives of the costs and revenues, respectively, from all decision variables must be equated. Type D changes add a requirement that the rates of return on the S_q expenditures be equated with some interest rate.

Fig. 7.1 shows the profit rates associated with various price (p) and quality (q) combinations set by a firm. The oblate spheroid lines are iso-profit contours, with the larger "circles" representing successively lower profits. The p* line gives the locus of profit-maximizing prices, with qualities taken parametrically. The q* gives the locus of profit-maximizing qualities with prices taken parametrically.(15) Profit maximization occurs at p_1,q_1 where price and quality are simultaneously optimal. The "heavy" iso-profit contour represents the minimum profit level required to induce entry.

Since we are dealing with conditions other than perfect competition, $p_1 > MC \geq AVC$ at the x_1 output implied by p_1,q_1. The departure from p_1,q_1 treated in the literature and in court decisions is a move to, say, p_2,q_1. With this combination, the price is lower than the profit-maximizing one, although the quality is the same as that which meets the full maximizing conditions; that is, quality change is ignored. Fig. 7.1 shows, however, that at p_2, the quality is higher than that which would be "best," given p_2. The move to p_2,q_1 produces a profit level lower than the minimum required to encourage entry.

So far as entrants are concerned, the same effect could be achieved by changing from p_1,q_1 to p_1,q_2, raising quality levels and leaving price the same. Obviously, any move by the focal firm to a p,q combination to the "south" and "east" of the p* and q* lines and below the entry inhibiting iso-profit contour stops entrants.(16) Price is so low, quality is so high, and profits are so low that entry is barred.

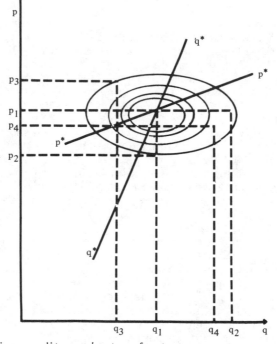

Fig. 7.1. Price, quality, and rates of return

Note that this is not the case for the p_3,q_3 combination and for other combinations in this area of the field. While the profits of the focal firm are low, this is the result of price being too high and quality too low for profit maximization. If an entrant expected the firm to remain with p_3,q_3, entry with lower prices and higher quality would be possible. The focal firm's demand curve would shift leftward as this occurred — raising substantive questions as to why the entrant might initially expect that firm to remain with p_3,q_3 set.

In general, moves from points such as p_3,q_3 toward p_1,q_1 by lowering price and/or raising quality, would be viewed by potential entrants and rivals as predatory. The moves would reduce their residual demand curves, constricting the p,q sets which they might select in order to enter or to remain in the market. Yet, as drawn, fig. 7.1 shows that entry would be possible as long as the focal firm does not lower price and/or raise quality beyond a combination such as p_4,p_4. Preda tion might clearly be charged by potential entrants faced with an existing firm having a set such as p_4, q_4 since there is no p_4, q_4 set available that would permit their survival. Unlike p_3, q_3, the low profits of the focal firm arise because price is "too low" and/or quality is "too high" — too low and high for profitable entry, but not necessarily for optimal welfare.

Actually, there is nothing about the p_1, q_1 point that has appeal in terms of welfare, despite the courts' attention to it. Where short-run profit maximization of the p_1, q_1 sort exists, price is too high and quality is too low in welfare terms.

Fig. 7.2 is drawn on the conventional p,x ordinates. Suppose that a firm has D_1 as its demand function and, without threat of entry, sets price at p_1, selling x_1 for profit maximization, with MC_1 as its marginal costs. When an entry threat arises, it lowers price to p_2, reducing the residual demand by enough to foreclose entry by selling x_2. Quality is left unchanged. The welfare gain (consumer plus producer surpluses) is shown by the shaded trapezoidal area, the integral under the D_1 demand curve less the integral under MC_1, both between output levels x_1 and x_2.[17] Profits at p_2, x_2 are, of course, lower than at p_1, x_1.

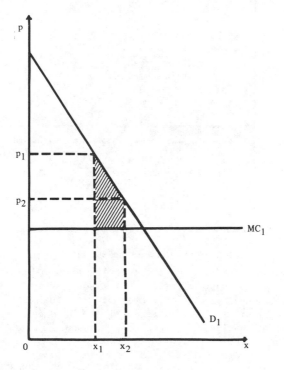

Fig. 7.2. Welfare effects of price decreases

Now consider fig. 7.3, where a Type A quality change is portrayed. Under threat of entry, the firm increases quality, but leaves price at p_1. The demand curve shifts from D_1 to D_2 and the firms sells x_2. The resulting welfare gain is now the difference between the integrals of the D_2 and D_1 curves from zero to x_2 plus the welfare gain from the price decrease in fig. 7.2 (the area with horizontal shading lines), less the difference between the integrals of MC_2 and MC_1 from zero to x_2, and less the difference in the integral of MC_1 from x_1 to x_2 (the area with vertical shading lines). If the initial p_1, x_1 (and q_1) set was fully profit maximizing, the incremental quality costs of the change would exceed the incremental revenues. Profits fall but total surplus rises. Welfare is improved even though entry may have been forestalled.

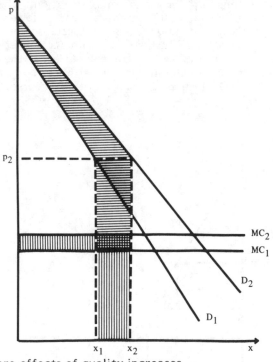

Fig. 7.3. Welfare effects of quality increases

Assuming no externalities and, more importantly, no changes in tastes, the p_1, x_2 situation in fig. 7.3 is not socially ideal. Price exceeds marginal costs at those levels of quantity and quality. Fig. 7.4 shows successive price and quality changes – price falling from p_1 and quality rising from that involved in p_1, x_1. Each increase in quality raises the demand curve, shifting it from D_1 across to D_3. Each increase in quality shifts the marginal cost curve upward (Type A change) from MC_1 to MC_3. At $x_3, p_3 = MC_3$ and marginal social gains equal marginal social costs.(18) This, of course, is the "competitive" equilibrium in an "ideal" world.

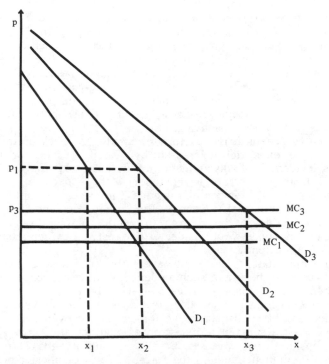

Fig. 7.4. Welfare maximization

Returning to fig. 7.1, it is clear that a rule on predation that prevents a firm – any firm – from moving away from the p_1, q_1 profit-maximizing position by raising quality or by lowering price does not comport with welfare criteria. Stated conversely, any policy that allows a firm to remain over long periods of time at the p_1, q_1 profit level or at lower profit levels attributable to prices that are too high or quality levels that are too low even for profit maximization does not comport with welfare criteria. A policy is needed that drives price lower and quality higher, aiming at an approach to the p_3, x_3 (and q_3) levels of fig. 7.4. This is generally true for all types of quality change, A, B, C, and D, although the graphical portrayal would vary somewhat.

QUALITY CHANGE AND PREDATION RULES

The failure of all of the proposed rules and tests explicitly to consider quality changes is an important failure. This is especially true of the "cost rules." Costs may rise or fall, prices may rise or fall, profits may rise or fall, and ratios of price to marginal costs of production may rise or fall if quality changes occur.(19) Nothing can be said from any of these facts, by themselves, about effects on welfare.

The most important of Williamson's arguments remains valid when quality changes are introduced. Stated considerably more generally than he puts it, the rule employed should aim at keeping the limit price low and the limit quality high even during periods when specific entry threats are not obvious. His output test is designed to achieve this by finding predation if a firm utilizes strategic responses to ward off entry, thus enabling it to keep in the long-run something like the p_1, q_1, x_1 position in figs. 7.1 and 7.2. The output test aimed at preventing only strategic responses would be as applicable to quality change as it is to price behavior.

An entry preventative pattern of strategic behavior <u>might</u> be the same as the exception expressed by Areeda-Turner for "clear and obvious evidence of disciplinary intent." Intent, that is, could be inferred from the strategic behavior with respect to price and/or quality, and the Williamson and Areeda-Turner tests would be the same. For Types A and B quality change, the "turning on" and "turning off" of a quality variable in the context of explicit entry threats or market share gains by rivals would, under either test, be evidence supporting a charge of predation.

It is important to note, however, the conjunctive conditions described above in the use of such evidence. Quality responses of a "quasi-permanent" nature have positive welfare effects just as "quasi-permanent" price reductions do. If entry does not occur when quality is increased — or if rivals' shares no longer rise or even fall — there is at the very least a substantial question of whether the "equally efficient rival" considerations stressed by Posner and Areeda-Turner are not relevant. <u>Permanent</u> gains in the form of welfare superior price-quality configurations should be encouraged, not discouraged, by the rule on predation.

When quality changes are necessarily of a discrete variety, rather sudden increases in the output(20) of the initiating firm are likely to be observed. By the Williamson output test alone, predation cannot be distinguished from competitive, welfare-improving behavior. In any case, a long-term pattern of price decreases and/or quality increases which persistently deny market opportunities to potential entrants is not obviously bad. Contrary to Judge Hand's dictum, progressively embracing every new opportunity may be welfare-inducing, even if it is, on its face, obviously exclusionary.

Still, such behavior is less justifiable in welfare terms if it is used strategically. It is preferable for the continuity in quality changes to occur when threat is <u>not</u> apparent as well as when it is. Generally, then, "artificial" barriers to entry should be discouraged, keeping open the continuing possibility of entry. This standard, one assumes, is in the corpus of existing law. What may not be in existing tests is any explicit consideration of quality, as well as price changes, and to their patterns through time. Where quality change is a significant fact of the market, a record of change when no rivals — actual or apparent — pose obvious threats is consistent, but not conclusive of, behavior that avoids the costs of the p_1, q_1 monopoly.

As noted above, the opportunity for strategic behavior in the Types C and D quality changes is less likely than for Types A and B. Time and costs are necessary to implement them and they are far less reversible. It is not surprising, nonetheless, that changes of these types, or the maintenance of the facilities and expenditures necessary to achieve them, are often regarded as entry barriers. From the view of rivals and potential entrants, they are just that. They increase the capital outlays necessary for entry and the current expenditures required to effect the quality changes. Yet it is precisely where this resource use <u>does</u> make it more difficult for any to enter or to maintain shares that <u>one</u> can have some confidence that moves toward welfare-inducing quality improvements (and often concomitant price decreases) are being made.

Repeated and successful moves of this kind by a single firm are likely to be reflected in high market shares by conventional measurement methods; repeated moves by different firms, in fluctuating market shares. Predation may be charged in either case. Actually, market share is a misleading indicator of predation save where size is obviously combined with repeated strategic forms of behavior showing "clear and obvious evidence of disciplinary intent." A high share may indeed reflect low price and quality demand elasticities in the short run. But where the firm behaves as though the short-run power deriving from a high share would be ephemeral if exercised, predation ought not be found. A firm that rather continuously lowers price and raises quality whenever technology permits it to do so may be demonstrating nothing other than the tenuousness of its market share at any point in time.

As Scherer argued in his response to Areeda-Turner, simple rules will not work in predation cases. Williamson's output test may be superior to the $P \geq MC$ test, but it too may be misleading, especially when large and discrete technological changes are involved. Complicated phenomena require careful consideration, not simple rules.

NOTES

(1) John S. McGee, The Defense of Industrial Concentration (1971); Harold Demsety, "Two Views on Monopoly," in H. Goldschmid, M. Mann, and F. Weston (eds.), Industrial Concentration: The New Learning (Boston: 1974).

(2) U.S. v. Aluminum Company of America, 148 F.2d 416 (1945).

(3) Richard Posner, "Exclusionary Practices and the Antitrust Laws," 41 University of Chicago Law Review 506 (1974). This article was prompted by Utah Pie Co. v. Continental Baking Co. 387 U.S. 685 (1967).

(4) Ibid., p. 518, emphasis added.

(5) Ibid.

(6) Brief of Appellants, California Computer Products, Inc. v. International Business Machines Corp., United States Court of Appeals, 9th Circuit, p. 54.

(7) Frederick M. Scherer, "Predatory Pricing and the Sherman Act: A Comment," 89 Harvard Law Review 868 (1976). See also Areeda and Turner, "Scherer on Predatory Pricing: A Reply," 89 Harvard Law Review 891 (1976), and Scherer, "Some Last Words on Predatory Pricing," 89 Harvard Law Review 901 (1976).

(8) Scherer, "Comment," p. 890.

(9) William J. Baumol, "Quasi-Permanences of Price Reductions – A Policy for Prevention of 'Predatory Pricing" (unpublished, undated).

(10) The extent of the shift in residual demand will depend on the price-quality set chosen by the focal firm. A price increase combined with an increase in quality can still reduce residual demand. It can be shown that even in the monopoly case no generalization is possible about whether the profit-maximizing price is higher or lower with different levels of quality. Specifications of the functional forms and parameters of the cost and demand functions are necessary to determine this.

(11) The marginal cost per passenger mile would rise if the load factor fell.

(12) The size and completeness of inventories would be another illustration of this kind of quality variation. Lower probabilities of outages and more complete stocks would be valued by customers, but would require outlays such as $K(y)$ and $\Gamma q_y y$ for ordering, carrying and control.

(13) See International Air Industries, Inc. v. American Excel. Co., 517 F 2d 714 (1975); Telex Corp. v. Int'l Business Machines Corp., 510 F. 2d 894 (1975); Hanson v. Shell Oil Co., 541 F. 2d 1352 (1976); Pacific Engineering and Products Co. v. Kerr-McGee Corp., 551 F. 2d 790 (1977); Janich Bros. Inc. v. American Distilling Co., CCH Trade Reg. Rep. # 61,826; ILC Peripherals Leasing Corp. v. Int'l Business Machines Corp., CCH Trade Cas. # 62,177 (1978).

(14) ILC Peripherals Leasing Corp. v. Int'l Business Machines Corp., supra, n. 19. See also Hanson and Int'l Air Industries, supra, n. 19, and TransAmerica v. Int'l Business Machines Corp., (1979).

(15) For Type D changes, in a more or less continuously changing technological environment, q might be better expressed dq/dt, the rate of change in quality over time. The demand for a firm's products in some cases may be strongly affected by its dq/dt performance as well as by q at any point in time.

(16) See note 10, however. The p*,q* lines in fig. 7.1 are drawn with iso-profit contours suggesting a positive relationship between the optimum price and quality.

(17) This assumes that the quality change, like a price change, does not affect consumer tastes.

(18) This is a necessary but not a sufficient condition for welfare maximization. Consumers presumably have marginal rates of substitution between price and quality. The MC function is an interaction term reflecting costs of output change of a given quality and the costs of quality change. For sufficiency, consumers' marginal rates of substitution between price and quality would have to equal the reciprocal of the ratio of the respective marginal costs of output and quality.

(19) It is tempting to argue that the ratio of prices to marginal costs should still be relevant. They would be if a total derivative could be used that includes interactions between cost differences due to output change and cost differences due to quality change. The usual partial derivative of costs with respect to output is not sufficient for the welfare test.

(20) On decreases in the rate of decrease, increases in the rate of increase, etc.

8 Comments on Part I
Roland A. Artle

In this brief review of the papers in Part I, I shall concentrate on the papers by Phillips, Preston, and Thompson. Certainly the characteristic that underlies all seven of the papers is the eloquent demonstration that the boundary between aggressive competition and competition-destroying behavior is a fuzzy one, indeed.

Narver strikes this note in his very interesting and illuminating paper on our fuzziness in measuring price and the apparent "nonresponsiveness" of market prices. I will make one passing comment about that paper before directing my main attention to the three papers listed above. The past decade has witnessed what one might call a strengthening of the microfoundations of macroeconomic theory. A central feature of this so-called "new-new microeconomics" has been the attempt to draw macroeconomic conclusions based on more detailed analysis and description of individual markets – under conditions where prices do not necessarily clear the market. This disequilibrium analysis has provided new insights into the relationship between Keynesian macroeconomics, on the one hand, and Walrasian general-equilibrium analysis, on the other. However, the new theory is rather short on explanations as to <u>why</u> prices do not adjust to clear all markets. This is precisely where I see John Narver making a contribution. His way of looking at the responsiveness, or lack of responsiveness, of prices to change is quite rich. However, his very understandable eagerness to illustrate his ideas, and in particular the concept of "effective price," has led him astray, I believe. Using equation 18 and assuming that "general economic conditions improve," Narver tries to show a "perverse" price movement. The problem is that with improving economic conditions and assuming, realistically, a positive income elasticity, the "reservation price" will increase. Hence, <u>both</u> sides of the inequality 8 will increase, and the author's conclusion is no longer valid. The form of Narver's analysis is qualitative; that is, the only possible conclusions concern <u>directions</u> of change. Section 4 ("Perverse" Movements of P_{sd})

128

of his paper implies that at least two variables will change. Since they change in opposite directions, with respect to their effect on $\pi* - \pi$, no qualitative conclusion can be drawn. This critical observation is added parenthetically, as it concerns only the brief section of "perverse" pricing.

Turning now to the papers by Phillips, Preston, and Thompson, let me begin by making an observation which perhaps all three authors consider superfluous – namely, that the very existence of threat of litigation restrains a monopolistic or dominant firm. Another factor leading to restrained behavior on the part of monopolies or dominant firms is the risk of new entries to the industry or – a phenomenon of growing significance in the United States – new competition by way of imports. A third reason why a monopoly or dominant firm is <u>not</u> setting prices and producing quantities consistent with profit maximization is linked to uncertainty, particularly in industries subject to rapid technological change. Firms do not know their demand functions and are hence unable to pick their profit-maximizing price-output combinations.

Phillips makes the point in his paper that the situation facing a court becomes even more murky, when it is recognized that quality of product is often a strategic variable for a firm. The classification of quality change into four different types that Phillips introduces is very instructive, and a reader would be hard put to disagree with his conclusion that "complicated phenomena require careful consideration not simple rules" (simple rules, that is, of the kind proposed by Areeda-Turner and Williamson). For pedagogical reasons, I presume, Phillips illustrates his analysis by means of a set of four simple diagrams. However, isn't the simplicity carried a bit far? Let us look at fig. 7.1. It shows the relationship between "Price, Quality, and Rates of Return." Yet, there are at least five variables operating in this diagram, and it is unclear how the omitted variables – the quantity of production, and the capital investments needed to vary both quality and quantity – influence the analytical result illustrated. Furthermore, the accompanying text refers to the level-curve variable interchangeably as "the rate of return" and as "the level of profit"; the two are not interchangeable. However, this is a minute blemish, a matter of exposition rather than substance.

Having learnt from Phillips's paper how significant variations in the quality of product are – significant, that is, in blurring the picture of conduct which may be appraised as "predatory marketing" – one feels at least hesitant about accepting Lee Preston's condemnation of IBM's conduct. Yet, it must be stressed, Preston gives an extraordinarily insightful and illuminating behind-the-scenes account of IBM's market responses to a variety of developments involving the manufacturers of peripheral equipment and the third-party leasing companies.   One aspect of the issue of aggressive (and acceptable) competition versus predatory (and unacceptable) competition deserves consideration. It concerns the existence in an industry of <u>decreasing</u> long-run marginal costs. A dominant firm in such an industry has a very great deal at stake in retaining its position in the market place. It must run fast merely to stand still. If it were to fall behind in the competition – even relatively in terms of its market share – the outcome might be a drastic drop in its rate of return.

A stroke of genius has placed Donald Thompson's paper next to Lee Preston's. Although Thompson does not address himself specifically to the issue of predatory behavior in the computer and related industries, some quotes from his paper are interesting in the context. Based on evidence that he has analyzed, he is inclined to conclude "that superior profitability in concentrated industries reflects efficiency rather than exploitation of market power." With specific reference to decreasing costs, he also writes: "Experience curve analysis suggests that concentration is the natural outcome of a process which confers on the leading producer a real cost advantage, and it is this advantage which produces superior profitability rather than exploitative behavior or restraints on competition."

As suggested by the last quotation, Thompson focuses his paper on what he calls the "experience curve phenomenon." He uses the term in a broad sense. It comprehends not only the "process of managers and operators learning from experience how to operate particular technologies and facilities more efficiently." It also includes many other factors which may lead to decreasing costs. Much new knowledge would be gained if these contributory factors could be disentangled in future analysis. One of these underlying factors is "increasing returns to scale" – or more broadly, any homothetic production function of degree greater than one. With constant input prices, such a production function possesses decreasing long-run average costs. Another contributory factor can be labelled a "public good" or (better) "collective good" effect. This is roughly what Thompson refers to as "sharing." The dynamic sequence of events which has become so familiar for example in the electronics industry, can be singled out as a third factor. In this "virtuous circle," through competition or otherwise, prices of new products fall, which increases demand, which in turn faciiltates new technological advances, through which costs fall, leading to another round of lower prices and/or higher quality of products, with the effect that demand increases still further and so on.

In this brief review, I have attempted to seek out a theme unifying the papers. The review would be very incomplete if I did not in conclusion note another property common to all the papers. They are of the highest quality and truly written in honor of, and with reverence for, our beloved "Greth."

II
Market Information

9 From Competitive Conduct to Buyer Information: The Problems of Consumers in Coping with Changes in the Marketplace

Francesco M. Nicosia

There are advantages and disadvantages in introducing the following four chapters written to honor my teacher, E.T. Grether. One of the advantages is that I had the opportunity to read these chapters more than once. The first reading showed a natural flow of issues, and how they related to those in the preceding and following parts; a Gestalt emerged. Further reading, however, allowed me to sense and to identify deeper issues – those that emerge only when we are willing to look at the realities of marketing activities by buyers and sellers.

In these introductory remarks, then, I would like to share my experience as to how the "information" content of these chapters may have different meanings. Accordingly, in the first section I shall briefly describe what I perceive to be the chapters' content, and in the following section I shall share my interpretation of the chapters' meaning for public policy.

A DESCRIPTIVE SYNOPSIS

The opening of Holton's chapter reminds us of at least two of the issues emerging in Turner's paper: How do we define the relevant product and price? As for defining products, public policy makers use the set of definitions of industries created by the Standard Industrial Classification, which emphasize the chemical and physical characteristics of inputs, technological processes, and so on. But in the 1930s Joan Robinson and other economists had already made it clear that it is a buyer's preference function that defines a product. And this is an empirical fact for those of us who apply psychology to the study of consumer and organizational buying behavior.

*I gratefully acknowledge the substantive suggestions by R. Artle and J. Carman.

133

A fundamental question for public policy is to decide whether to continue to define the "relevant" product in terms of the chemical and physical attributes of the inputs necessary to make a product (SIC) or in terms of the buyer's own utility (economics) or perceptual (psychology) maps.

Holton begins with the realistic assumption that consumers define what a product is. He then concisely argues that to perceive a product, a consumer must know something about it — must have at least some information about the product's attributes. He completes the argument by showing that the conditions under which a consumer can get a "complete" set of information about a product's attributes are not easily satisfied in the real world. As an illustration, Holton describes at length the case of purchasing life insurance.

The life insurance illustration also reminds us of the issue of defining price and quality (as discussed in Turner's and especially in Narver's chapters). Even though we may agree with economics that price is a measure of the perceived value of a certain good (the perceived attributes of the good), we find in the chapter that it is rather difficult to establish what is the objective value of a life insurance policy. In fact, Holton forcefully shows that not even the sellers of life insurance can agree among themselves on an industry "method" to measure such value!

So how can a consumer get all the information about a good (the good's attributes) that approximate the case of "perfect" competition, as defined in that area of economics usually called industrial organization? This very same question, incidentally, also applies to industrial buying. Behavioral studies have shown that an organization of persons — e.g., a business firm — experiences exactly the same problem: How to get perfect information. All the conditions making for imperfect information, as listed by Holton, apply to both small and large business firms. Individually or in groups, humans are presumed to "compute" the worth of additional information, and it appears that they stop far short of attempting to buy perfect information.

There remains, however, the problem of formulating public policy. If, in fact, public policy believes that a society of individuals and organizations is most "effectively" and "efficiently" organized only when all decision makers tend to have perfect information, then the task is indeed formidable, for, as Holton concludes, we should apply the same rules to selling cars, stocks, homes, tires, pharmaceuticals, medical services, appliances, and even ". . . many supermarket items as well."

The Thorellis' chapter takes on this central issue of Holton's. If decision makers (i.e., consumers) want and, in fact, use information, in how many ways can they go about acquiring information? And, in how many ways can public policy supply, and facilitate the supply of, information? The Thorellis have extensive experience in observing how this and other societies are attempting to answer the second question. Thus, they set forth a sketch (see fig. 11.2) of what public policy could do in the formation of future consumer information systems.

This sketch is the most valuable aspect of their chapter, for it offers something tangible about designing information systems. Although only a sketch, it at least guides our attention to the things we and public policy should know. For example, Mayer and Nicosia (1976) interviewed a number of federal agencies and independent consumer organizations and observed how these two sources of consumer information tend to interact not in a synergetic fashion; and from such observations they were able to derive suggestions for improvements.

The Thorellis' design for future consumer information systems indicates the need for public policy to observe and evaluate the relative impact of different sources of information and how they interact with consumers' own responses. For instance, at the micro managerial level, it has been found over the past 30 years that mass media advertising has the relative lowest impact on choices ranging from breakfast cereals and movies, to farm machinery and farm practices, and to ethical drugs when compared with the impact of personal selling and that of "peers."

Do these findings hold at the societal level? Forthcoming studies by Ashley, Granger and Schmalensee, by Jacobson, and by Jacobson and myself strongly suggest that changes in advertising expenditures tend to follow changes in consumption expenditures. Accordingly, a practical policy question is: To what extent, and how, does this commercial source interact with the present independent consumer information programs?

And can new technologies for the production, transmission, and reception of information indeed provide the basis for constructing viable consumer information systems? The Thorellis respond affirmatively, and proceed with considerations of organizational design — namely, from centralized to decentralized systems of production, transmission, and reception.

In my opinion, the Thorellis' description and discussion of future systems signal a potentially sharp departure from the most typical view of human life espoused in that branch of economic theory called industrial organization: that perfect markets are not only the most efficient but also the most effective (desirable) way for all decision makers to operate and live a human life. The Thorellis, however, accept the fact that ecological variety also applies to human life. From their early statement that the main stream of consumerism is an expression of classical liberalism (in the European sense) and democracy, to their concluding "revealed" preference for a highly heterogeneous social system of consumer information, the Thorellis imply that public policy, in attempting to structure a society of humans along the line of perfect markets may — perhaps unknowingly — force "unidimensionality" on individuals and social groups. And we do not need to refer to the writings by Marcuse to appreciate the various human costs that must be paid by the creation of unidimensional mankind!

As I finished reading the Thorellis paper, with its refreshing stress on the rich variety of human life, I could not avoid asking whether the most pressing problem facing public policy is to come to terms with the irrepressible multidimensionality of mankind. If perfect markets and perfect information do not fit consumers, then public policy may first need to study and understand how humans function, and then to develop social designs that may help humans to function the way they, the consumers, want.

The construction of the ecologically sound consumer information systems envisioned by the Thorellis depends at least on two key factors: technology and the willingness of public policy to experiment as well as let people experiment.

Mary Gardiner Jones focuses on these two key factors. Although my academic and professional interests make me to be somewhat aware of the ferment in R&D, engineering, and production of new technologies for gathering, storing, distributing, and retrieving information, I was simply fascinated by Jones' ability to sum up all that is going on in the area of communication technologies. Her paper must be read directly, without any middleman!

Jones' paper also discusses the other key factor: public policy willingness to experiment and to let people experiment. From the very first page, she skips over the tradition of industrial organization and goes directly to basic economy theory: that is, information is not free; it is an economic good. More importantly, it is not a homogeneous good, for the meaning of information does vary across individuals. This is a well recognized fact in pure economic theory, from its birth to the recent elaborations by Lancaster. It is also established in practically all branches of psychology. And of course, the poet (Goethe) knew it before economics and psychology were invented: each of us sees only what he or she knows (or wants).

Evolving new technologies have the potential of making it possible for each member of a society to interact with all other members. If this evolution cannot be stopped, then public policy makers (legislators, regulators, and courts) will inevitably have to choose: Either public policy will assume the authority to shape the development and uses of communication technologies (for the good of the people, of course), or it will help people search for a society-wide institutional arrangement of consumer information systems that fits the variety of human needs for different kinds and amounts of information. Jones' paper goes on to describe some current experiences with this search for institutional designs that fit the heterogeneity of consumers and organizations.

The chapter concludes with a sensitive analysis of the different vested interests that may shape the development and uses of new communication systems and the role of public policy in allowing flexibility in the current historical experiment, in which we are all participants.

Much of these three chapters' stress and illustrations deal with consumers. The chapter by Moulton reminds us that organizations also may want to have information. In fact, for those of us interested in observing human behavior, it has not come as a surprise to find that the buying processes of a consumer and of an organization are equivalent (not analogous).

Although Moulton focuses on a particular industrial sector – agriculture and agricultural commodities markets – he faces exactly the same questions that Holton has raised for consumers. To illustrate, Moulton reminds us that price does not contain that much information (it is, at best, a signal). It is the variety of product characteristics, terms of trade, services, and so on that make each specific offer a distinct set of "qualities." Accordingly, two offers may be equal as far as price is concerned and yet be substantially different in their own configuration of qualities. Useful information is that which concerns each of these qualities.

Let me further argue that when we observe exchange activities, we can conclude that knowledge of price and quantities sold/purchased cannot possibly be a case of perfect "competition," of perfect "information." I am told that Ricardo was a stockbroker. The fact that on the stock exchange floor he saw, and may still be seen today, price and quantity does not mean that buyers and sellers have perfect information at all. On the contrary, the economic good being exchanged is not a stock or a bond but information – that is, two different sets of information (and expectations) about the attributes/qualities represented by the certificate that lead someone to sell and someone else to buy. And, by his willingness to observe the reality of selling and buying activities in agricultural commodities, Moulton discovers that the participants do indeed withhold information. It is refreshing to see that some scholars are willing to observe how humans function.

Just as in the consumer goods case, Moulton brings to the fore the reality of "imperfection" in the markets he studies. There is an implicit question raised by Moulton that could just as well have been raised by Jones. Presumably, imperfect markets create costs for society. But, providing the information to eliminate these imperfections creates at least two other social costs: those of collection and disseminating this information, and those of a unidimensional society mentioned above. Just how cost efficient, then, are public expenditures for providing perfect information to market actors? Moulton experiences the same dilemma I have noted earlier. Should public policy try to fit life to the schema of perfect markets, or should it instead observe, understand, and then try to facilitate the vitality of the ecological variety imbedded in human life?

I have certainly not done justice to these four chapters in sketching what I perceive to be their content. At the very least, I have tried to share with the reader the excitement I have experienced in reading them. Here we have authors with different academic training, professional experiences, and, most likely, visions. And yet, as they look at the realities of marketing, all of them bring to the fore the role of information in human behavior and attempt to set information in the context of public policy. On the basis of what I have experienced in the areas of public policy, and being rather biased toward observing and modeling human behavior rather than fabricating "models" that prescribe human behavior, I more than welcome these four chapters, for they do open new visions and pose new questions about the tasks and responsibilities of public policy.

AN INTERPRETATION

My first exposure to public policy and marketing was in some seminars taught by E.T. Grether. On the one hand, he showed us how useful it is to observe the rich variety of human activities that we call "exchange." On the other hand, he demonstrated how some public policy is necessary to keep the unfolding of a society within boundaries of efficiency and perhaps even effectiveness.

As the seminars unfolded, the question became: What kind of criteria do we have to "measure" efficiency and effectiveness, and the boundaries within which a social aggregate can function? Historically, it would seem that the first criteria were mainly drawn from legal constructs. Later on, public policy began to draw increasingly from the thinking of a new branch of economic theory: industrial organization. The growth of this branch was probably due to the increasing demands that public policy placed on it.

Somehow, public policy came to accept the following vision of the world of exchanges. First, exchange activities can occur in about four types of structures: perfect competition, monopolistic competition, oligopoly (homogeneous, heterogeneous), and monopoly. Second, information is perfect; i.e., it is free, and thus it is not an economic good. And finally, for a society and its members, the most efficient and effective structure is that of perfect competition. For about 40 years this vision has prevailed, and it has been used by public policy makers.

Yet the chapters I have reviewed, as well as others, are not at ease with this vision of the world of exchange activities. They seem to call our attention to the new vistas emerging from economic theory and behavioral sciences. Let us turn to economic theory.

Just about 40 years ago, economic theory realized that the word "competition" may have two very different meanings. In industrial organization, competition is the name of one of the four types of market structures. But economic theory realized that the word competition may also refer to those realities where "if I win, you lose." Thus, in this ecological sense, in the market structure of perfect competition no one actor competes with anyone – by definition; and, in this ecological sense, competition takes place "among the few"; that is, in the market structure called oligopoly. Almost concurrently, game theory captured this very essence of life with the concept of zero sum games.

Economic theory evolved, and by the late 1950s it bravely faces the reality that information is not free at all – there are demands and supplies for such a thing. From Telser's and Stigler's theoretical work and from the early simulation systems by Shubick, Balderston, and Hoggatt – to name a few – information acquires a central role. In addition, economic theory gradually incorporates the reality that, individually or in groups, humans have a cognitive limit to how much information they can process anyway (H. Simon).

And by the late 1960s, the construct of utility (preferences) finds its application for both industrial(1) and consumer goods (e.g., the work by

Becker and Lancaster). Individual and organizational buyers perceive, evaluate, and choose in terms of configurations of attributes (characteristics) – there is no such thing as a product, as Joan Robinson had already told us in the 1930s!

This historical evolution in economic theory must be compared with several other events, I believe, for this comparison allows us to detect some fundamental choices for public policy makers. One such event is that no changes have occurred in the thinking about, and typologies of, exchanges developed in industrial organization, as used in public policy. At the very minimum, one would expect improvements such as explicit consideration of both demand and supply functions simultaneously (see David Grether's chapter). In industrial organization, information is still free.(2) Or one would expect explicit consideration of the "budget constraint" (at the very least, a la Hick's of the mid 1930s). Last but not least, there have been no attempts to define a product in terms of buyers' and sellers' perceptions. But how can industrial organization describe selling and buying events when that which it defines as the object of exchange (the SIC product) is in fact different from what buyers and sellers do exchange?

Another key historical event is the learning about the buying processes by consumers and organizations in a variety of behavioral sciences. This learning almost parallels the evolution of economic theory I have just described. In fact, I have argued elsewhere that we are witnessing a convergence in understanding how people function – not how they "should" function. A case in point is the empirical work in hedonistic pricing (economics) and conjoint measurement (psychometrics), as they both describe what buyers define to be a product in their own terms, rather than in SIC-based definitions of products. Another case in point is the realization both in economic theory (e.g., team theory) and applications of behavioral sciences that there is no such thing as the entrepreneur who, sitting at the top of an organizational chart, has the ineffable ability to absorb all sorts of information and compute how to maximize profit and even returns on investments!(3)

The final key event is that legislators, regulators, and courts have consistently relied on the schema offered decades ago by industrial organizations. The questions, issues, and stresses raised by the authors of the four chapters I have reviewed and by Narver, D. Grether, Thompson, Phillips, and Carman, are caused to a large extent by a simple and yet basic dilemma.

On the one hand, marketing scholars observe selling and buying activities, often relying on the conceptualizations of economic theory (not industrial organization), the behavioral sciences, or both. They observe the fundamentally human variety of life. On the other hand, when called to examine society in its entirety, they see public policy diligently trying to fit multidimensional life into the historically frozen unidimensionality of life portrayed by industrial organization. To focus on this dilemma may lead to clear and hopefully socially useful results.

Let me paraphrase a point made by Roland Artle in his chapter: It may be that the reality of exchange activities as perceived in marketing, economics, and the behavioral sciences is different from that of neo-classical theory as used in traditional industrial organization. And let me add: To the best of my knowledge, price theory was constructed for solving problems of interest to economic theory; e.g., the formation of value.

At some point in past history, the use of price theory to understand some exchange activities and regulate them accordingly may have been appropriate. But to insist in its use when marketing, economics, and the behavioral sciences have offered newer visions and models is rather dangerous. For example, from the points of view of these three disciplines, there is no such thing as monopoly. Of course, it is true that railroads were monopolists of the rail and the locomotive – a set of physical, chemical, and technological attributes. But such attributes are rather weakly related to the evolving behavioral predispositions of mankind. The failure to acknowledge this in regulating railroads has certainly cost society a rather large misallocation of natural and human resources.

Roland Artle also reminds us that, under certain assumptions, price theory might be used to conceptualize the efficiency of a social aggregate. But he also reminds us that price theory cannot be used for thinking about the effectiveness of a social aggregate. How come then that public policy tries to fit – in fact, force – human activities into the efficient structure of perfect competition? Is the public policy's interest and task that of obtaining efficiency only? Or has it made the assumption that we – sellers and buyers – are all alike and all equate efficiency with effectiveness?

If all individuals in our society are alike, if all of us share only one value (efficiency), then efficiency is equal to effectiveness, and individual choices and social choice are identical. Yet, for 40 years public policy has not succeeded in eliminating all the imperfections in the markets that our authors observe and in a few other markets with which I am familiar.

There may be a few reasons for this lack of success. First, there is the possibility that public policy has been inefficient in its pursuit of efficiency. To begin with, as noted earlier, efforts to shape a system of exchange into the mold of perfect markets imply individual and social costs. If these costs have been greater than those of imperfect markets, then public policy has been inefficient. Unfortunately, I find no evidence that public policy has at least raised this question for consideration. In addition, public policy has not considered another question – namely, that there are individual and social costs implied by nonmarket failures associated with the creation and implementation of public policy (laws, regulations, and court decisions).(4) My work on consumers and issues of safety, pollution, and energy conservation, leads me to agree with the idea that demand for government action may be politically efficient,(5) but to doubt that government action has been efficient in economic terms.

A second reason for this persistent lack of success may be associated with a point of view – a vision – of mankind. This view has been captured by a metaphor of a sailing vessel reported in the First Paul F. Lazarsfeld Lecture by Hans Zeisel.(6) "The market economy keeps the vessel moving, and the government at the rudder keeps it on course by its taxes and expenditures and its regulative powers. The metaphor goes far; a sailboat does not move at all unless somebody holds the rudder."(7)

The image of a "government" keeping a group of people on course by controlling the rudder may imply for some that government chooses the course. It is possible that during the last 40 years public policy has assumed that all of us passengers want to go to the same harbor, by the same route. This image is certainly different from that guiding the efforts of the Thorellis (that of European liberalism) and from that E.T. Grether taught me. Public policy may have failed to reach the perfect markets, for it has not considered that different people may want to go to different harbors, and choose their own course.

If culturally and psychologically we are not identical, if we are a pluralistic society, then individual and social choices cannot be equated, and efficiency is not effectiveness. As I look back at the scenario discussed by the Thorellis and Jones, I do wonder whether public policy makers are at least aware that the stream of their future decisions will ultimately amount to a simple, but historically crucial, choice:

1. by pushing society and each individual into the frame of perfect "competitive" market they equate individual and social choice; if they succeed, it will be the first time that humans have become unidimensional; or
2. by accepting the intrinsic variety of life, they will have to change their frame of reference from industrial organization to those being worked out in marketing, economics, and the behavioral sciences.

This latter choice implies that public policy makers have accepted that individual choices do differ form social choice in all ecological systems. And in so doing, they have learned the lesson I learned from E.T. Grether in his seminars I had the privilege to attend.

NOTES

(1) In addition to the pioneering work by Griliches and Adelman, see the empirical progress reported in R.J. Gordon, Energy Efficiency, User Cost Change, and the Measurement of Durable Goods Prices, National Bureau of Economic Research, Working Paper No. 408, quoted in the NBER Digest, January 1980.

(2) For a review of industrial organization studies of information in the form of advertising, and for some new findings, see F. Nicosia and R. Jacobson, Advertising, Consumers, and Public Policy: The Macroeco-

nomic Effects of Advertising, forthcoming; and R. Jacobson, Consumption and Advertising: A Multivariate Time Series Approach, Ph.D. dissertation, Department of Economics, University of California, Berkeley, 1980.

(3) For an inkling at the rich variety by which a group of persons organizes itself to deal with information in buying processes as well as selling processes, see, e.g., a summary of current knowledge in Nicosia, F.M. and Y. Wind, "Emerging Models of Organizational Buying Processes," Industrial Marketing Management, 6 (1977), and some new findings in Nonaka, J. and F.M. Nicosia, "Marketing Management, Its Environment, and Information Processing: A Problem of Organizational Design," The Journal of Business Research, September 1979.

(4) For a discussion of the issues and literature concerning the costs associated with nonmarket (public policy) failures, see C. Wolf, Jr., "A Theory of Nonmarket Failure: Framework for Implementation Analysis," The Journal of Law and Economics, April 1979.

(5) Ibid., p. 138.

(6) H. Zeisel, "Austrian Socialism, 1928 and 1978" (Philadelphia, Pa.: The Center for Research on the Acts of Man, October 1978).

(7) Ibid., p. 11, quoting from W. Leontief, "Sails and Rudders, Ship of State," Op-ed page, New York Times, March 16, 1973.

10 Public Regulation of Consumer Information: The Life Insurance Industry Case

Richard H. Holton

Fifteen years ago, President Lyndon B. Johnson startled the business community by appointing a Special Assistant for Consumer Affairs, the first time in history that a President had given such status to consumer problems as a matter of public concern. Most if not all of President Johnson's actions in the two months following the assassination of President Kennedy had assured businessmen that he would be a more sympathetic spirit than President Kennedy. Establishing this new staff position, and especially appointing to it Esther Peterson, long affiliated with the labor movement, was seen as a major danger signal by corporate executives across the land. In retrospect, most businessmen no doubt would say that those premonitions were justified.

The resurgence of the consumer movement, after years of desultory existence, can probably be dated from that event. Although President Nixon had no difficulty controlling his enthusiasm for consumer affairs as a matter of presidential interest, by that time a number of congressmen and senators had developed a full appreciation of the voter appeal inherent in the consumerism issue. Initiatives in this area shifted from the White House to Congress, where they remain. Concern about improving the functioning of the markets for consumer goods and services continues to be highly visible today.

Much of the debate in this area turns on the nature and extent of information which is to be provided to consumers. In this paper I would like to focus on this consumer information problem, to put forward a point of view about the problem in general, and then to examine how the problem is manifested in the case of the life insurance industry.(1)

A VIEW OF THE CONSUMER INFORMATION PROBLEM

I have argued elsewhere that the markets for many consumer goods and services are quite imperfect, and likely to remain so, simply because the consumer has neither the time nor the knowledge needed to become an expert buyer of everything.(2) So the consumer advocates who say that consumers do not have enough information miss the point, as do the businessmen who respond that consumers do not use the information which is already available. Both reactions fail to recognize the nub of the problem – namely, the inability of any given consumer to obtain and comprehend all the relevant information needed for each purchase to be a wise selection among the available alternatives.

The consumer information problem varies significantly across markets. The traditional, non-technical description of the virtues of competition in the marketplace says that if a consumer buys a particular brand and is dissatisfied with it, he buys a competing brand the next time. If the manufacturer or the first brand fails to please enough people, he must either improve the product or go out of business. Thus the competitive process, we hear, leads to a winnowing out of the brands which do not please consumers. This is saying that the consumer's information, gained through experience in the marketplace, works to assure that only those sellers who are satisfying at least some minimum percentage of the buyers will survive the competitive race.

The consumer's own experience can be a useful source of information if certain conditions are met, namely: (1) the product is one which the individual consumer buys frequently; (2) the product's quality and performance characteristics can be readily perceived either before the purchase or soon after the product is put to use; (3) the rate of technological change is slow, relative to the frequency of purchase; and (4) the terms of sale are fairly stable between purchases. Illustrative products which might at least come close to meeting all these criteria are razor blades and scouring powder. The individual consumer buys them frequently and their performance characteristics are readily perceived. When one returns to buy these products again, normally the available alternatives have not changed significantly in their technical characteristics since the time of the previous purchase; the consumer's information gained from the prior experience is not yet obsolete. And the terms of sale, although subject to specials, perhaps couponing and the like, are reasonably stable from purchase to purchase.

At the other end of the spectrum are such products as automobile tires. The individual buys tires infrequently, and the performance characteristics are difficult to perceive prior to purchase or even after use. (If a tire seems not to have worn well, what motorist knows whether he had inadvertently subjected it to particularly severe conditions?) Even if one were to experiment carefully with the various brands over time, the rate of technological change in the industry is fast relative to the frequency of purchase, so one's experience provides information which becomes obsolete by the time one is back in the market. One's own experience as a source of information suffers from the same inadequacies to a greater or lesser degree in a variety of markets; e.g., those for automobiles, for appliances, furniture and most hard goods, for repair services, medical services, and others.

For those goods and services which do not meet the four criteria I have suggested, the consumer must rely on sources of information other than his own experience. Advertising, the advice of friends, point of sale information from the retail clerk or point of sale material (including the label), and such publications as Consumer Reports immediately come to mind. But all of these sources of information have their own shortcomings; we need not take time to explore these here since they are fairly apparent. Most important for this discussion is the recognition that using these sources of information takes time. The consumer therefore incurs a cost of searching. Presumably, the consumer will extend the search until the incremental costs of further search are seen as no longer exceeding the probable gain from further search. (Stigler, 1961, p. 216) But using any of the sources of information about a product effectively requires that the consumer know what attributes of the product are important for a proper assessment of the product's value, and what weights are appropriate for each of the attributes. If the product embodies technical complexity, this is expecting a good bit of the consumer.

Viewed in this light, it is apparent that the consumer's acquisition and use of information about the goods and services in the market of necessity will often fall far short of providing the information conditions we assume necessary if competition is to approximate the description in our models of competition. The consumer simply does not have the time or expertise to become an expert buyer of everything.

We can go further and argue that the consumer information problem is surely getting worse. With increasing income per capita, the consumer can buy more goods and services; more alternatives are available every year and the rate of technological change, some would argue, is accelerating. Particularly troublesome, if true, may be that technological developments may cause more attributes of a product to be below the threshold of perception. Thus, the consumer cannot use any of the five senses to determine, for example, the vitamin content of a packaged food product or the value of an additive in his gasoline.

It is worth noting, incidentally, that this worsening of the consumer information problem arises because of the success of our economic system. Most observers would say that higher income, more choice in the marketplace, and continuing technological change are all good. This may well be, but the point here is that one cost of such change may well be more imperfect markets because of a worsening state of consumer information.

If the consumer's direct use of information is in fact increasingly complicated by the developments noted above, we would expect to find consumers resorting to greater use of two proxies for information which are available. One such proxy is the retailer; the consumer who favors a particular department store, for example, is in effect saying that that department store is a satisfactory purchasing agent. Thus, the department store buyer in a sense is being asked by the consumer to engage in the search for products and to screen the alternative brands which are offered. We can question just how well this process works, especially if the department store buyer is most interested in what sells, rather than the inherent quality of the product alone. In other words, does he apply the screening criteria the consumer would have him apply?

Another proxy for information is the brand, the reputation of the manufacturer. If the consumer cannot take the time to learn about all the mechanical intricacies of the competing brands of automobiles or washing machines on the market, or if he or she lacks the background required to comprehend and assess this information if exposed to it, we can appreciate that individual's tendency to give much weight to the general reputation of the manufacturer. So the consumer is using the brand name as a proxy for information. Scitovsky has argued that this can lead the manufacturer to emphasize advertising and product differentiation, thus increasing the inelasticity of the firm's demand curve and permitting higher prices (Scitovsky, 1950, p. 49).

If what I have been saying here is an accurate view of the consumer information problem, we should be careful in our assessments of reports that consumers are "satisfied" with their purchasing experience in particular markets. They may be satisfied because they do not know enough about the product or the characteristics of alternative brands to be able to judge the wisdom of a given purchase. As one author has stated, "Satisfaction is partly dependent on the perceived alternatives" (Hunt, 1977, p. 253). And given one's understandable reluctance to admit that a particular purchase was too hasty or unwise, any given level of satisfaction reported in a consumer survey is likely to be biased upward.

CONSUMER INFORMATION IN THE MARKET FOR LIFE INSURANCE

The market for individual life insurance seems not to meet, very satisfactorily, at least, the four criteria I have suggested must be met if the consumer's own experience is to provide good information. Life insurance is not bought frequently by the individual consumer, so what may have been learned in the course of one purchase can readily be forgotten, in whole or in part, before the next purchase. The "performance" of a life insurance contract is not readily perceived, since the mortality of man prohibits repeated deaths in order to see if the insurance pays the promised benefits promptly. The rate of technological change is fast relative to the frequency of purchase, in the sense that modifications of the product seem fairly frequent, thanks to the imagination of the life insurance companies. And the terms of sale, if this can be distinguished from the "product" in the case of life insurance, are not stable over time.

The life insurance industry is rather interesting on a number of counts. It is a large industry by most criteria; life insurance premiums account for a not insignificant percentage of disposable personal income; life insurance is widely regarded as a necessity; a large number of companies are in the market; and it is already regulated. Of particular interest here are the unique features of consumer demand for life insurance, the type of distribution system commonly used, and especially the complex consumer information problem which is involved.

The scale of the life insurance industry is impressive; the total assets of life insurance companies in the United States came to about $352 billion in 1977, having risen from $64 billion since 1950.(3) This is about equal to the total assets of the top 20 companies in the "Fortune 500." Expenditures for ordinary life insurance premiums in 1977 were just over $24 billion, or about 1.8 percent of total disposable personal income in that year,(4) so we are not talking about insignificant amounts of money in the consumer budget. Surveys have consistently shown that consumers generally consider life insurance to be a necessity, and 88 percent of all families have at least some life insurance coverage.(5) This large market for life insurance has attracted many firms, now about 1,750 in number, up from only 649 in 1950.(6) So to the extent that the number of sellers in the market is relevant to assessing the state of competition in a market, the life insurance industry would appear to be competitive. Finally, the insurance industry is regulated by the individual states, so this, too, might lead one to expect, or at least hope for, the market to operate quite satisfactorily.

I wish to focus here on only one segment of the life insurance industry – namely, the market for ordinary life insurance bought by the individual. In part because it is such a special market, I will exclude the so-called "industrial" life insurance market.(7) The group life insurance business is also excluded since the employer or trade association is a middleman in the sale of this product. And credit life insurance is excluded because it is sold not by itself but as part of another transaction. In 1977, of the total life insurance premium receipts of U.S. life insurance companies, 72 percent was for ordinary life policies, 20 for group life, 4 for credit life, and 4 for industrial life.(8)

Consumer buying behavior in the market for ordinary life insurance is unique in at least two dimensions. First, to use the language so commonly heard among people who know this market, life insurance is "sold, not bought." Obviously, anything that is sold by one party must be bought by another or it is not sold; what is meant here is that the initiative in a life insurance transaction in the market we are concerned with comes typically not from the buyer but from the seller. Rarely does the buyer say to himself, "I need some life insurance," and then proceed to shop around for a policy the way one might shop for an automobile or for furniture. We can only speculate about the reasons for this. Perhaps life insurance is the ultimate in the postponable expenditure. In the case of an automobile, the consumer might be reminded daily of the need for a new car because of the deteriorating performance or appearance of his present car. There is no such daily reminder of the need for life insurance. Perhaps the difficulty of understanding the specifics of the product are a deterrent to the buyer. Or the buyer may assume that life insurance salesmen are ubiquitous and that one pesky life insurance agent or another will approach one with sufficient frequency to provide the useful reminder of the need for life insurance.

The second noteworthy aspect of consumer buying behavior in this model is that the buyer, after having been exposed to a life insurance salesman, typically does not check with agents representing other companies to learn what alternative policies and prices might be available. According to one survey, only four out of ten buyers compared policies across companies.(9) Since respondents in such a survey must recognize that wise buying requires comparison shopping, respondent bias probably causes this percentage to be overstated. Again, one can only speculate about the cause of this. In part, it may be because buyers perceive all life insurance policies to be about the same. Or perhaps it is so time-consuming to learn just what is involved in buying a particular policy that the buyer assumes that the probable gain from shopping does not warrant the additional time and effort. Maybe the life insurance agent is successful at persuading the buyer that the policy he offers is the best in the market and hence shopping is not deemed warranted. According to the survey just cited, consumers reported being more interested in such things as whether the agent seems interested in helping the buyer select the best policy for the buyer's needs, whether the agent appears to be well-trained, etc., than in whether the cost of the policy is lower than the alternatives.(10)

A third and particularly troublesome feature of consumer behavior in the life insurance market is the high lapse rate. The lapse rate is defined as the percentage of new policies for which the second year premium is not paid at the end of the 13th month in the life of the policy. Thus, a lapse rate of 10 percent means that the second annual premium was not paid by the end of the 13th month on 10 percent of the policies sold. For the life insurance industry, the lapse rate is in the range of 20 percent. So much life insurance does not "stay sold"; the contract is frequently broken, in effect. Since personal selling is a relatively high priced means of selling life insurance in the first place, the high lapse rate inflates an already large expense of operating an insurance company which uses the agency system.

Most individual ordinary life policies are sold through the agency system. Certain characteristics of that system can be mentioned here, since they are relevant for our later discussion. First, the agent typically represents but one life insurance company. There are insurance brokers, however, who can place life insurance with any of several companies whom they are authorized to represent. Second, since the product, or more explicitly the product alternatives, are complex, considerable personal explanation is normally required before a policy is sold. Third, the valuable agent is one who advises the client about just what type of policy is best suited to the client's needs, so the agent can be thought of as providing an advisory service as well as the product itself. Finally, one should note that the agent is typically paid on a commission basis. Although the compensation formula varies by company and by type of policy sold (and by the age of the client), a common formula applicable to whole life policies calls for the agent to receive an amount equal to 50 or 55 percent of the first year premium, 10 percent of the premium in each of the next four years, and 3 percent for the sixth through the tenth year. In the case of term policies, the first-year commission is generally in the 35 percent range. It is worth noting that typically the agent has no vested rights in his continuing commission; when he leaves the company, he does not continue to receive the commissions on policies which he has sold in the previous ten years. This presumably works to minimize the turnover of life insurance agents.

Perhaps the most troublesome aspect, although in some respects this is a virtue, of the market for individual ordinary life insurance is the complexity of the product. Since the life insurance policy is a financial contract, the innocent observer might expect it to be relatively straightforward. Unlike many consumer goods, which can vary in appearance, styling, function, taste, aroma, and the like, and thus permit wide variations in price even in a market characterized by perfect information on the part of the buyers, the life insurance policy might at first seem to be only a matter of cold numbers: the face amount of the policy, the premium, the cash values, the dividend, etc. But two sets of complexities immediately arise when one looks even momentarily at the problem. First, authorities disagree about the best means of measuring the net cost of a whole life policy. In the Hart committee hearings on the life insurance industry, no fewer than 21 different methods of computing the net cost of a whole life policy were presented.(11) So there are important conceptual problems to be overcome, and at least some of the measures which are more conceptually attractive to the expert are relatively unattractive in a public policy sense because they are too complex for the average life insurance buyer to comprehend readily. But a second difficulty lies in the unavoidable fact that any net cost calculation is based on forecasts of the company's return on investment, operating expenses, lapse rates, mortality experience, and dividends, with these variables of course being interrelated. Since net cost is a function of a company's future performance, it is impossible to develop a true net cost figure for a life insurance policy when it is being sold to the buyer.

When the most common net cost methods are applied to the policies offered by the larger life insurance companies, it is common to find that comparable policies — i.e., $10,000 whole life for a 35-year old male — will vary substantially; some policies, for example, are twice as costly as others.(12) Thus, it would seem to be apparent that the market for individual whole life policies is indeed a very imperfect market. And given the complexities of life insurance contracts, one is led to believe that much of the imperfection in this market is because of inadequate consumer information.

THE PUBLIC POLICY ALTERNATIVES

One rather heavy-handed approach to the problem of improving the state of consumer information in this complex market might be to permit life insurance companies to offer only a set list of standardized contracts so that comparisons among companies would be simplified; this is reported to be the solution adopted in Germany.(13) The social cost of this approach would be to prohibit, or at least retard, innovation in the industry and to make it more difficult for the industry to meet the needs of particular groups of prospective buyers. And, as we will see later, one could ask whether buyers would shop for life insurance even if only a limited list of contracts were available in the market-place. It is interesting to note that none of the critics of the industry who testified in the course of the Hart subcommittee hearings suggested this approach to the problem. I am prepared to assume that this solution, if it can be called that, is not considered attractive in the United States.

In this country, the critics of the marketing of individual ordinary life insurance have focused their attention on disclosure. The most recent manifestation of this attention can be found in the December, 1978 report of the Subcommittee on Oversight and Investigations of the Committee on Interstate and Foreign Commerce of the House of Representatives.(14) Briefly put, the subcommittee concluded that the market for ordinary life insurance "does not generate sufficient information for consumers to make intelligent purchasing decisions," that "many consumers do not, or are not able to, purchase life insurance products on the basis of suitability, quality, and cost," that there is "significant consumer loss" in this market, and that the "serious failure" in the market mechanism can be "corrected only by deliberate regulatory action."(15) The subcommittee is particularly exercised by what they interpret as the life insurance agent's bias toward selling whole life policies rather than term policies since the commission is greater on whole life policies. They recommend an information disclosure system which would consist of an individualized policy summary and a standard buyer's guide; both of these should be presented to the prospective buyer before the product selection is made. To avoid going into full detail, we can cite just two of the types of information proposed for the policy summary. One set of information would show "how the cash value increase compares to a 'term plus side investment' plan. The 'side investment' would be funded by the dollar difference between the term premium and the higher whole life premium." The second set of information worth noting here consists of one or more cost index numbers. The subcommittee recommends either the company retention index or the net payment and surrender cost indexes.

The life insurance industry spokesmen object vociferously to the argument that it is proper to compare a whole policy with a term policy plus side investment by the policyowner. The argument is that the cash value of a whole life policy, unlike a bank savings account, can be used to purchase extended or paid-up insurance benefits, to provide a life income to the insured or the beneficiary, and to provide collateral for a relatively low cost policy loan. Income taxes are not payable on any interest that might be imputed to the owner of a whole life policy, whereas interest received on a savings account would be. A bank cannot provide the long-term investment guarantees which are inherent in whole life policies, nor would a savings account provide the counterpart of the waiver of premium in the event of disability. Also, the whole life policy for at least some policyowners would be preferred to the term policy plus side investment alternative because the annual premium instills a discipline which might be absent were the side investment program alternative chosen. Finally, it is argued that an individual might well find it quite a challenge, as well as time-consuming, to manage a portfolio of private investments in such a way as to earn an after-tax return which exceeds the return on the funds he has placed with the insurance company. The subcommittee's rebuttal to all this is essentially that the individual's alternative of a term policy plus side investment can yield, over time, enough assets so that the term life insurance can be terminated when the insured reaches the age range where term insurance becomes prohibitively expensive.

Providing cost index numbers appears to be less objectionable to industry spokesmen. But one can legitimately ask how many prospective buyers are going to recognize that one company is using one cost index while a competitor is using another. Furthermore, there is room for manipulation of at least one of the cost indexes, if a company wishes to engage in "window dressing." The problem of consumer comprehension of the life insurance purchasing decision is reflected in the results of two surveys on consumer use of the buyer's guide prepared by the National Association of Insurance Commissioners. The subjects responding gave the buyer's guide high marks for "understandability," but did poorly on an objective test of the key cost information. Only 38 percent, for example, knew about using the index numbers to compare the cost of policies, and only 21 percent knew that the lower a policy's index, the lower the cost. A similar survey revealed that of those who read the guide, only 33 percent could explain the difference between term and whole life.(16)

We need go no further with the subcommittee recommendations for disclosure in order to see the nature of the problem here. The public is well served if our markets for consumer goods and services approximate the competitive ideal; at least we can agree that competition works best in those markets in which buyers are knowledgeable about the alternatives they face in the marketplace. Ordinary life insurance is a complex product for most prospective buyers to contemplate. Objective students of the subject disagree over the appropriate concept of net cost. The alternative types of policies have different sets of attributes, and these attributes can carry different weights in the minds of the prospective buyers. Furthermore, the buyer normally does not shop for life insurance to any significant extent; perhaps the complexity of the product causes the individual to trust one agent, or the buyer simply might not realize that there are major differences in cost, however measured, within the life insurance industry. Thus, price competition seems not to work as effectively in this market as one might wish.

I would agree that here we have a clear illustration of my earlier point − namely, that we cannot expect the consumer to be an expert buyer of everything. So markets are going to be quite imperfect, simply because buyers have neither the time nor the expertise to become professionals at purchasing. Given the complexities of the life insurance market, we should not be surprised to find major differences in prices across the sellers' offerings of comparable products.

The state regulators of the life insurance industry are clearly being goaded by Washington to require more complete disclosure, so conceivably competition in the industry will come closer to the competitive norm over time. But I am not optimistic, simply because of the basic intransigence of the problem.   In short, not every problem necessarily has a satisfactory solution.

In closing, I would like to make a few points which may be worth noting. First, the subcommittee and the Federal Trade Commission both propose that the life insurance agent present the buyer not just with a buyer's guide which explains the differences between term and ordinary life in a general way, but also with the comparison of the ordinary life policy and a "term plus side investment" for the prospect's specific case. The industry people object because this suggests that the "term plus side investment" alternative is a perfect substitute for the ordinary life policy, which it is not. I would add that requiring this much detail about alternatives open to the buyer would be a departure from most selling situations. We assume that the prospective automobile buyer, for example, learns about the various alternative models the dealer has to sell — we do not require the salesman to bring the available alternatives to the buyer's attention. When the stock broker calls a client, we do not require him to tell the investor about alternative ways to use his money. When the individual is buying a house, we do not require the real estate agent to show alternatives. The subcommittee report states that "The problem we find in the market is that the methods used to sell life insurance do not ensure adequate and accurate understanding by consumers of the available product alternatives" (p. 13). If one were to look carefully at the automobile market, could we not say that "The problems we find in the market is that the methods used to sell automobiles do not ensure adequate and accurate understanding by consumers of the available product alternatives?" The same statement could surely be made for quite a list of products and services; e.g., tires, pharmaceuticals, medical services, appliances, repair services of various sorts, and some would include many supermarket items as well.

A second and closely related point is that in most markets we expect the consumer, through his or her own shopping, to develop the information which would "ensure adequate and accurate understanding . . . of the available product alternatives." We do not expect the salesman or the seller to do it. Perhaps the state of information in the life insurance market is so much worse than in other markets that we should expect the seller to engage in consumer education as well as the selling effort. But if that is the route we choose to take in the design of public policy, we should recognize just what we are dong. And it is not easy to do in a market in which even the professionals can disagree about how net cost should best be calculated. Alternative cost indexes can be provided, of course. But even the advocates of more disclosure recognize that "If there is too much information . . . the whole purpose of disclosure can be defeated."(17)

Third, from a public policy standpoint one can be excused for being singularly unimpressed with the industry-sponsored surveys which generally show that life insurance policyowners are "satisfied" with their life insurance purchases. This may be true, but the market might not be working well nevertheless. Would the respondents in these surveys have been "satisfied" if they were all expert buyers of insurance? A survey of owners of the Firestone 500 radial tire or the Pinto with the reportedly faulty gasoline tank design might have revealed that they were "satisfied." The point is that in a market where consumers know relatively little about the details of a product, they might be satisfied because of ignorance, not knowledge.

Finally, one cannot help wondering how many life insurance purchasing decisions would be affected if more disclosure were provided. Obviously much depends on just what kind of disclosure, and especially how objective it would be. Given the complexities of the product even with full disclosure, the life insurance agent surely would still be relied upon, rightly or wrongly, by the prospective policyowner for advice on what total package of insurance he should have. Given that any life insurance agent expects to return to any given policyowner for future sales, it would appear that the agent's reputation with the prospect would be enhanced if it were apparent that the prospect was being given the information needed to make a wise purchase. Since "best industry practice" now in existence appears to make at least a reasonable compromise with what the FTC and the subcommittee have in mind, we can probably look forward to some improvement in the state of consumer information in the market for life insurance. But substantial imperfection in the market will surely remain.

NOTES

(1) The reader suspicious of biased analysis should be alerted that the author is a member of the Board of Trustees of the Northwestern Mutual Life Insurance Company.

(2) Richard H. Holton, "Advancing the Backward Art of Spending Money," in Regulating Business: The Search for an Optimum, Institute for Contemporary Studies, 1978, pp. 125-153.

(3) American Council of Life Insurance, Life Insurance Fact Book, 1978, p. 69.

(4) In the national income accounts, the personal consumption expenditures for life insurance are shown as $11.1 billion for 1977; but this is just the total operating expenses of life insurance carriers and noninsured pension plans, whereas the full premium includes monies which

flow into the life insurance company reserves. The $11.1 billion would also include costs not associated with ordinary life policies alone, which are our principal concern here.

(5) American Council of Life Insurance, p. 35.

(6) Ibid., p. 89.

(7) Industrial life insurance policies are defined as being sold typically with small face values, normally less than $1,000, and the premiums are collected personally by an agent every week or every month. Of the total life insurance purchases of $367 billion in 1977 (ordinary, group and industrial), only $6.5 billion was accounted for by industrial insurance. (American Council of Life Insurance, op. cit., p. 13.) By its very nature, this type of insurance is expensive. The state of consumer information in this segment of the life insurance market must be very bad indeed.

(8) American Council of Life Insurance, p. 57.

(9) Life Insurance Consumers: A National Survey of Cost Comparison Attitudes and Experience, Institute of Life Insurance and Life Insurance Marketing and Research Association, August, 1975, p. 7.

(10) Ibid., p. 15.

(11) The Life Insurance Industry, Hearings before the Subcommittee on Antitrust and Monopoly of the Committee on the Judiciary, United States Senate, 93rd Congress, 1st session, (hereafter referred to as Hearings) p. 930 ff.

(12) See Best's Flitcraft Compend, 1977, A.M. Best Co., p. 26 ff; also Hearings, pp. 1088-89.

(13) See the testimony of Spencer L. Kimball, Hearings, p. 1087.

(14) Life Insurance Marketing and Cost Disclosure. Report by the Subcommittee on Oversight and Investigations of the Committee on Interstate and Foreign Commerce, House of Representatives, Ninety-Fifth Congress, Second Session, December 1978.

(15) Subcommittee report, p. 3.

(16) Reported in the statement of Albert H. Kramer, Director, Bureau of Consumer Protection, Federal Trade Commission, before the Oversight Subcommittee of the Committee on Interstate and Foreign Commerce, House of Representatives, August 7, 1978, p. 11.

(17) See Kramer, p. 12. Kramer also pointed out that "Providing six different index numbers poses a great risk of confusing consumers and defeating the purpose of cost disclosure," p. 13.

11 Consumer Information Systems of the Future

Hans B. Thorelli
Sarah V. Thorelli

This essay is concerned with strategic planning for the consumer information systems of the future. This is a vital area of consumer policy, private and public. It also happens to be a vital part of any realistic policy aimed at retaining and improving an open market economy in an era of product complexity and proliferation and consequent consumer information gap.(1)

Planning in general involves three principal elements: diagnosis of the present, forecasting the future, and providing for the future (see fig. 11.1). On the assumption that readers are familiar with the present, the first part of the paper gives a very brief diagnosis of the situation. Applying an ecologic view of social institutions, the forecasting element of strategic planning is the futurology of the environment – the second part of our essay – while providing for the future is the programmatics of consumer information systems, which constitutes the last part of the paper. As institutions interact with their environment, it is clear that no iron-clad distinction can be made between futurology and programmatics; certainly, this paper is the result of many "feedback loops" between the two. Our time horizon may be anywhere from five years to the end of this century.

Strategic plans aim at the realization of the main objectives of an organization or system of organizations. Objectives in large part are derivatives of the environment in which the organization finds itself, but they also reflect the values of the planners. The values of the authors are restated in capsule form in the epigraph of this essay.

THE PRESENT CONSUMER INFORMATION SYSTEM:
A BRIEF DIAGNOSIS

All the sources of information about market offerings (be they products or services) available to consumers as well as the actual flows of such

STRATEGIC PLANNING	INFO SOURCES
*Diagnosis	*Commercial
*Prognosis	*Personal
*Programmatics	*Independent

INDEPENDENT CONSUMER INFORMATION (CI) PROGRAMS

Current:
*Comparative Testing (CT)
*Informative Labeling (IL)
*Quality Certification (QC)

Future additions:
*Computerized CI Bank
*Combo IL + QC Program

RELEVANT CONSUMER TYPES AND APPROX. PROPORTION IN EUROPE & NORTH AMERICA

The Information Seekers (IS)	10-20%
Average Consumers (AC)	55-75%
Underprivileged Consumers (UC)	15-25%

TARGET AUDIENCES OF CI PROGRAMS

	IS	AC	UC
CT	X		
IL	X	X	
QC	X	X	X
CI Bank	X	X	X

Fig. 11.1. Consumer information systems of the future.

information constitute the elements of what may be called the consumer information system (CIS). Sources are generally divided into commercial, personal, and independent (see fig. 11.1). Of the many commercial sources (including owner's manuals, warranties, fairs, demonstrations, etc.), advertising is by far the most important. Although many would say that the subjective (persuasive) component of advertising is too prominent, it is nevertheless probably true that due to its enormous volume advertising constitutes by far the most important single source of objective information about products. In addition to the fact that many consumers are unable to separate the subjective and the objective elements in the information conveyed by advertising, it is a fact that the objective parts of advertising typically inform us about only a fraction of the characteristics of interest to a consumer intent on intelligent decision-making. This is not necessarily a criticism of advertising – business may well be right in its obvious assumption that most consumers do not want to spend the time, money, and effort necessary to obtain the "best" buy. Human beings may well be "satisficers" rather than optimizers. However, it is also clear that the information requirements of the satisficer are increasing and, certainly, that advertising falls far short of satisfying the consumer elite in Western industrial democracies whom we have identified as the Information Seekers (IS).(2) We also know that consumers in most of these countries consider misleading advertising as the single most objectionable feature of the marketplace.

Personal information sources include our own past experience of market offerings, personal examination of them, and advice by relatives, friends, neighbors, and other individual consumers. Independent consumer information programs (hereafter CI programs) is the third major set of product information sources. CI programs have no direct commercial interest in the promotion of the offerings about which they provide consumer information. It is important to realize that there is a subjective component involved in information emanating from personal sources and CI programs as well as from commercial sources. If on personal examination of a product we find we like it, the propensity is there to "rationalize" away any deficiencies it may have. What friends tell us about their experience with a Ford or Volkswagen automobile tends to be subjectively colored indeed. CI programs have major subjective components by virtue of their emphasis on functional characteristics of a product at the expense of psychosocial ones and in their buying recommendations and/or minimum thresholds. While it seems difficult to generalize about the relative mix of objective and subjective components in personal and commercial information, it is probably fair to say that both of these sources tend to have a greater subjective component than does CI.

CI programs are, of course, less well known than commercial and personal information sources. Many of these programs are narrow-scope, in that they relate only to a single characteristic (energy consumption, wool contents) or only to a single product or related group of products (life-vest certification, food nutrition labels). The great problem with such programs is that their proliferation tends to add to the "noise" characteristic of Western cultures, thereby tending to enhance rather than reduce consumer confusion and frustration. Of much greater principal (and, we believe, in the future also practical) interest are multi-product, multi-characteristics programs. Currently, there are some 50 broad-spectrum CI programs in the 20-nation North Atlantic community.(3) As all such programs are based on the testing of products and services our collective term for them is The Testmakers. Sponsorship of such programs may be quite diverse: consumer groups (Association des Consommateurs in Belgium, Consumers Union in the

United States), government (Stiftung Warentest in Germany, Institut Nationale de Consommation in France) or pluralist (DVN – the Danish informative labeling bureau, Association Francaise de l'Etiquetage d'Information). At present, comparative testing (CT) programs as run by the four first-named organizations dominate the field, followed by informative labeling (IL) programs as illustrated by DVN and AFEI.

Less attention has been given to quality certification (QC) programs. The pioneering group in this area is Qualite France. AFNOR, the French standards organization, also has a quality marking scheme, with its NF symbol, as does the British Standards Institute with its Kitemark. In its pure form, a QC program involves the marking of products with a symbol (such as a star), indicating that products thus marked have been tested and found equal to or better than a certain minimum standard or threshold defined by the certifying organization. Clearly, this represents a stark simplification of information dissemination as compared to CT reports (IL is in a middle position in this regard). Yet there are many indications there is a need for simplified point-of-purchase information.

We may observe in passing that almost by definition voluntary IL and QC programs require the cooperation of industry for their success. Another passing remark of great practical significance – amply documented in our own research – is that CI programs themselves must be given large-scale advertising and promotion in order to be successful.

The CIS of any given country, then, consists of a certain "mix" of commercial, personal, and information sources and flows. It would carry us too far here to inquire into the determinants of the local mix in any given environment. We may merely observe that at the present time there is very little effort made anywhere in the world in the direction of conscious coordination of the elements of the local CIS.

FUTUROLOGY

The view of the future environment relevant to CIS to emerge here is based in part upon analytical material from our own research, in part derived from other sources. In several instances we are projecting and evaluating trends already at work. However, many pieces of the puzzle are necessarily based on mere assumptions, whose credibility must be left to the reader to evaluate. At least we have tried to make them explicit.

Environmental Trends and CI Aspiration Levels

Open market economy

This essay focuses on industrialized countries with open market societies. In communist economies, the consumer has a hard time making his voice heard, and choice is drastically limited. Few, if any of the less developed countries have well-behaved open market systems, and the situation of consumers in these nations, too, is quite different.

There can be little doubt that there is a global leftward trend, in the sense of increased government coordination and regulation of the economy. But even if "market socialism" will make some headway in parts of Western Europe, one seems fairly safe in predicting that most industrial nations will continue to be based on open market systems with local modifications.(4)

Economic progress will continue in these nations. Contrary to the "zero growth" gospel, they will not voluntarily lower their growth rates under the influence of environmental pessimism or some introverted flight from things material. True, resource constraints may force a slower rate of growth, which may also result from a decline of the old work ethic. At the same time Mr. Average is still interested in a higher standard of living (forever a major part of his definition of Quality of Life). While one may doubt that the quest for material progress will diminish in an absolute sense, it is clear that it will decline in importance relative to other elements constituting the quality of life, such as cultural pursuits, the return to nature, and "doing your thing" in other ways than by conspicuous consumption.

Consumers, values, and life styles

With increasing affluence and growing emphasis on self-actualization and "personalismo" will follow greater differentiation in life styles. Differences in consumption patterns will remain an important means of expressing individualization. The psychosocial characteristics of products will not diminish in significance relative to the functional ones as a greater part of all spending becomes discretionary.

Everyone will place an increasing premium on time – we shall have more and more "harried consumers." Even those of us with a conservationist or nonmaterialist bent will come to realize the importance of good CI systems precisely as means of resource conservation (the right purchase for the right purpose) and of minimizing input of personal time on those purchases which even the most frugal nonmaterialist must make.

More Information Seekers, higher CI aspiration levels

The proportion of Information Seekers (IS) in a society is closely related to levels of education and income. Barring war and other catastrophic events, we may confidently predict growth in general education as well as in income. Possibly of even greater significance will be the emergence of consumer education as a major social influence. But many aspects of "consumer civics" will also be broadcast on a scale hitherto unknown by consumer advice bureaus, voluntary consumer groups, business and its trade associations, by government agencies, and by the media. Nor should it ever be forgotten that a vital ingredient in CI systems themselves is consumer education – about functions performed, properties of component materials, and so on.

The intensification of consumer education in our view will have major effects. The single most important effect will be greatly enhanced information-consciousness as more citizens become aware of what intelligent decision-making is all about. Where the average consumer in the past blithely reported that he had all the information needed when he bought his car or refrigerator, his ambition for solid data will be much greater in the future. In response to these new demands, the quality of all product information sources will improve.(5)

Marketplace changes

From our point of view, the most critical aspects of the emerging marketplace is the continuing proliferation of products and brands and the ascending complexity of the average product. The open spaces in the "product spectrum" will be filled increasingly with new types and variants. Product proliferation will mean much greater interproduct competition, cases where different products may meet the same period. This will increase the importance of interproduct and cross-functional tests. Pre-sales service will be an important new concept, comprising product information, information on warranty and on what the customer may expect in terms of after-sales service, as well as access to owner's manuals and assembly instructions before purchase.

The prime characteristic of post-industrial society is that the service trades are outgrowing physical production. To meet the demands of the times, CI programs will have to come to grips with how to evaluate services, the local and personal nature of many of these trades notwithstanding. A similar challenge is confronting us in the rapidly growing area of institutionalized or "collectivized" consumption, such as in the health, postal, transportation, and public utilities areas. There is a great need for CI in these "managed markets," a need presently poorly met. When, as is often the case, these services are provided by government or under close government regulation, it is especially important that CI programs be conducted by independent organizations.

Developments in retailing may actually be rather favorable from a consumer information viewpoint. In the vital food area, the trend in leading countries is clearly towards the extremes of "hypermarches" and neighborhood convenience stores. A large part of the superstore assortment will be small appliances, housewares, and other nongrocery items. By and large, the convenience store will carry strictly routine items for which the need for CI (beyond conventional packaged goods labels) is fairly limited. A major function of the superstore, on the other hand, is precisely to permit choice based on in-store comparative shopping. This is vastly facilitated by the large sales volume, which permits the store to carry a great number of brands of individual food as well as nonfood items and to make use of such devices as unit pricing, open dating, consumer corners, etc., at surprisingly low margin cost.

Consumerism

"Consumers' liberation" will gain full recognition as a movement of urgency similar to women's liberation and ethnic-group liberation in the civilized part of the world. The ultimate driving force will remain the tension between consumer aspirations and the capabilities of the economy to satisfy them as well as the Consumer Information Gap characteristic of affluent economies. Sweden and the United States are likely to remain the precursor nations for the foreseeable future, though there is no reason to believe that their approaches to consumer policy will always be the same.(6) The mainstream of consumerism is perfectly compatible with – indeed but a contemporary expression of – classic ideas of liberalism and pluralist democracy.

Future of Commercial, Personal, and Independent Information Sources

The current product information system is dominated by sellers. It is estimated that producers in the United States spent $64 billion on advertising, sales promotion, and personal selling in 1970. Total expenses of the two leading independent CI programs were around $12 million; that is, less than 1/5,000 as much. Many reservations surround these data, but they do give a perspective. It is impossible to place a dollar tag on the cost of personal (consumer-to-consumer) information; even if it were, we are fairly certain that the impression of producer dominance would remain. Estimates have been made suggesting that the average American gets 100 to 200 or more seller "cues" a day; it may be doubted that he has as much as half a dozen product-oriented conversations with other consumers in the same time.

No one could seriously question the legitimacy of advertising and sales promotion in an open market economy. Nor is there much doubt that advertising in various forms will remain the most important single source of product information in such economies. Personal experience – be it our own or that of our friends – seems likely to continue its relative demise, assuming that the pace of change and proliferation will remain brisk. It is important to note, however, that rising standards of education will make everyone both more information-conscious and more capable of evaluating data, regardless of source.

The future of CI programs will be bright. Their core audience of Information Seekers will grow. Their natural advantage – saving the consumer time in comparative shopping – will become increasingly important. The need for greater transparency in the marketplace will be recognized in ever-wider circles. As average consumers become more information-minded, and as IS become more harried, simplified, point-of-purchase oriented CI programs will be especially vital. If CI programs can be given a local anchorage (see below), they may even supersede commercial and personal information sources as the most important element in the product information system at the community level as regards such vital matters as local prices and availability of offerings, the after-sales service of various dealers, etc.

We think the media will become more interested in product information. There will be market overviews (based on producer specifications) and independent product reviews in the daily press. Additional hobby magazines will appear, publishing market overviews and perhaps even comparative tests of their own. In affluent countries where the daily and/or specialized press fails to seize this kind of opportunity to serve consumers, CI groups will themselves fill the void. Handyman Which?, Holiday Which?, and Money Which?, published by Consumers' Association in Britain, and specialty issues produced by several continental CT programs, demonstrate that this is no idle talk.

The last paragraph illustrates the gradual and informal, even subconscious, emergence of a product information systems approach. We shall have more to say about a deliberate systems view in this area.

Technology Assessment   Computerized CI Utility
Localized CI

We need only think of the role of TV advertising in countries in which sellers are free to use this medium to realize that technology impacts the product information system, just as it permeates most aspects of modern life. The makings of a technological revolution in the CI area are already on hand; the problems in harnessing these technical advancements are primarily economic and institutional. Pending the fusion of these forces, the scenario here will be impressionistic and suggestive rather than specifically prognostic.

The pressure of time will make buying from the home increasingly attractive. Home buying will be greatly facilitated by such developments as the picture-phone and by two-way cable TV. Sales presentations may also be made on videocassettes, which the potential customer can play back through his own TV set. It may soon be economically feasible for individual households to be linked to large central computer facilities by means of input-output terminals attached to their telephone or TV. As most of these developments have built-in feedback capability, they also provide new opportunities for the consumer to "talk back" to sellers in market surveys, product tests, satisfaction studies, on so on. Furthermore — and this is of special interest here — all of this communications technology has tremendous potential for the creation of new types of CI programs. From a CI point of view, however, even more important is the capability of large computers to store, and instantly retrieve, astronomical quantities of data.

We predict that the next breakthrough in CI programs will be the computerized CI utility. Independently of each other, this grand vision was conceived by Consumers' Association of Canada (CAC) and Sweden's VDN in 1968. Consumers Union in the United States sponsored some exploratory work shortly thereafter. A pilot module of a computerized CI utility based on a VDN experiment was developed at

Indiana University. This embryonic Consumer Enquirer Program, which takes the form of a dialog between a perspective buyer of a tape recorder and the computer, is admittedly a primitive creation. Yet it does demonstrate the technical feasibility of computerized CI banks.(7) Large-scale experimentation is currently going on both in Britain and France. For a fee, a couple of American firms will give any consumer a computer printout of the automobile's actual cost to the dealer for the basic car plus any accessories specified by the consumer.

We confidently foresee a bright future for a properly conceived computerized CI utility as a supplement to existing programs due to some powerful inherent advantages. The greatest of these is the dialog feature, which literally makes possible information – and advice, if so desired – tailored to the personal needs and preferences of the individual consumer. Even our primitive program demonstrates two other important advantages. It incorporates basic consumer education about tape recorders, not merely brand comparisons. The consumer who already has sufficient background knowledge can simply bypass the educational program routines. The program also carries data about local availability of various brands of tape recorders and corresponding service facilities in Bloomington, Indiana, thus combining education and product information with highly desirable local data. Pending the everyday availability of the communications devices discussed earlier, access to a CI utility might be arranged by calling an intermediary operator at a time-sharing terminal from any telephone.

Obviously, there are also certain weaknesses in the idea. At present, there is no easy way for the computer to arrange an actual viewing of the product. The logic of computers is also to focus on one characteristic (buying criterion) of the offering after another in staccato fashion, leading the prospect down an orderly decision path. However, in this way the consumer may lose sight of the forest for the trees. Like so many other phenomena, a product has Gestalt; that is, it may appear different when viewed as a whole from the impression gained by examination characteristic by characteristic. Care must also be taken to achieve a distinct separation between factual information and buying recommendations.

One may wonder why we do not already have a computerized CI utility system. There are at least two good reasons. First, no data bank can be any better than the information which is fed into it. Even assuming the willingness of The Testmakers to cooperate, it is a formidable effort to prepare all their information in a format suitable to the computer, not to speak of attendant programming of education and dialog routines for all products involved. It is also a fact that for hundreds of products the requisite data do not yet exist. Here one would have to make do with market overviews based on manufacturer catalogs pending neutral testing data. It will also be a very big – and costly – job to keep the information up to date. There would be some scale economies, in that product information would have national – in some markets international – validity. Yet it is self-evident that to be successful a CI utility system would have to be extensively decentral ized, so that in any given community it would include local availability, price, service, and perhaps even complaint data.

Second, the economics of this kind of venture is still highly uncertain. The Consumer Association of Canada (1969) speaks of a nonprofit, nongovernmental venture (which philosophically has our own preference), while E. Scott Maynes (1975) talks in terms of either user (subscriber?) or local government financing. The main point in favor of the latter alternative would be the public-goods (externality) nature of the information provided by the utility.

Obviously, computerized data banks are not to be viewed as alternatives to comparative testing, informative labeling, and quality certification. Being based on the tests underlying these types of CI programs, such banks are to be viewed as large-scale extensions and supplements to them. Each of the four approaches has some unique characteristics. They are all needed to span the consumer information gap in concert with advertising and other aspects of the total consumer information system.

PROGRAMMATICS

Having thus attempted to forecast the operating environment, we turn now to the policy conclusions and recommendations part of our exercise in strategic planning for CI systems.

Attending to the Information Seeker

In open market democracies, the Information Seekers are the shock troops in the perennial struggle to maintain and increase consumer sovereignty. We know that the IS, more than average consumers, will:

- personally enforce consumer rights
- personally exercise consumer responsibilities
- keep suppliers on their toes by pinpointing poor service, deficiencies in products, out-of-stock conditions, misleading advertising, and other malpractices
- voluntarily finance CI programs
- disseminate information and advice to fellow consumers
- serve as proxy purchasing agents for many less information-conscious and planful consumers

The IS do perform the role of St. George; they are the vigilantes of the marketplace. Indeed, IS themselves constitute a public good in more than one sense! It has been said that we have spent the last hundred years perfecting producer institutions, but that unlike the firm, the average consumer has no purchasing agent, quality control system, or expertise on hand to enforce sellers' contractual obligations. There is much truth in this notion. Due to the diseconomies of scale involved, we can never hope that the average household will reach similar degrees of professionalism. Nor could (or, we think, should) public policy ever be expected to do this job in full. Consumer education will be an important assist. So, it will be seen from the above, are the Information Seekers. They, more than others, are indeed professional consumers.(8)

The IS are most effectively assisted in their public functions in the marketplace by greatly enlarged and diversified CI programs of the variations discussed in this paper. But in a democracy everyone must be free to become an Information Seeker. An indispensible part of this upward thrust is a comprehensive set of policies aimed at the emancipation of underprivileged consumers. Average consumers are most readily helped along the way by consumer education and simplified CI programs.

What Business Can Do

The number of transactions between sellers and individual consumers in the affluent democracies of the world may well exceed one billion per day. It appears that in a clear majority of these transactions, consumers are at least fairly well satisfied. To say that the open market system is a failure seems to us grossly unfair. Yet we are singling out business, among all consumer-policymaking groups, for separate discussion here as there is so much more that it can do that is yet undone, or done to much less than perfection. Much of this can be accomplished by voluntary action, in the spirit of free societies. It must also be admitted that not until the last few years has business received any strong signals from its operating environment that it needed to view its activities from a CI perspective. A further reason for such a discussion is a conviction that individual firms in the future may secure an important differential advantage by adopting superior information as a competitive strategy.(9) Finally, it seems clear that business in general stands to gain by being proactive rather than merely reactive in dealing with the modern consumer, his needs, aspirations, and problems.

Business should make advertising and sales promotion more informative. An excellent way of making ads and mail order catalogs more informative is to use material from CI programs to the extent this is permissible (e.g., referring to test reports and reprinting informative labels as done by the German mail order house Quelle). Let the package inform, not deceive. Facilitate comparability by sensible and fair comparative advertising, by unit pricing, by providing an assortment that offers real choice, by participating in fairs, collective displays and multi-brand outlets. Most retailers could vastly improve sales training to upgrade clerks into consumer consultants, and large retailers should make much broader use of consumer corners for advice, information, and education materials. In providing consumer education materials, business should scrupulously avoid promotion. Owner's manuals and assembly instructions could be markedly improved. Warranties could be made more specific and yet more understandable.

This brings us to some of the things business could do in cooperation with others, notably consumers. In the past decade or two of consumerism, we have witnessed a kind of "fighting on the barricades" in most affluent countries. We firmly believe the time has now come when both business and consumer groups are ready to sit down for problem-solving of mutual interest, just as management and labor have learned to do after an initial period of mutual suspicion. As part of this process consumer affairs management must be given much more weight in corporate affairs. (Fornell, 1976) Also, through this channel and/or by means of consumer sounding boards, panels, and surveys, consumer inputs may directly benefit product planning, advertising, and other aspects of marketing strategy.

Whether in the interest of long-term survival of the open market system, or as a matter of social responsibility, or as an element of a superior competitive information strategy, it behooves business to do what it can to promote voluntary CI programs, together with consumers and perhaps other interested parties such as independent experts and government. The most crying current need among average and underprivileged consumers is simplified point-of-purchase information of the IL and QC varieties. Until now, where such programs have coexisted, they have generally been entirely separate. This is a major advantage from the viewpoint that we certainly need more experimentation as regards CI programs. Even more important, as subjective elements can never be entirely eliminated even from independent CI programs it is indeed crucial that the administration of such programs does not become a monopoly — regardless of what bodies, private or public, are sponsoring them.

Yet we are firmly recommending a combined voluntary IL-QC program open for all consumer products and services. Participating firms (be they producers or distributors) would themselves decide whether they would like the tags attached to their products to carry only the label, only the quality mark, or both. Separate committees — composed on a pluralist basis — should decide on the characteristics and measurements to be declared on the label and on the minimum performance threshold required for the quality mark. (Incidentally, one might well consider two levels of quality, such as the green and gold seals used by the Dutch IVHA). Other circumstances equal, customers will naturally be served best when a seller uses both the label and the seal on his tag (and in his advertising). Mary Gardiner Jones places this proposal in the realm of "familiar" approaches — yet it must be clear that we have absolutely nothing by way of an IL-QC program in the United States at present, or even a separate multi-product labeling or certification program for that matter.

Apart from the fact that a common, easily identified type of tag would be used whether a product would be given a label, a mark, or both, there are three other areas in which major gains will be obtained by a combined IL-QC program. Great common economies may be secured by joint testing, joint performance control, and joint promotion. Testing is an expensive and yet indispensable activity for both IL and

QC. Even if most performance control is delegated to producers themselves, any independent CI agency must occasionally conduct performance control audits by repeat testing and/or a review of the quality control procedures at the factory level among participating producers. This is also costly. Promotion of the CI program itself to both consumers and producers requires a great deal of money. Our research indicates that a prime reason for the failure of many IL and QC programs in the past has been insufficient promotional and educational effort. The requirements here are hundreds of thousands, or in larger countries millions, of dollars. A single promotional program for IL and QC, therefore, is a major economic advantage.

Industry, consumer groups, and independent laboratories should cooperate much more intensively than at present in the development of standard methods for measuring performance (SMMP). This is also an expensive activity. Decentralized experimentation in the development of testing methods is desirable, but presently a great deal of unnecessary duplication is taking place in almost all countries as well as internationally. This is indeed a shame, as there is still a crying unmet need for SMMP for many products and performance characteristics. National and international standards organizations need plenty of stimulation in this area.

A reward of more straightforward product information will be fewer complaints. But better CI will also increase consumer satisfaction. In the long run, consumer satisfaction is the single most important determinant of business survival, both at the firm and at the system level (Thorelli, 1977).

There are several CI-related causes at the community level inviting business cooperation, such as local business-consumer review boards for misleading advertising and other malpractices. Pending computerized CI banks as discussed earlier, business could help by publishing community catalogs of model and brand availability, service capabilities, etc. of local dealers, preferably in cooperation with consumer groups or community organizations. (Telephone catalog directories are, of course, inadequate in this regard.) Constructive business initiatives for underprivileged consumers should also be more common.

Business may elect not to engage in the kinds of CI and consumer policies illustrated here, or do it only in a perfunctory way. If so, we have to put aside our programmatics and go back to prognostics. The scenario then likely will be quite different. It will likely involve obligatory information requirements, counter-information programs, mandated corrective information, an advertising tax to finance government CI programs, etc. — all these measures adopted in an atmosphere of animosity toward business. Some of these things may come anyway, but then likely in less severe form, and with business-proposed amendments incorporated with due respect for a legitimate viewpoint.

Further away on the horizon of that type of scenario are such prospects of questionable merit in an open market system as censorship of new products, mandated economy models, and such detailed controls and regulations at every step of managerial activity that we shall have to accept zero growth whether we want it or not.

CI international

Internationalization of CI programs. In the past, next to nothing has been done in the direction of true internationalization of CI programs. This has been a failure of the EEC, the International Standards Organization, and by CI groups themselves. As far as we know, the Woolmark is the only "global" consumer products symbol in existence! Yet the world is becoming increasingly interdependent, and we now know that in the Information Seekers the affluent democracies have in common a highly cosmopolitan clientele. For many more products than is the case currently, it should be eminently feasible to conduct joint testing – gaining both common economies and division of labor.

The greatest promise for multinational CI programs is in the IL area. A label format could be standardized for the entire universe, as long as a firm using the label would only have to indicate the performance of its brand on the characteristics identified on the label. Theoretically, QC programs could be made universal even more readily. However, in this case, one runs into the problem that national member groups might wish to establish different minimum thresholds. (Italian men want their suits to be cool, Norwegian men want them to be warm – both groups with good reasons.) Even so, the mark itself could well be standardized internationally.

International organization of CI programs. The International Organization of Consumers Unions needs drastic revitalization in terms of quality of personnel, monetary resources, and active support of members. Perhaps IOCU should also invite IL and QC organizations with adequate consumer representation to join. In the fragile field of international relations a unified organization would surely do a better job than several splinter groups. For IOCU to become effective – which it currently is not – influence on the policies of the organization must more faithfully reflect the contributions by member groups than in the past. Also, non-CI consumer lobbies should be excluded from full membership. If not, IOCU is likely to evidence the same inexorable trend towards ineffectuality as the United Nations in recent years.

Should it prove impossible to reorganize the IOCU along the lines suggested, our best advice is that the members interested in an effective grouping form a separate organization. This is really no more remarkable than the creation of the OECD at the level of international economic policy.

Wanted: Decentralized Pluralist CI Systems

CI program development

Strategic planning for CI programs will benefit from:

- adopting an ecologic perspective
- viewing CI as part of consumer policy
- viewing CI as part of a pluralist marketing communications system
- taking into account a ten-fold operating challenge

The essence of an ecologic perspective is simply stated: to attain desirable performance (P), organizational resources (O) must be matched up with environmental opportunities (E) by means of appropriate strategy (S). This is easier said than done, to be sure, but in Consumer Information Systems there is a wealth of conceptual and empirical data which provides a fair indication of how P, O, E, and S variables are related.

It is also important to view CI as part of consumer policy. The numerous tradeoff and reinforcement opportunities between education, information, and protection should be especially considered. So, it should be emphasized, should the tradeoffs and reinforcements between different types of CI programs and different groups of consumer policymakers.

Related areas of private and public consumer policy include the following:

- consumer education
- standardization
- advertising
- sales training
- product safety
- complaints handling and redress mechanisms
- antitrust and competition policy
- environmental protection

In the past, few CI programs have looked upon themselves as integral links in a product information network. However, to do this must again be a major guidepost in strategic planning. Fig. 11.2 gives a highly simplified, integrated view of a pluralist market communications system. Here, CT represents all varieties of CI, manufacturers represent distributors as well, and underprivileged consumers, government agencies, educational institutions, etc. are excluded for reasons of practicality. Even so, the figure points to several lacunas in current systems and to other opportunities for improvement and cooperation.

The last guidepost in strategic program planning to be emphasized here involves the consideration of operating problems. We have tried to summarize them in a ten-fold challenge.

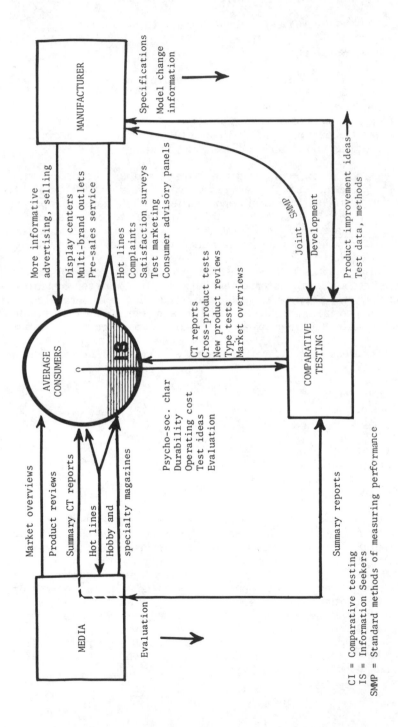

Fig. 11.2. Simplified view of pluralist market communications system

CI = Comparative testing
IS = Information Seekers
SMP = Standard methods of measuring performance

170

1.   The Challenge of Takeoff
2.   The Challenge of the Audience
3.   The Challenge of Relevance
4.   The Challenge of Quality
5.   The Challenge of Product Service, Price, and Availability
6.   The Challenge of the Product Image
7.   The Challenge of Ratings and Thresholds
8.   The Challenge of Product Systems
9.   The Challenge of Services
10. The Challenge of Credibility

For a detailed discussion of these critical challenges in CI program operations the reader is referred to Consumer Information Systems and Consumer Policy.

Systems development

The need of viewing CI programs as parts or extensions of consumer policy, marketing communications, education, and other social systems has been emphasized. But there is also need to think of all CI programs existing in a given culture as constituting a CI system (CIS). The opportunities for synergy and reenforcement are great — as are the somewhat opposite needs of independence and experimentation. We are convinced that in a pluralist, decentralized system the benefits of both competition and cooperation can be obtained without incurring an overdose of either.

Consumers' liberation

The rationale of CI programs is simple. It is the liberation of the citizen in his role of consumer. That role is a major one, whatever our interests or stations in life. CI is in and of itself an instrument to enrich the quality of life. It helps us free time and resources for concerns other than purely material ones. It helps us save on material resources for society as a whole. It has virtually nothing to do with inculcating or reenforcing materialism as such.

Incompatible it is with the idea of a free society to prevent anyone from spending his money foolishly, but it is quite within the scope of this ideal to assist people in spending their money less ignorantly. The costs of doing this are miniscule relative to the costs of everyday commercial information.

In the end, it may well be that the principal effect of such programs is not the dissemination of information in itself, but rather the renewal of consumer trust in business, of consumer faith in the integrity of products and their makers. Inevitably, CI programs will tend to reward the purveyors of "value for money." Thus, they are an instrument of perfecting the open market system. Let it not be forgotten that in a free society the market itself is the greatest comparative testing agency of them all!

We have argued the need for integration of CI programs into an overall Consumer Information System. To the extent that the parts of the system reenforce each other and the wastes of overlap are avoided, this will be all to the good. However, care should be taken to decentralize the units of the system and to encourage different sponsorship of the parts – and for two reasons. First, the field is still in need of free-wheeling experimentation and innovation. Second – and most importantly – only by decentralization and differentiation in sponsorship can we guard against the ever-present possibilities of abuse.

After all, knowledge is power. A monopoly on information would be worse than one on a product. Hidden informers would be worse than hidden persuaders, and we do not want our testmakers to become our tastemakers. Freedom of consumer information is quite as important as freedom of the press.

NOTES

(1) This paper builds upon the last chapter of Hans B. Thorelli and Sarah V. Thorelli, Consumer Information Systems and Consumer Policy (Cambridge, Mass.: Ballinger, 1977), the last volume in a trilogy also comprising Hans B. Thorelli, Helmut Becker, and Jack Engledow, The Information Seekers - An International Study of Consumer Information and Advertising Image (Cambridge, Mass.: Ballinger, 1975) and Hans B. Thorelli and Sarah V. Thorelli, Consumer Information Handbook: Europe and North America (New York: Praeger, 1974). For a detailed analysis of the existing consumer information gap, see ch. 1 of the first-mentioned work.

(2) For an in-depth comparative study of the Information Seekers in Germany and the United States and a review of related research elsewhere, see the Information Seekers.

(3) For a detailed analysis of almost all of these programs see the Consumer Information Handbook, op. cit., selectively updated in Consumer Information Systems, Appendix E.

(4) Consumer information gap would also be a challenge under market socialism (though it might be smaller due to less choice, restrictions on advertising, etc.), although the means of bridging the gap – assuming the task would be undertaken at all – would likely be different from those discussed in this essay.

(5) The reader will note that the discussion is based squarely on the prognosis that education in general and consumer education especially will play an ever-increasing role in the future. We think this is a pretty safe prediction. Should it be false, much of this chapter would have to be rewritten in a scenario based on consumer protection and immensely intensified government regulation of markets instead of the education-information approach which we (perhaps wishfully) believe will prevail.

(6) For a detailed case study of consumer policy and philosophy in Sweden, see Consumer Information Systems, chapter 7.

(7) The Consumer Enquirer Program is reproduced in Consumer Information Systems as Appendix F.

(8) Naturally, this does not necessarily mean that IS are obsessed with materialism.

(9) In a study of 3,400 business executives, it was found that no less than 62 percent at least somewhat agreed with the statement that, "Marketers should make a sincere effort to point out the failings and limitations of their products as well as their strengths." Stephen A. Greyser and Steven Diamond, "Consumerism and Advertising: A U.S. Management Perspective," Advertising Quarterly (Spring 1976): pp. 5-9.

12 The New Telecommunication Technologies: Answer to Consumer Needs?

Mary Gardiner Jones

The most significant characteristic of the United States economy today is the increasing dominance of the service industries in the economy and the concomitant emergence of information as a major product of this service economy. These service industries include the electronic and print media, advertising, education, telecommunications services, and banking industries, and an embryonic information producing/disseminating industry. Of equal importance to the information service industries are the telecommunications hardware industries which provide the essential terminal, computer, microprocessor chip, etc., infra structure for transmitting and processing information to the user communities.

To date, the chief beneficiaries of these information and communications technologies are industrial and commercial users. Business applications are coming on stream in ever increasing abundance and variety. Yet the significant potential of these technologies lies in their capacity to transform the quality and scope of the information which can be made available to the individual members of our society. With the coming of age of the information and telecommunications technologies, the challenge of the 1980s will be to channel their use for the service of society.

This paper will explore the potential application of these technologies to provide information for individual and social uses, to examine the steps taken to date to apply these technologies to the home market(1) and to analyze some of the more important issues raised for society in developing the social uses of these technologies.

INFORMATION: AN URGENT NEED

The importance of information as an essential resource and critical basis for self-actualizing power for individuals has long been recog-

174

nized. "The management of modern complexity" has been the name given to the information problems confronting citizens today by British cyberneticist Stafford Baer. It has been said that each year 10,000 new chemical compounds are discovered which impact our lives; each year 50,000 new local, state, and federal laws are enacted and each year 75 billion new documents are produced by society. If citizens are to be active participants in society, and not sink into an information poverty with almost as drastic results to their humanity as the more familiar economic poverty, then the information and telecommunications technologies must be harnessed to their use with even greater urgency than the need to harness them for business use.

The consumer movement and the explosion of how-to books provide vivid examples of the public's demands for information in order to make intelligent decisions about goods and services in the market place. The popularity of TV interview and talk shows, the Op Ed page topics, letters to the editors section, and the expansion of major newspapers to a variety of nontraditinoal news-feature sections illustrate the public's wider interests in a broad range of quality of life concerns. On the other hand, much of the public's current alienation, apparent political apathy, and disaffection from the major political, economic, and intellectual institutions in our society attest to their growing sense of helplessness and inability to grapple effectively with issues respecting the impact of the human and environmental externalities of the marketplace on the quality of their lives.

The information and telecommunications technologies coming on stream today can empower citizens and consumers to call up a limitless range of information on a virtually unlimited range of topics and subject matters.   Moreover, the information can be provided to individual citizens on their demand, at times of their choosing and, to a large extent, in a form corresponding to their needs and interests.

THE PRESENT STATE OF TELECOMMUNICATIONS

Satellites, high-speed switching exchanges, laser beams, coaxial cables, and small dish antennas all provide the capabilities to bring electronically together into one accessible market economically significant groups of users with widely disparate interests in the same geographic market or with the same interests in widely-dispersed geographic markets. The capabilities are important both because of the economies of scale they permit and also because of the opportunity they provide information vendors to differentiate their data to meet the different needs, education levels, and interests of their available markets. Information of interest to relatively small population segments in different communities can now be economically disseminated because of the networking transmission media which tie these disparate groups into a viable market. For the first time, therefore, information vendors and providers do not need to predetermine the audience to whom their information materials will be directed. No longer need they give up reaching the smaller segments of the population who would require a different writing style/format or information content. Consumers Union, for example, can provide a software package which enables the sophisticated and the unsophisticated, the specialist and casual browser, the price conscious and the quality or environmentally conscious consumer to pick the content and scope of information which corresponds to their needs.

There are still significant economic and institutional restraints which need to be overcome in order to make a telecommunications-based, publicly available, in-home information system operational.

The major economic barriers are already on their way to being overcome. Today, the economics of simple home terminals are already at a level ($500 to $600) which make them largely accessible to significant segments of the population. More complex interactive home terminals are on the market for $2000. Every indication exists that as the market grows these costs will decline. Desksize computers which cost $30,000 in the early 1960s are now being replaced by postage stamp-sized microprocessor chips costing $15 which can perform simple user directed tasks. More complex multi-purpose microprocessor-based computers are already available to the computer hobbyist for under $1000. Printer attachments today would add substantially to current terminal costs but these, too, it can be reliably assumed, will also come down in prices as larger numbers of industrial users come on stream. Video discs are already on the home market commercially at prices fully affordable by the more affluent segments of the population and these can be expected to decrease as the market develops.

Transmission media to interconnect the householder either with various consumer information data banks or with live interactive educational, medical, or other information-oriented dialogues are also already technically available and in the process of development. Because these media have immediate commercial and industrial markets, their development does not depend on the viability of the consumer market and can be expected to proceed as quickly as the industrial markets open up.

The National Research Council's 1978 report, Telecommunications for Metropolitan Areas: Opportunities for the 1980s, believes that the new technologies can be achieved by offering to the householder a flexible, multi-purpose information and communication system. This system could encompass not only information, education, and entertainment services but a series of remote control applications to adjust home temperatures, energy use, a variety of types of intrusion, fire and hazard alarms, as well as record keeping, accounting, and bill paying systems.

In view of the varied applications for which a home communications and information center can be used and the rapidly developing industrial demand for the basic components which are also necessary for the home system, there seems little doubt that consumers can have in place the requisite hardware system to give them access to the benefits of the information society.

The existence and nature of consumer demand for the products of our information-based society and the institutional mechanisms best suited to meet that demand have up to very recently been largely a matter of wishful thinking and speculation. Today, the institutional barriers, in the sense of who will exercise the leadership in applying these telecommunications technologies to the information needs of individuals, are beginning to break down.

HOME INFORMATION EXPERIMENTS

There are several ongoing projects designed to test consumer/public information demands in realistic hands-on modes. Information in the sense of these experimental projects is used in a very general sense to encompass factual data, TV games, and opinion polling, as well as transactional activities such as banking, teleshopping, and electronic mail. A brief description of these projects will illuminate the potentialities of the new technologies to serve home information needs and point up some of the problem areas for future resolution.

The most popular of the current experiments to provide information to the public are two home information systems using the viewer's TV as the information terminal. These systems known as Teletext and Videotext are being widely experimented with both in Europe and the United States.

Teletext

Teletext is essentially a one-way broadcast information system using the vertical interval on the TV screen to display text and graphic information frames selected by the viewer from a limited data bank of some 100 frames continuously "beamed" at the screen in a rotating fashion. The number of frames available is limited by the per page recycling time — about one-fourth of a second — and the viewer's anticipated wait time tolerance, estimated to be about 17 seconds. Given these two parameters, a likely "magazine" of 150 pages is possible. One way of expanding this data base, used by the British CEEFAX system, is to change the content during the course of the day to accommodate different viewers' interests.

The system has the attraction of being simple to use, requiring viewers to select one or more frames from a listing of information frames available. Moreover, it is well adapted to providing current up-to-date information in view of the ease with which frames can be changed on an hourly, daily, or weekly basis, as needed. Current applications of teletext systems envisage providing viewers with weather, travel schedules, entertainment offerings, and other similar "almanac" directorized types of information. Teletext need not be limited to directorized type information. It can also be used for reading ordinary textual material. The viewer has control over the "read" time desired for each frame and simply presses a button when another frame is desired.   Current payment modes vary from providing TV viewers with free access to charging a per frame rate.

Currently, two teletext systems are operational in Great Britain (CEEFAX and Oracle). These systems, developed by the BBC and the British Independent Broadcasting Authority respectively, are free to the viewers. Estimates place the number of set owners at around 30,000 to 50,000 in 1979 in Great Britain.   Similar systems are being experimented with in France, Sweden, Germany, and Canada. In the United States, several TV stations – KSL-TV in Salt Lake City and, more recently, KMOX-TV, in St. Louis – have been testing teletext systems during the past year. WETA-TV in Washington, D.C., in cooperation with New York University's Alternative Media Center is engaged in a two-year planning study for the Corporation For Public Broadcasting on the use of teletext in public television. The study envisages an "information bank" of about 75 to 100 pages of information on subjects to be drawn from such categories as public services, health, consumer information, local (bulletin board) type information, news, personals, and entertainment. One of the interesting features of this project is its experimentation with making the system available through the TV screen not only in the home but also in designated public places such as local libraries, federal buildings, bars, hotel lobbies, and other areas frequented by the public.

One major advantage of teletext systems is their relatively low cost. For a viewer to use the system, it is necessary only to purchase a decoder at a current cost of approximately $100. No estimates exist of the cost to the system owner in creating the data bank necessary to fuel the system.

Control over editorial content in these systems is divided between broadcasters and press interests. So far as is known, none of these systems envisages a right of access by information providers in any form, nor have these systems utilized independent providers. While the full potential of teletext systems has not yet been tapped, many people regard these systems as essentially limited to offering primarily new features of TV programming rather than providing a medium for new uses for TV to meet home information needs.

Videotex systems

Also using a home TV receiver, these information systems are essentially interactive. They link the user/viewer by telephone with data banks and offer a whole variety of new information uses for TV quite unrelated to today's TV programming. TV owners are provided access to data banks which can potentially offer 70,000 pages of data provided by independent information vendors at a fixed rate. These information vendors or providers can range from governmental or private social services, citizens, or consumer organizations to newspapers, travel agencies, advertisers, or other commercial entities who wish to sell and disseminate information to the public. The viewer pays for the information called up unless it is made available by the information provider at no charge. The amount of information available is constrained only by the capacity of the computer's magnetic store. Moreover, the scope of information can be infinitely increased by simply networking a hierarchy of locally, regionally, and centrally established data banks or computer centers.   The degree of sophistication with which the information can be probed is theoretically equally unlimited, depending upon the type of search mechanism used, whether key words or tree-type indices which allow searching in varying degrees of depth, depending on the searcher's interest and need.

Currently, there are several videotex systems on stream or in the process of being designed in Europe, Canada, and in the United States. The British Post Office has the most advanced videotex system operational. Known as View Data or Pestel, the British system reportedly has a list of some 100 organizations willing to load the View Data computers with information for users to access. They include the Stock Exchange, Reuters, local newspapers, travel agents, consumer associations, retail chains, publishers, and entirely new "electronic publishing" companies formed to use the new media. The information topics currently offered include news, sports, radio and TV, going out, holidays and travel, tourist guide, education, hobbies and pastimes, jokes, quizzes and games, home and family help, marketplace, cars and motoring, houses and mortgages, facts and figures, money and insurance, jobs and careers, business services, stock markets, messages, and View Data Index. Under the British Prestel system, seven hierarchies of information are available with ten options at each point. Essentially, the British viewer is assigned an identifying "answerback" number which identifies the subscriber to the system. Entry to the system's services is by keyboard via tree-structure search. Directories are published listing the data bank's offerings. Subscribers are charged for their telephone call to the system, the value of the "pages" of information searched and a small connect time fee.

The British View Data system also has industrial electronic mail type uses. It can be linked to the telex network to enable business users to transmit cheap messages and communicate with each other without interfacing with the system's data banks. Closed user group systems using special access pass words and private specialized data bases have also emerged in the British system. These applications open up an intriguing potential of these systems not only for business users but for special membership groups or nonprofit users who wish to communicate with their members using this "public" information network.

Current costs of the British terminal are in the $1600 range above the ordinary cost of the TV terminal, although the original estimate of $300 above the set cost is still regarded as a realistic target.

Almost every European country has launched some form of videotex pilot program with hands on market trials scheduled for 1980 and 1981. Essentially, these pilot programs involve the collaboration of national PTTs and information providers, usually publishers and newspapers. In Germany and France, the information component of these systems is being correlated with transaction/directorization type services which may provide interesting financing possibilities as additional revenue sources.

Unfortunately, it is still too early to be able either to evaluate these European projects or even to know whether they will succeed in evoking public acceptance and meeting the public's information needs and concerns.

In the United States, several teletex systems are being developed.

Rights to market the British View Data system in the United States have recently been acquired by General Telephone Electronics Corp. – reportedly for the business market. Home application of a teletex system is now currently being readied for launching in the Miami area by the Knight Ridder newspaper chain. Knight Ridder is planning a two-year market test to provide 150 Miami home viewers with both hardware and software necessary to use the system. Knight Ridder expects to offer a full range of information services, including local, national, and international news, sports results, lists of adult education classes, product ratings, local amusement schedules, boating and fishing information, and other data bases.

While the UK Post Office which runs Britain's View Data systems has opted for a type of common carrier stance towards information providers, the European PTTs have rejected such editorial neutrality. They expect to be the prime control authorities in ensuing the quality of both the indexing and the data base on which their systems depend. The European systems envisage an interesting mix of interactive networks of locally or regionally created data banks. Their plans contemplate creating distributive data centers with small computers located at major telephone exchanges tied together presumably by satellite or microwave systems.

Another set of pilot programs on stream in the United States utilizing cable TV focuses on using the new telecommunications technologies to reflect direct viewer expression of attitudes or choices. In Columbus, Ohio, Warner Cable Corporation's Qube, a two-way interactive television service, records viewer votes on political issues, can accept purchase orders for merchandise displayed on the viewer's TV receiver, administer educational tests, and perform a variety of other interactive transactions. Older citizens in Reading, Pa., have used their local cable TV system to originate their own programs or entertainment, talk with local political figures, and discuss issues with other members of the population. While not strictly "information" dissemination applications, these experiments are important illustrations of the flexibility of these new technologies to meet public interests and needs.

Current experiments with home information systems are not restricted to TV display terminals. An independent commercial enterprise, Telecomputing Corporation, has designed such an information system utilizing separate home terminals which are available for sale or lease. Known as the Source, Telecomputing Corporation offers subscribers an information system linking the user's terminal by telephone with a series of data bases created or purchased for the system. While home terminals are available at a purchase cost ranging from $600 to

$2000 depending on their complexity or at a rental cost starting at $21, the Source is also currently available to consumers at a franchised retail outlet in McLean, Va., the first of many such franchised outlets being planned. A one-time subscription charge of $100 is levied by the system plus user charges that vary, depending on whether the data banks are utilized at night or during the day. Evening and weekend usage is billed at $2.75 an hour in one-minute increments and at $15 an hour for daytime access. On stream or in the planning stage are data bases containing current news, dining out guides for major cities, toll-free 800 numbers, business and financial information, travel schedules, consumer affairs, and the like. The Source has made arrangements to access such existing data bases created by the New York Times and UPI. It plans to tap other nationwide data bases.

A second experimental home information system, "Operation Green-thumb," is also scheduled to be operational this year. The experiment, designed for 200 farm households, is being sponsored by the Department of Agriculture's Extension Service in cooperation with the United States Weather Service and administered by the University of Kentucky, using micro-processor hardware developed by Western Union. The system envisages providing farmers with access to a variety of farm-oriented data bases concerning weather, markets, crop diseases, commodity prices, local farm news, and other similar topics. A listing of the information available on the system will be provided to the farm households participating and will also appear in the county newspaper. The information is free and financed by the state. Decisions on what to include in the data base are made by the University of Kentucky and the county agent. The farm household calls the computer by telephone and the requested information appears on the home television set. The uniqueness of this system is its Greenthumb Box, a hand-held, calcu-lator-like device connected to the TV and the telephone in the farmer's home. The farmer will be able to dial a local phone number which ties the box into a micro-processor chip in his county agent's office which will send the information desired for storage to the user's "box." This permits the farmer to page the information on his TV screen at his own pace without incurring costly long distance telephone costs. The house-holder may also input material into the system. Assuming a successful trial, the system will be expanded within Kentucky and perhaps to other states as well as to a wider variety of existing data bases geographic-ally dispersed throughout the country.

KEY QUESTIONS

Daniel Bell heralds the new information service economy as one characterized by an increasing multiplication of interactions between persons and of personal transactions between persons. According to Bell (1979, p. 20), while the earlier preindustrial and industrial societies were set apart by their struggles first with nature and then with fabricated nature, the post industrial society is "a game between persons, between teacher and student, doctor and patient. . ." excluding nature except as recreation and things except as hobbies.

There will be serious challenges to Bell's characterizations from those who fear the electronic world as creating ever widening opportunities for human isolation. Home application of the new telecommunications technologies is seen as simply providing more incentives for people to remain at home and thus confining their interactions more and more with the world to their TV screens, remote from the warmth – and hostilities – of human contact. Obviously both views may be accurate. That society is evolving electronically is unassailable – and unstoppable. That we can influence and perhaps shape how it will, in fact, impact human beings and their society is also unassailable if there is a will or demand to do so. This is the challenge which the information and telecommunications technologies pose to business leaders, government officials, academics, and citizens groups. To do so, we must have a clear understanding both of the technologies and their potential and also of the options and alternatives which we have in their application to home and social uses.

To date, little has been done to analyze the important potentials and problems associated with any widespread application of these technologies for broad social purposes.

Academic, institutional, and nonprofit communities traditionally concerned with information are just beginning to grapple with the impact of the new communications technologies on their traditional missions. Librarians and information specialists are meeting this fall under the aegis of a White House Conference to discuss these issues. Marketers and consumer behavior specialists have shown only modest interest in exploring the potential of these technologies to meet the information needs of consumers or the promotion and marketing goals of consumer products companies.

The inherent dynamics of these technologies and of the market system into which they are currently being introduced are powerful forces. If unattended, they can shape the long-term development and applications of these technologies to the service of individuals and of society in fundamental and perhaps irreversible ways. It is essential, therefore, to be clear on our goals for the development and use of these technologies in the service of individual information needs. If consumers and citizens are to reap the full benefits and potentials of these technologies, the key questions influencing that goal will be to determine who should become the producers and vendors of information and how should the communications technologies be employed to disseminate this information to the public.

It is clear that two distinct approaches to serving the home market are currently being experimented with: (1) the British Prestel View Data system utilizing essentially a common carrier public utility approach, separating carriage and content, and (2) most of the other systems utilizing either government or the media as administrators of the system and, more importantly, selectors of the information content of the system. Each carry very different implications for the future development of these information systems. In the United States, with the exception of Operation Greenthumb, the Teletex systems in operation are operated either by media or by private industrial interests. Where the media are the system providers, the selection of the information to be made available will in all likelihood follow the traditional media concepts of media's constitutional right of program and content accountability to the public for the way in which they discharge their role. It is unlikely that these media would be receptive to any concept of a right of access to their media-based information systems by independent information providers. Hence, information systems developed along these lines will not be calculated to create incentives for the emergence of a strong independent information provider sector in the information society. Nor will these media-directed information systems be as likely as nonmedia systems to innovate wholly new information resource programs given their newspaper/TV backgrounds and traditions. Indeed, the tentative information menus planned by both Knight Ridder and WETA read essentially like electronic newspapers delivered through the TV medium. Telecomputing Corporation's the Source, while a more open flexible system, is influenced by the traditional profit incentives of any private sector corporation. Like the media, Telecomputing Corporation is also the sole determinant of the nature and content of the data bases to be made available. Utilizing traditional marketing concepts rather than any tradition of public service responsibility, the responsiveness of Telecomputing's information offerings to individual needs will depend essentially on the size of the demand, the ability of the consumer to pay, and the respective profitability involved in offering one data base over another (assuming as we must that the size of Telecomputing's potential data base capacity has some finite limits).

While it is, of course, important, for diversity reasons alone, for all types of enterprise to participate in creating new home market information systems, it is essential, in my view, that as a society we make certain that other nonmedia and nonmarket driven elements in our society also participate in the creation and operation of these systems.

The dynamics of profitability and of media public service responsibility may not be sufficient to ensure that the full potentials of the information society are in fact effectively available to all citizens for their full range of applications. Telemedicine and tele-education, to mention only two, have never traditionally been applications which society has been willing to leave entirely to the private sector. A range of community services has similarly been confined primarily to the public sector as social services available to the public without regard to their ability to pay. Even market place information and documentation about most public policy issues, such as nuclear energy, energy conservation, environmental costs and benefits, carcinogen and other health hazards in foods, drugs, pesticides, and the like have not regularly been made available by the traditional information providers in our current society. There is no reason to believe that this situation will change drastically if these same sectors of society remain the information providers under the new technologies.

It would seem essential to create incentives for the emergence of new types of information systems providers whose primary function will be to act as a type of common carrier to broker the dissemination of information between users on the one hand and independent information vendors and providers on the other hand. Whether such data bank utilities will emerge on their own or whether they will need some type of government impetus cannot be foreseen at this point. What is important, in my judgment, is to explore the potentiality of this type of information resource in terms of the goal of providing all segments of society with access to the full range of information required by them in order to function as fully effective and participating citizens.

Another range of questions which need to be answered concern the mechanisms for consumer/citizen access to information resources once they are created. The first order of importance concerns the search techniques, indexing mechanisms or entry facility offered by the information resource to the individual. Critical to the effective use of these resources will be the care with which all citizen groups can manipulate the data for their purposes. Tree-structure indexing systems will be appropriate for certain groups of users and for certain types of information – key word entry systems may be more appropriate and usable for other groups and uses. Whatever indexing system is used must respond to the intended user's sophistication, interest level, and ability to pay. Creation of these indexing systems will demand an expertise which is largely unavailable today. Whether government intervention in either a funding or direct training role will be necessary must again be high on our national information agenda in order to ensure that the system develops in direct response to individual needs and capabilities. Parenthetically, the ultimate success of many of the current pilot programs may be directly influenced by the sensitivity of their program managers to this critical key to consumer interest in and the use of these new systems.

Finally, of course, is the critical question of the quality of the information content of these new information resource systems. Unfortunately, the projected content of the experimental programs reviewed above shows only a modest grasp of the exciting potentials of the new technologies and of the real information needs of citizens today. Perhaps not surprising, albeit disappointing, these new programs seem to do no more than "electronify" existing information sources now available in other media. Whether consumers and citizens can be expected to switch their current information search and listening habits from the print and TV media simply to get the identical information on demand, especially if an extra charge is incurred, seems to me unlikely. The success of these new technologies in meeting consumer/citizen information needs will depend on the extent to which their needs can be identified and responded to with entirely new type and formats of information inputs.

Some of the key questions which I believe have to be answered about the form and structure of the information systems needed in order to ensure their use by the non business sectors of our society include the following:

1. Should consumer information data banks be structured as profit market driven organizations or as nonprofit organizations administered and operated by a board broadly representative of the major interest groups in the generation and use of the information service performed by the data bank?

2. Should consumer knowledge and data banks be funded and administered under the aegis of government agencies with the private/nonprofit sector creating the information and knowledge data bases, or should we look to a mixed system of profit and nonprofit, government and privately owned, created, and administered data banks as well as data bases?

3. Should society provide that data and knowledge banks may not be a monopoly, or should it permit monopolistic structures and provide instead for a legal right of entry for creators and packagers of information and for other standards of operation?

4. Should we look to establishing a central data bank containing information about essential consumer products and services as well as about medical care facilities, educational opportunities, recreational areas, and community and public services, or should we move towards promoting establishment of different data banks? What are the cost and accessibility implications of either route for vendors and users?

5. Should vendor access to data banks be: (1) as of right, (2) conditioned through some system of publicly mandated quality assurance, or (3) subject to other public review and entry standards (administrative or judicial)? Should computer utility managers have total discretion to admit or reject vendors, subject only to normal government regulation of accuracy and truthfulness of item descriptions?

6. Should all of the data in the data bank be available on line, or should merely indices or abstracts of some of it be available on line for display and browsing purposes and available either for viewing or for ordering written copies of the specific data desired by the consumer?

7. Should a pricing scale to the user be designed in terms of the essentiality of the product, service, or basic information with minimum price ceilings established for basic data, or higher prices paid to the vendors providing priority data as designated by the board?

8. Should there be some percentage of data bank capacity specifically reserved for or allocated to information of special concern to specific consumer groups in our society such as the elderly, the poor, ethnic, rural, urban, etc.?

9.   Should capacity be specially allocated or reserved for specially designated product and service categories corresponding to the principal income expenditures by citizens with appropriate incentives to information vendors to design relevant data about the products and services accounting for these expenditures?

10.   Should government fund the generation of information materials falling into the categories referred to in questions 8 and 9 if they are not otherwise produced? Is accuracy of information best assured by competition coupled with standardized compulsory disclosure of information source and identity of the disseminator?

11.   Do consumers need information in the form of basic data organized for easy manipulation and levels of complexity as well as the more traditional textual forms of articles and analyses? (The former is most typically referred to as data banks and the latter as knowledge banks)

12.   Should data be retained in the data base permanently and should distinctions be made in on line availability in terms of frequency of use? Could safeguards be provided to prevent use frequency standards from being manipulated by vendor, advertiser, or product service provider interests?

13.   In today's information world, users of data are aided in their use and reliance on the data through their familiarity and past experience with the gatekeepers involved; i.e., the author and/or publication. Publishers, advertisers, independent consumer information suppliers, and media columnists act as both gatekeepers and "insurers" of the "bias" of the data. How can this function be preserved in a computer utility, or will competitive data banks emerge which will perform for users this gatekeeper function for the data provided in each particular data bank?

The answers which we give to these questions can in large measure be a determining factor in the extent to which our democratic and economic system meets the needs of consumers and of our society. It will not be easy to find the right answers, but our failure to try will be far more serious than any errors in judgment which we might make. We must, for example, thread our way between the use of government subsidies and other public and private incentive programs and the risk of premature freezing or standardizing of technology at a time when maximum flexibility is essential. We must encourage and test consumer acceptance and demand without finally determining the form in which the information system finally comes on stream. Thus, government could take the leadership in promoting the establishment of a variety of "home use" type information systems to evaluate the size and type of information demands of small nonindustrial users.

Shopping centers offer an ideal community center to provide shoppers with a variety of specific and "browsing" type information about the products and services available in that shopping mall. "Ordering" consoles could be installed as well to enable shoppers to simply place their order at the shoppers' information center and skip the crowds. Consoles could be installed providing general Consumers Union type information as well as consoles with specific price information, ordering facilities, and the like. Some information-providing sources could be telephonic, some visual, and others a mixture of audio-visual. Some would be one-way, some interactive with varying degrees of complexity as to information retrieval. The data bank could be interconnected with other shopping centers so that a broad test sample could be obtained. Careful records could be kept on usage of all types, peak loads, and the like. This approach would serve both the user and the two types of vendors involved: the information vendor and the product and service vendor. Most importantly, it would serve to provide individuals with realistic experience in the use of this type of service and would accustom them to see computers work for them and appreciate the benefits they can provide.

At the same time, model community public service type information demonstration centers could also be created in order to determine their ideal placement, as well as the type and content of the information required by consumers about these service offerings.

A second range of policy issues underlying the answers which we should give to these questions concerns the basis on which the development and quality of the software – the information content of the home delivery information market is to be made available to the individual consumer.

In designing our educational system in this country, we have never accepted the notion that education should only be available to those who can afford to pay for it; nor have we accepted the notion that even free education should be geared only to the levels and abilities of the majority. Today, we insist that handicapped children, slow learners, children with learning defects, as well as the gifted, must be served by our educational system to the point of developing special classes and schools for each special segment of the learning population.

In the commercial world of entertainment, we have not used our educational philsophies as the model but have been willing to accept the commercial tenets of the market system as the sole determinant of what shall be produced and whose interests shall be served.

I am convinced that a different model must be developed for the information society – a model which will perhaps borrow from both the educational and commercial worlds and which will probably require a mixed system of government and private industry to administer. Mixed government and private industry models are in no way a new phenomenon in our country. Government has been subsidizing private industry research in the computer and telecommunication fields for years in a variety of interesting and imaginative ways. The entire space program with its fascinating spilloff of products for private industry has been an openly applauded government-industry joint venture. Investment credit policies and indeed the entire system of taxation is a familiar, more indirect shotgun technique by which government has used its taxing powers to achieve certain goals through private sector activity. It is my sense that the policies which will be required to ensure that the resources and benefits of our information society will be available to meet the needs of the smaller individuals and nonprofit organizations will have to be much more overt and thoughtfully planned than many of the existing models of government/industry joint ventures. Government is comfortable in dealing indirectly with ventures from which the benefits for industry and government are clear. While I believe that the information telecommunication industry will indeed benefit from serving the needs of individual consumers, I am well aware that at least initially these benefits may not be as apparent as serving the large industrial users. While the consumer information data bases are more likely to emerge from both nonprofit and commercial sources, the establishment of the computer utilities pose far greater economic problems.

This suggests that the establishment of central or decentralized community data banks may only come about as a result of government action. Whether these banks are commercial or governmental in origin is less important than: first, that they are established; and second, that they operate under carefully defined conditions of vendor access, user access and assurances of quality, either by pre-screening which would rightfully raise first amendment problems, or by insuring proper identification of source and other qualifying disclosures about the information being vended. If free data bank access for information creators were assured, we would be taking a giant step toward meeting the objective of insuring that the needs and interests of all of our citizens were likely to be responded to.

Democracy requires a new capability on the part of citizens and consumers to reassert their primacy over the government and over the economic institutions in our society which exercise such power over the quality of their lives. Knowledge is a central national resource and access to it a critical source of political and economic power. We cannot hope to reverse and eliminate current feelings of alienation, cynicism, and mistrust of authority which are so deeply engrained in consumers and citizens today until we confront and redress the current information and communications imbalances in our society.

This is the challenge of the consumer information systems of the future and the challenge of the consumer leaders today. How we respond will determine the health and ability of our political and economic institutions to serve the needs of their constituents. It will critically determine whether individuals will be empowered to define more clearly and purposefully the essential dimensions of their lives and to pursue their life's goal on as informed and as involved a basis as they desire.

NOTE

(1) It is not intended by using this term to imply any perceived necessity that the information products be disseminated to individuals on their home receivers or terminals. Indeed, community centers, libraries, and other publicly located information centers may be the most felicitous way, sociologically and economically, to ensure the availability of this resource to individuals. The term "home market" is used here, therefore, to denote the application of these technologies generally to the noncommercial needs of individuals.

13 Market Reporting and Its Public Policy Implications
Kirby S. Moulton

The preceding chapters in this section relate primarily to problems of consumer information where information asymmetry exists and where dysfunctional competitive results are believed to occur. These markets have private information systems with varying coverage and content but relatively little in the way of public information services. The remedies suggested to reduce asymmetry focus on government as a facilitator for information systems or as a direct supplier of information. It is agreed that the technology exists for supporting sophisticated systems. There is disagreement about which agencies, either public or private, should bear primary responsibility for operating the systems, and who should bear the cost.

This chapter examines a sector of the marketing economy where extensive public information systems have existed for a long period. Conclusions are derived from this examination which have implications for the policy and operational changes proposed for consumer markets in the preceding pages.

The following analysis is of the agricultural commodities markets and their public information systems. The first sections consider relevant theoretical and empirical studies and describe the existing system and its deficiencies. The ensuing section examines several issues raised in preceding chapters which are also pertinent to extensive public information systems. Succeeding sections consider the corrections needed in information programs and their public implications.

ASYMMETRY OF INFORMATION IN AGRICULTURAL MARKETS

Several factors hinder the equitable distribution of information in agricultural markets. The greater frequency of market involvement by buyers relative to sellers gives buyers better access to current and comprehensive market information. This is particularly important for perishable commodities, such as lettuce, where market conditions are highly variable. Buyers establish extensive information networks through telephone contact and other electronic means, and are generally better able to interpret available information.

A superior location in the channel of distribution provides buyers with a more comprehensive view of market conditions. Wineries, for example, are informed about conditions in the grape market by virtue of their raw product acquisition program and also about conditions in the wine market by virtue of their wine sales program. Information gathered in the latter market provides a competitive edge for negotiations in the former market. An information advantage is also gained through the marketing "funnel effect" which places the buyer in contact with a multitude of potential sellers from numerous producing areas while sellers are able to negotiate with relatively few buyers.

The larger size of buyers relative to most sellers permits them to achieve economies of scale in information search and interpretation. This augments the informational advantage of channel location and frequency of marketing activity. Buyers also tend to gain an informational advantage through product diversification. Buyers of barley, for example, are often buyers of related commodities such as corn, sorghum, and other feed grains. Their knowledge of these markets facilitates their buying decisions in the barley market.

The changing character of agricultural markets has contributed to information asymmetry and dysfunctional competitive effects. The substitution of contract buying for open market transactions has reduced the flow of public price signals. Increased vertical integration has internalized transactions which formerly generated public market information. The conglomeration of many buying organizations has created an aggregation of statistical data which does not yield the same information as the disaggregated data supplied by single commodity buyers.

COMPETITIVE EFFECTS

An extensive body of theory supports the critical role of information to the competitive performance of markets. Perfect knowledge by market participants is a necessary condition for perfectly competitive markets. The imperfect state of information and its interpretation is a key element in theories of oligopoly and monopolistic competition. Excellent reviews of inquiries into the economic impact of information are presented by Eisgruber (1978) and by Fama (1970), among others.

The general social welfare model uses neo-classical concepts to provide a comprehensive evaluation of information. Changes in the state of information created by search or by free discovery cause shifts in commodity supply and demand schedules as buyers and sellers change their decision rules. These shifts create changes in social welfare and social cost and in their derivative: net social benefit. Imperfect information leads to reduced social benefit.

Hayami and Peterson (1971) used the general social welfare model to specify the value of benefits achieved by a government information program which reported crop conditions. The program clearly provided a net social benefit. Devine and Marion (1979) used a similar model, among others, in evaluating a retail food price information system and showed that social value was well above social cost. Severe data limitations impair the usefulness of this model and others in evaluating the benefits and costs of information systems for complex marketing channels involving extensive vertical linkages and numerous nonmarket users of information (Moulton, et al. (1974); Rothschild (1973)).

Empirical studies have tended to focus on the link between information and pricing efficiency. Devine and Marion showed that average retail food prices were lowered and inter-store price differentials were reduced after a retail price reporting system was initiated. Fama explained inefficient prices as a result of information restrictions and inadequate interpretation. Similar relationships in nonagricultural markets are reported by Kryzanowski (1978), Grossman (1977) and Hirschleifer (1971).

Few studies investigate the link between market information and other elements of market structure. This lack is unfortunate because of the impact that structure has on market performance. Two types of structural change are encouraged by inadequate or unequally distributed information. One is the growth in size and market power of firms able to obtain more information than competitors. The other is an increase in vertical integration as firms seek to reduce the uncertainties created by insufficient market information. The implications of the link between market information and market structure are discussed in a subsequent section.

Economic theory and its validating empirical studies demonstrate that information asymmetry is incompatible with a competitive marketing system. Early recognition of this relationship undoubtedly contributed to the establishment of the agricultural Market News Service, although the actual political rationale for its establishment has become obscured by time.

THE AGRICULTURAL MARKET REPORTING SYSTEM

The reporting of market transactions has been an important program of U.S. agricultural marketing policy for over 60 years. In 1915, the first reporting program was initiated in the strawberry market of Hammond, La., in order to improve the adequacy and timeliness of market information. Since then, the program has expanded extensively and is currently administered by the Agricultural Marketing Service of the U.S. Department of Agriculture. This administrative relationship emphasizes the marketing orientation of information policy rather than its competition orientation.

The Market News Service has the responsibility for reporting conditions in numerous agricultural markets throughout the United

States. It operates, in cooperation with agricultural states, an extensive reporting network covering markets for cotton, dairy and poultry, fruits and vegetables, grain, livestock, and tobacco. The degree of financial participation by the federal government in the reporting system depends on the national impact of a particular market and the availability of public information from other sources. The frequency of reports and the means of their dissemination depend on the volatility of the reported market. Fresh produce market conditions are generally reported daily and disseminated by radio, private wire, telephone, newspapers, and mail reports. Reports include information about prices, volumes, quality standards, and other factors which influence market results.

The agricultural market information system focuses on the needs of market participants. Its activities are considered as a marketing service. At least two factors suggest this. This first is the criterion for the establishment or disestablishment of market reporting activities. Although loosely defined, the criterion is the needs of the market as perceived by industry members and reporting agencies. The needs relate to market decision making rather than to regulation, research, or other nonoperational needs. The second factor is the justification given by public agencies for establishing fees for market news services. This justification is that market users benefit and therefore should pay. Those who will not or cannot pay for market information will not receive it. Little attention is given to the implications for market performance and public competition policy of such an incomplete distribution of information.

DEFICIENCIES OF THE PRESENT REPORTING SYSTEM

The present market reporting system has been operating over a long period of time and yet continues to be deficient in meeting the needs of market policy and competition policy. This may well be the result of confusions between the two policies and the physical impossibility of collecting and disseminating adequate information about an extremely complex set of markets. Whatever the cause, the deficiencies need to be examined prior to implementing new public information systems.

A notable failing is the lack of cost reports suitable for judging pricing efficiency. This is privileged information. Yet, agricultural costs of production throughout the United States are continually reported and provide added information to buyers for their bargaining purposes. Sellers, however, are in the dark about relevant buyer costs.

Market reports often fail to clarify the relationship between price and quantity sold. Numerous transactions escape reporting because of incomplete market coverage. Many small markets are not covered, and few vertically related markets are reported in a way which permits margin calculations.

In some instances, buyers refuse to report transactions or report on a highly aggregated, hence less useful, basis. Cooperators can be selective and report only prices favorable to themselves or data over several grades in order to obscure price differentials.

Structural changes have reduced the flow of market information. Newly evolved private markets utilizing contracts and transfer pricing create no public market signals as did the nonintegrated markets they replaced. As currently structured, the market news system cannot effectively identify the terms of trade or other characteristics of transactions within this "closed system."

In some markets with both cash and contract sales, contract prices may be tied to reported cash prices. As a larger share of market volume is transacted by contract, the cash market becomes less reliable as a true measure of supply and demand conditions. Examples of this are found in the Chicago corn market, where cash prices are based on about 5 percent of the corn sold in Chicago; and in the California wine market where contract prices were (before regulatory changes) often based on cash prices based on less than 10 percent of the total market. Marketing and policy decisions based on such "thin" prices are risky.

ISSUES AND THEIR IMPLICATIONS FOR CONSUMER INFORMATION SYSTEMS

An analysis of agricultural market information programs raises the same issues as identified in prior chapters concerning consumer information systems. This occurs despite differences in the vertical level of markets being reported, the economic motivations of market participants, and the availability of publicly reported market information. The issues discussed in the following paragraphs include those concerning the adequacy of price as a signal of market performance; the ability of market participants to utilize information; the incentives for private information services; the equity of information distribution; and the influence of information systems on market structure.

Narver, Preston, Phillips, and Holton have questioned the adequacy of price as a signal of market performance. Their question is based on the extreme variations in product characteristics which may not be known to all market participants and which are not adequately reflected in price differentials. Each transaction appears to have numerous dimensions which may differ (similar to Cox's concept of the market "proposition") and these are not adequately conveyed in price signals.

In its simplest form, this is exhibited in the pricing of fresh produce where numerous perishability factors may influence prices so that they are not strictly comparable. The complexities of meat grading or the diversity of grape varieties and characteristics, for example, make price aggregation and averaging – often a necessity for reporting purposes – extremely misleading.

On a more rigorous level, recent investigations have cast doubt on the likely empirical validity of the theory that market prices convey to uninformed traders all the information known to informed traders. The doubt is raised because of the strict assumptions (absolute risk aversion, for example) upon which the theory is based (Kobayashi, 1979; Grossman, 1977; Leuthold and Hartmann, 1979). This implies that public or private reporting in a market with a very well specified commodity (such as a futures contract) does not guarantee efficient prices as measured by information content. If this situation exists in such well-defined markets, it is not likely that government or private information programs, at least at current technological and budgetary levels, can improve the quality of price signals in the far more complex consumer markets.

The inability of market users to effectively interpret and act upon market information impairs market efficiency. Yet, many discussions of information are based on the assumption that users are equally (and fully) capable of interpreting information. Clearly, participants in both producer and consumer markets have unequal abilities to deal with information as suggested in earlier chapters and in other studies (Capon and Lutz, 1979; Carter, 1979; Gorham, 1978).

The well-established agricultural market reporting system has not overcome this difficulty. Therefore, it is likely that an extensive consumer oriented information system will have similar problems. To improve the situation will require a change in information policy to include an educational component as an adjunct to information programs.

The question of adequate incentives for the establishment of private market reporting systems is raised in the preceding chapter. Classical economic theory suggests that if information has a value, then profit opportunities may exist for information "middlemen." The issue is whether barriers exist which discourage the establishment of private market information services.

An important impediment to information gathering is the incentive to market participants to withhold information. This incentive has been demonstrated theoretically and tested empirically by Hirshleifer (1971) and by Grossman (1977). Further evidence is found in the difficulties encountered by the Market News Service in obtaining appropriately disaggregated data from market participants (Moulton and Padberg, 1976). Private news services seem to thrive best where open public markets are important (financial markets), where public market reporting exists (agricultural commodities), or where trade associations are active in information dissemination (the petroleum industry). Market characteristics are important determinants of the success of private information systems. An analysis by Gorham showed that private services anticipated market movements more accurately for soybeans, a relatively stable crop in terms of yields, than for corn and wheat, crops with more variable yields. This type of predictive difference was also found by Rausser and Just (1979).

Some of the following implications are relevant for consumer information systems. The absence of significant "public" markets in consumer goods will discourage the establishment of private news services, just as it has in certain agricultural industries (processed food, for example). Private reporting seems to do best where public reporting also exists. This suggests that private information in the consumer market might most readily appear for food products, where public reporting, at least at the wholesale level, is important. Countering this implication is relatively poor record of private reporting in interpreting highly variable markets. This should narrow the likely areas of successful private enterprise to stable consumer goods with significant public reporting at some point in the distribution channel.

The difficulty in estimating how the benefits and costs of information systems are distributed through the economy creates difficulty in establishing new publicly funded information programs. This issue is raised in the relatively mature agriculturally related markets with a long history of public market reporting activity. It suggests that efforts to estimate information impacts in complex consumer markets will be formidable.

There are important aspects of market information systems which need study. One aspect concerns the dispersion of information through a vertical marketing system and the evaluation of its impact. This is particularly necessary for the determination of all benefits resulting from market reporting. Additionally, a comprehensive evaluation is needed of the benefits to nonmarket users of information such as regulatory agencies, research organizations and service firms.

The knowledge and data necessary for an accurate evaluation of the benefits of market news reporting is still lacking. Consequently, the benefits of market information systems must still be accepted on faith. Conclusions can be made about bits and pieces but not about the entire system. Specifically, what is measurable relates to market efficiency and the well-being of market participants. What is not, relates to the specifics of structure, the efficiency of regulation, and the other public activities related to marketing, such as research. This tends to focus policy and research attention on the relationship between information and market participants and not on other more complex relationships which may be important to public competition policy. The implication for consumer information systems is that concentration only on consumer benefits, which are measurable, may distract attention from other potential benefits which could adequately justify the system.

Underlying much of the discussion of market information systems is the belief that such systems will result in an improved market structure. However, the link between information and market structure has not been well demonstrated empirically even though the theoretical arguments are sound. The paucity of studies in agricultural and financial sectors, where information systems are prevalent, suggests difficulty in justifying consumer information systems based on expected benefits to market structure.

Most studies concentrate on the relationship between information and efficiency because the theory is well developed and because the improvement in market efficiency is a generally accepted objective of market information systems. Few studies carry the argument forward to relate changes in efficiency to changes in structure. From the standpoint of public competition policy as it relates to consumer marketing, the link between efficiency and structure is important because of its subsequent implication for market performance.

Some studies have examined this link. The interesting market simulations of Balderston and Hoggatt (1962) showed that wholesalers, as the hub of an information network between producers and retailers, were able to gain larger shares of the marketing system's capital when producer prices were highly variable. Figlewski (1979), in examining futures markets, demonstrated that market participants obtaining market information that was unavailable to others tended to grow in size and to increase their information gathering capacity. The net result was an increase in market concentration and also an improvement in market efficiency due to better interpretation of market information. Hirshleifer's evaluation of the incentive for withholding market information from others indicates the potential for a nonefficient market structure. Added studies of this relationship are reported by Rothschild (1973).

The beneficial effects of market information on the structure of the food system is not readily apparent. Despite the long history of commodity market reporting, concentration in the food industry has increased. An important hypothesis for future testing is that the forces which favor concentration (e.g., financial or marketing barriers) have offset the "competitive" effect of market information systems. In testing this hypothesis, it may be discovered that information systems have preserved a competitive fringe of firms within the industry or, at least, impeded the rate of concentration.

This hypothesis needs to be raised because it recognizes that information provides an environment for increased competition, but does not assure its existence. The structural issue revolves around the equitable distribution of both public and private information in a way that gives equal opportunity for competitive success, other things being equal. Market performance is more likely to be competitive in the presence of equitably distributed information than in its absence.

ADJUSTMENTS NEEDED

The preceding discussion describes an insistent public policy dilemma: market imperfections obviously exist although their cost is not established. Without knowing costs, the value of remedial public policies becomes a question. However, there are adjustments needed to the agricultural reporting system if it is to meet the demands of efficiency and public competition policy. No attempt is made at this point to establish the costs of such adjustments. The problems of adequate market coverage, the reporting of contract markets (such as exist for consumer durables), and use of a voluntary reporting system are particularly relevant to the establishment or expansion of consumer information programs.

Some substantial changes in the agricultural market reporting system are needed to meet public policy requirements. These include the expansion of coverage to new markets, the reporting of contract transactions, the improvement in reporting accuracy, and the reporting of vertically related markets.

Moulton and Padberg identified a hierarchy of information needs as goals for an information policy with the objective of restoring information flow to that of an open market economy. The hierarchy includes:

1. Adequate reports in cash contractual markets for agricultural commodities, for domestic use and for export; and for relevant production input markets.
2. Coverage of comparable markets at the next higher and lower level in the distribution chain.
3. Analysis of processed product movement in order to evaluate requirement trends for raw products.
4. Line of business reporting by conglomerate firms.
5. Data concerning transactions within vertically integrated market organizations.

Such adjustments cannot be achieved simultaneously and some of them may require a mandatory rather than voluntary reporting system. The political feasibility of returning to an "open market" information system is not high because substantial questions of government infringement in the private sector are raised. However, such changes are a logical extension of a competition policy which seeks to attain competitive market results.

IMPLICATIONS FOR PUBLIC POLICY

The deficiencies of the present market information system relative to public policy needs are significant, and the corrective measures are costly. Since benefits of such a system cannot be measured in total, the political will to make the required adjustments may be lacking. This is particularly true when the system is viewed solely in relation to the benefits gained by market users of information. It is not surprising that the market reporting system is deficient in meeting the information requirements of public competition policy since that system is viewed as a function of marketing policy rather than as a function of competition policy.

Explicit incorporation of the market reporting system within the competition policy of the United States might well provide the justification of system changes which will benefit both market and nonmarket users of market information. In such a situation, the criteria for changes in market reporting systems would then include their impact on public policy information needs.

The issue of charging for market information may be more easily resolved if market information services are a component of our competition policy. Three factors are important in this regard: First, the market information needed to assure efficient market operation may not be the information for which users are willing to pay; second, a user fee policy may lead to legitimate concerns about controlling the flow of information; and third, smaller enterprises which are important to a healthy economic system are likely to be at a competitive disadvantage because of higher information costs per unit of output.

CONCLUSIONS

A common concern of the preceding chapters is the asymmetry of information and its dysfunctional competitive effects. Suggestions for change center on government's role as a facilitator, or as a generator, of market information at the consumer level.

The technology is available to support vastly improved consumer information systems. Government has a role in establishing consistent ground rules which will facilitate the use of such technologies. Private information systems, utilizing modern technology and operating under a consistent set of government policies, can make a significant contribution to an improved information flow in U.S. markets.

Serious questions need to be answered about the role of government in resolving information deficiencies. As Phillips contends in his chapter in this volume on antitrust policy, the government should seek to report market conditions (the price-quality relationship, for example) in such a way as to enhance competition and inhibit predatory pricing practices. Both theory and related empirical studies suggest that improved information flows can result in more efficient markets and may reduce information asymmetry. Whether or not such systems can improve other elements of market structure remains to be proved.

Experience in the agricultural sector, where market reporting is prevalent, suggests that expectations concerning the efficacy of information systems should be tempered. Asymmetry of information continues to exist in these markets and continues to have dysfunctional competitive effects. Further, these systems have not adequately resolved issues raised in earlier chapters concerning consumer information systems: the inadequacy of price-quality reporting; the varying capabilities to interpret information; and problems of evaluating complex information programs.

An important conclusion about information policy is that it should incorporate programs to improve the utilization of information. Studies of agricultural and nonagricultural markets show that improper use of information is a serious barrier to market efficiency.

A careful analysis of agricultural market reporting programs shows that they are logical elements of competition policy. The implication is that consumer information programs should be considered a part of the same policy rather than as an element of national marketing policy.

This approach relates information systems, both external and internal, to market performance. Thus, the criterion used in establishing or abandoning an information system is the impact that such action would have on competitive market performance. Further, it considers the ability of the system to provide the data necessary for defining relevant markets, for evaluating cost-price relationships, and identifying other competitive performance. This policy approach recognizes that program costs are balanced against benefits to market and nonmarket users, including the policy agencies themselves. Explicit incorporation of the market reporting system within the competition policy of the United States might well provide the justification for system changes which will benefit both market and nonmarket users of market information.

III
Competitive Structure

14 Vertical Systems, Regional Systems, and Relevant Market: Some Structural Issues

James M. Carman

A major recurring theme in Part I of this book was that a major problem of managing any public policy toward competition concerns our inability to determine the relevant product market. If oligopoly is the predominant market structure and competitors use product differentiation to flee from homogeneous oligopoly, then this problem is guaranteed to be a serious one.

David M. Grether introduced this problem in his review of the literature on the relation between market structure and the level of research and development activity. Is investment in R&D a reasonable competitive strategy in particular market structures or are certain preconditions of the underlying technology a necessary condition for satisfactory returns from R&D? The PIMS data analysis shows a high return from R&D to firms with dominant market shares (Schoeffler, Buzzell, and Heany, 1974). Such firms are also more likely to diversify. Because the directions of cause and effect here are not well understood, the public policy implications of these relationships remain elusive.

This fact became immediately apparent from a reading of the chapter by Lee E. Preston in which one of the issues is whether product differentiation and new product development by a dominant firm can constitute predatory marketing conduct. One cannot begin an analysis of this issue until an operational and measurable definition of relevant product market can be determined.

Almarin Phillips' chapter helps to clarify the problem by making the distinction between a quality change or line extension and a new product. His Type D quality change involves new technology, a different cost structure, and a different demand function (although it may have a high cross-elasticity with the original product).

The usual guidelines for defining relevant market all place great emphasis on the substitutability (cross-elasticity) of one product for another as actually exhibited by the behavior of buyers. Sullivan (1977,

p. 41) says a relevant market "is the narrowest market which is wide enough so that products from adjacent areas or from other producers in the same area cannot compete on substantial parity with those included in the market." The phrase "compete on substantial parity" needs to be given operational meaning. Marketers could probably agree that this substitutability should be proven by the behavior or behavioral intentions of actual buyers. Relevant markets are defined by buyers, not by sellers, raw materials, or production processes.

Part II of the book develops a major complexity for this seemingly straightforward idea. Simply, can buyers be counted on to exhibit behaviors that will perform this market defining task? It was pointed out in the Holton and Thorelli chapters that when products are technically complex, when technology is changing rapidly, or when products are purchased infrequently, it is usually not possible for buyers to be well enough informed to conduct allocatively efficient market transactions. Information asymmetry becomes a serious problem and a market failure can result. The public policy questions that emerged concern the extent and form of public resources to be allocated to provide buyers with the information required to redress this symmetry.

In this section of the book, the problem is pursued still further. Two new complexities are added to the problem of defining relevant market. In this chapter is discussed the complexity created by the presence of vertical market systems. Most products reach final markets through a manufacturing and distribution system. From many, but perhaps not all, perspectives the public policy concerns of the marketing system can focus on one level in that system. However, our public policy for maintaining competition is focused on markets. In so far as the vertical delivery system involves intermediate markets, it is not obvious that a pro-competitive public policy in each intermediate market will necessarily result in the socially optimal solution for the entire vertical system. Some of the complications that result are developed here.

In the next chapter, Reavis Cox continues this theme of whether the relevant unit of competition is the establishment, firm, or vertical channel. Much of that essay develops the measurement problems involved in attempting to deal with the vertical system's complexity and suggests that point-of-sale computer terminals may result, at last, in our ability to collect the data required to conduct analysis of vertical systems.

In the following chapter, Professor Ronald Savitt introduces the second of the two complexities – relevant geographic market. Professor Savitt shows that in order to formulate public policy, one must first have a theory of inter-regional marketing. He traces the development of that theory and Professor Grether's contributions to it. He then shows how the definition of relevant geographic market has developed in antitrust law and how this definition is less than optimal when compared to one that might have been evolved from Grether's approach to inter-regional marketing.

In the last chapter, Huff and Moyer review the case law on relevant market with reference to one particular product – coal. They then present a procedure and an example for defining the relevant geographic markets for coal, utilizing the contractual linkages between suppliers and users to delineate coal markets. Their analysis also points out that even with a commodity such as coal, the definition of relevant product market is still an issue.

VERTICAL MARKETING SYSTEMS

Products get to final users through vertical channels of distribution. The system may start with an extractor or grower, include the processor, convertor, or packer who actually transforms the product physically, the middlemen to whom they sell, and the buyers in the final market for the product. In some cases, only the organization performing the last form change would have to be included. For example, in the analysis of the soft drink industry, it may be useful for some purposes to include both bottlers and syrup producers and in other cases to include only the bottlers. In some cases – for example, agent middlemen or Professor Preston's computer leasing companies – it may also be useful to consider the facilitating marketing agencies who may never hold title to the product.

It is often difficult to classify organizations absolutely as being at one particular level in the channel. Wholesalers often sell to consumers and hence also are engaged in retailing; retailers often take over their own wholesaling functions for some part of their product line. Thus, single firms are operating in markets at different levels. Another reason the vertical system is a reasonable choice for the unit of analysis is that a set of marketing and production functions need to be performed in order to get the product into the hands of final users. The managerial problem is to determine which are to be performed, where, and by whom. The entire vertical system may be members of the same corporation or may be composed of a large number of independent firms. Given the characteristics of the member organizations and the markets they serve, not all vertical systems for the same product will have the same structure.

It is reasonable and useful to analyze the manner in which vertical systems compete against one another and to analyze the welfare implications of one channel structure as contrasted with another. The existence of even perfect markets between channel intermediaries does not guarantee that such a channel will yield more social benefit or allocate resources more efficiently than one which contains imperfect markets or is vertically integrated. Classical economic theory does not arrive at this conclusion because of its assumption that each firm operates at maximum internal efficiency. However, intermediate markets in one relevant geographic market are virtually guaranteed not to have sufficient buyers and sellers to have "large group" competitive characteristics.   Actors in such a system are more likely to be concerned with their relative power to influence the other actors.

Members of the same vertical system can be joined by five types of linkages: (1) market linkages; (2) leadership linkages; (3) contractual linkages; (4) decentralized, vertically integrated systems; and (5) centralized integrated hierarchies.   Each of these five structures deals somewhat differently with conflicts and power among channel members. For example, the leadership linkage differs from market linkage only in that one member of the channel systems possesses the power, by trust or coercion, to have other channel members do what the leader wishes. In contractually linked systems, the parties agree to a contract or franchise that spells out the nature of the linkage and specifies how conflicts are to be minimized.

In all three of these first types of linkages, the organizations are under separate ownership and management. Title to product is transferred. In the vertically integrated systems, ownership is common.

THE PUBLIC POLICY CONUNDRUM

Two issues for public policy toward the regulation of vertical marketing systems emerge from this classification. The first concerns the danger that antitrust enforcement could push a firm to an inefficient linkage system. The second concerns the problems of how to determine an efficient normative channel structure. In discussing these two issues, these five types of linkages will be compared and contrasted.

RESTRAINT OF TRADE VERSUS VERTICAL INTEGRATION

The statutes governing the regulation of channels of distribution (Sherman Act, Sec. 1 and Clayton Act, Sec. 3) and, in fact, the whole of our antitrust law are based on a foundation of strong private property rights. For example, certain provisions concerning exclusive dealing or price setting in a contract with a manufacturers' agent who does not take title would be legal while these same provisions in a contract with a dealer who takes title would be illegal.

Why are such provisions so often the subject of public policy concern? Obviously, because in most vertical channel systems some member of the channel believes that the organization, and perhaps all members of the vertical channel, can maximize their profits by coordinated efforts. This coordination often takes the form of setting resale prices, specifying the breadth of product line carried, and restricting the geographical coverage of channel members.   The motivation for channel leadership may come from any channel member who has the power to exert leadership. In the United States these are usually manufacturers or large retailers. The formalization of a suggestion from a leader into a written, binding contract between channel members is nothing more than an evolution of coordination being exercised by the leader so that the guidelines for decisions are more explicit and routinized. These are the contracts that are often held to be in restraint of trade.

Putting that point aside for the moment, what is the next step in the evolution of the coordination being exercised by the leader? It is another kind of contract – an employment contract. Under this arrangement, the follower avoids the risks and investment requirements of entrepreneurship and receives a guarantee of a salary in exchange for services performed. These services are at the command of the leader. The leader now has effectively subverted the individual goals of the follower and has achieved the power to have the follower perform marketing functions as the leader dictates. In most, but not all, organizational situations, organizational coordination should be more efficient under the command (employment) allocation mechanism than under the leadership (market) allocation mechanism.

Put more sharply, vertical integration is the end result of a natural progression toward tighter coordination over the activities of a vertical marketing system. It also creates a public policy dilemma. Since with vertical integration no title passes, commands by leader to follower are largely exempt from the reach of the antitrust laws. If such commands are contrary to the public policy, then it will fall to the statutes governing vertical mergers to prevent these restraints of trade. Integration without merger is exempt except in cases where Sherman Act monopolization can be proven.

Why then don't more channel leaders turn to vertical integration in order to achieve better system coordination and avoid the antitrust laws concerning vertical restrictions? Five reasons are frequently cited in the literature. The first two are financial; the next two are situational and therefore exogenous; the fifth is organizational.

1. The investments associated with vertical integration or the risks associated with those investments are often too great. It is common for a channel leader not to want to commit massive investment to a single vertical channel. Much of the franchising activity one observes comes about because small entrepreneurs can invest and risk that investment in a location without tying up the franchisor's capital.

2. The expected return on investment from vertical integration may not be attractive. There are many situations in which an existing distributor is making sufficient return to remain in business. However, the return expected by the leader is not attractive when compared to alternative investment opportunities. I want to distinguish here between this situation where distributor's return is unsatisfactory to the leader because of the competition in the intermediate market and the situation where the leader believes the vertically integrated organization would actually have higher costs. This latter situation will be discussed below.

3. The product may require intensive distribution or small-scale production. This discussion of vertical integration has presumed a small number of buyers and sellers in all intermediate markets. Many products require sales through a large number and variety of middlemen. A manufacturer of convenience packaged goods – e.g., gum, bread, soap – cannot vertically integrate with all of the retailers who might sell such products. Almost as unlikely is the possibility that a

larger retailer would try to purchase small-scale producers for its total supply of products such as raw milk or produce.

4. The existing infrastructure of intermediaries (distributors or producers) has sufficient capacity and high barriers to entry. This situation could occur in regional markets for products where only a few distributors are required, where they are well established, and where the barriers to a new entrant are great. Thus, many examples exist of firms that are vertically integrated in some regions and utilize dealers in others.

5. The vertically integrated system may be less efficient than the market, leadership, or contractual one. The arguments concerning this possibility will be developed in more detail in the next section. The point here is that rigorous enforcement of the laws on vertical restrictions and on vertical mergers that cause organizations to alter structure on grounds other than efficiency could lead to vertical marketing systems which are not as efficient as they might be if left in the hands of the participants in the system.

What Is An Efficient Organizational Structure for A Vertical Marketing System?

The previous sentence suggests that somewhere in business practice or the theory of marketing there exists a formula for how to determine the structure for a vertical system that maximizes efficiency. Unfortunately, no such formula exists. Here again we face a situation where public policy makers would like to have simple rules or benchmarks, but none exist. Professor E.T. Grether would argue that one must analyze the effectiveness of an organization or system in order to determine if a specific structure or behavior is socially desirable or undesirable. How can we begin an analysis of that effectiveness when we have no normative model? To repeat Professor Phillips' closing thought: "Complicated phenomena require careful consideration, not simple rules." In order to help in these considerations, the following thoughts are offered.

First, I want to argue that the differences in linkages among members of a vertical system from (1) market to (2) leadership to (3) contrast to (4) decentralized authority integrated systems to (5) centralized authority integrated systems is one of degree and not kind. This is not to deny that the leap from the anonymous transactions in competitive markets to the negotiation in bilateral contractual arrangements is not a long one. Nor is it to deny that the leap from title transfers in contractual systems to simple ownership integrated systems is any shorter. It is to point out that here we are studying the linkages in a system. As such, we can focus more on the internal organization of that system and less on the characteristics of the environmental setting like private property rights. Further, we have already suggested that, for this discussion, we might usefully break our system at any competitive market linkage. Thus, we will compare and contrast these five different linkage systems, assuming the same dimensions for comparison apply.

Second, we will use for this comparison of the five structures some dimensions from my "systems/exchange paradigm" (Carman, 1980). The dimensions selected are those most useful in identifying efficiency differences; they are not inconsistent with the constructs suggested by Zald (1970) and Arndt (1979).

Goals of the system

In the paragraphs that follow, the focus of the analysis will be on allocative and technical efficiency. However, public policy toward marketing has often invoked other goals as well. Some possible examples are listed to remind the reader that their inclusion could add substantial complexity to the analysis:

- maximum competition in all markets involving the system
- maximum competition in final markets only
- minimum concentration of economic power
- preservation of small business
- socially desirable wealth redistributions
- no undesirable externalities
- allocative efficiency in all goods used or produced by the system
- technical efficiency, which may be usefully subdivided into:
  Functional efficiency (minimum cost in the performance of all production and marketing functions performed by the system-internal allocative efficiency)
  Transactional efficiency (minimum transactions costs for all exchanges conducted within the system and between the system and outsiders)
  Administrative efficiency (minimum cost for running the system – these costs sometimes may be measured as transactions costs)

Control (incentive) mechanism of the system

The incentive mechanism clearly changes when one goes from independent to integrated systems. The independent distributor and manufacturer each may be assumed to be profit maximizers. It would be unusual indeed if joint profit maximization suggested the same behavior as individual profit maximization. Yet, the theoretical optimum equilibrium solution in many such situations suggests the channel leader should try to urge joint profit maximization. Note, however, that the opportunity for excess profits through hard work, shrewd bargaining, and clever decisions exists for all participants.

In the integrated system, advancement and recognition including salary increases are the key elements in the incentive mechanism. Notice that performance-based incentives can be offered by the leader in either case. (However, the Robinson-Patman Act outlaws some types of incentives in market linked systems.) Also, the need for holding some power exists in either case. The power structure within hierarchical organization may be just as significant as for the entrepreneur.

As mentioned earlier, the risk associated with the two systems is a major difference. Risk-averse persons would gravitate to integrated system; risk-attracted persons, to independent systems. It is not obvious that an individual's attitude toward risk has any bearing on system performance.

Characteristics of the participant organizations

More dimensions than incentive systems and risk aversion are required to describe the actors in the various linkage systems. Goal structures are more complex than financial goals. Are the individual goals of a manager in an integrated system any more likely to be at odds with that of his organization than are the individual goals of the manager of a small firm? Williamson (1975, p. 257) argues that the large hierarchical system may have internal control systems which create specialization in decision-making so that the freedom of individual action is bounded. Such specialization is not only administratively efficient but it reduces the likelihood of suboptimal decisions.

On this dimension, one might be willing to make a distinction between the decentralized integrated and centralized integrated systems. A price paid for decentralization is clearly the increased risk of suboptimization by individual units or managers. To overcome this increased risk of suboptimization, organizations employ control systems involving information structures, transfers, resource rationing, and management incentives. A transfer pricing guide is only one element of such control systems.

The nature of the demand structure is different in an integrated system than in a market structure. The bilateral monopoly or oligopoly structures are subject to market failure. The bargaining may result in a socially undesirable bargain. The command based transfer is much more likely to be at a clearly specified transfer price and come complete with instructions for handling every contingency in an efficient manner. Nonoptimal transfer prices may change with a lag, but at least they exhibit stability.

Value assignments

How are those transfer prices determined and do they lead to greater allocative efficiency than would bargain prices in the independently linked systems? If a free market exists for the good, the chances are that the contract price and transfer price are going to be similar to one another and to the market price.

If there is no comparable market price, a generalization is more difficult. There is no shortage of stories about nonoptimal transfer prices, but there is also no shortage of long-term purchase agreements that have gone sour. At least in the former case, it does not require a legal battle to settle disputes.

Transaction costs

Beyond the allocative correctness of the value assignment, we must also consider the transaction efficiency connected with achieving the exchange. Clearly, conflict resolution costs favor the command hierarchy over the bargaining arrangement.

In decentralized integrated units, bargaining may still be permitted to take place between operating units of the organization. However, the atmosphere and singleness of organization probably make for more efficient bargaining and for conflict resolution by quick mutual agreement or by command.

Level of information

The level of information available and usefully managed in each of the five linkage arrangements may be one of the most interesting constructs. Williamson (1975, p. 257) claims hierarchies will make better use of information because (1) they are more likely to have planning procedures that deal with uncertainty in a more rational manner than would organizations without systematic planning; and (2) information is managed better in hierarchies than in autonomous organizations.

Most advocates of profit-center, decentralized organizations would argue that decentralization adds a third advantage; that is, the focus on a single business activity by the decentralized units makes them even more efficient collectors and responders to information about change or unique local conditions.

When one jumps across the autonomous linkages, generalization is more difficult. A firm in bilateral monopoly or oligopoly may be just as good an information manager as a decentralized unit of a vertically integrated firm. However, the chances are that the latter spends more money on information support staff than does the former.

Certainly, the market linked firm is going to have less motivation to manage information than the other structures. Such a firm is far more likely to count on the information content of price to meet the needs of the organization.

Rules governing exchanges

This is because in a competitive market linked system, the price system is the market clearing mechanism. Buyers and sellers can often make decisions after they know the levels of market prices.

In the bargaining situation, participants will have some plans before negotiations take place, but the outcome of the bargaining may be difficult to forecast. The rules or mores of the bargaining process can influence its outcome and the efficiency with which it is conducted. Clearly, this is the linkage structure that requires the most time and effort to achieve exchange. Even if every exchange is not fully negotiated, the negotiation of the original contract can be very labor intensive.

In contrast, the authority rules in the integrated command hierarchies are clear. Exchanges are coordinated with a minimum of managerial interaction.

Strengths of Various Linkage Structures

If we accept the idea that the five linkage structures can be arranged along a single continuum, what generalizations can be made regarding their relative allocative and technical efficiency? When interpreting this summary, remember that investment requirements, expected return, the nature of the product, and the existing marketing infrastructure all could impose restrictions that would limit which of the five linkage structures are, in fact, available. Also remember that the goals of public policy are often more complex than simply maximum efficiency. Given these caveats, table 14.1 identifies six criteria on which at least some weak generalizations can be made. The five structures have been combined into four and each of these four ranked on each criterion.

The results are too close to call. As in any multiple objective situation, tradeoffs must be made. The rank order judgments of the table do not provide a level of measurement that is precise enough to make these tradeoffs. On the technical efficiency criteria (the first four), hierarchies seem to do a bit better than markets. On allocative efficiency and distribution criteria, market linkages appear to be superior. Decentralized hierarchies come out a bit ahead overall. Undoubtedly, the best structure, and indeed the availability of a structure, depend on the ideosyncrasies of the situation. These idiosyncrasies could vary among geographic markets for a single product and firm.

There are far more factors that will influence which linkage structure is best than we have mentioned here. Absolute size is one; cohesiveness of the management team is another. Vertical marketing systems are indeed complicated phenomena. Very careful analysis is required to formulate or interpret public policy concerning them.

Table 14.1. Ranking of Types of Linkage

(Highest Rank is 1)

Criteria	Market	Leadership/Contract	Decentralized Hierarchy	Centralized Hierarchy
Monopoly profit incentive	3	1	2	4
Efficient specialization of labor and internal control system	3	3	2	1
Transaction efficiency	2	3	1	1
Efficient collection and innovative responsiveness to information concerning changes or local conditions in demand	3	2	1	2
Allocative efficiency	1	3	2	2
Socially desirable wealth and power distribution	1	2	3	3

213

15 Establishments, Firms, and Channels as Units of Competition

Reavis Cox

The immediate stimulus for this paper comes from a consideration of what the growing computerization of checkouts in retail stores may do to the understanding, organization, management, and control of marketing channels. In the background, as evidence of the spread of interest in the subject among students of marketing, stands a rapidly growing literature concerned with channels. Still further back lies a conviction some of us have long held that channel analysis offers a promising but largely undeveloped instrument for gaining new insights into the nature of managerial problems raised by marketing for businessmen and academics alike. Finally, there is reason to believe that some important problems of social policy may be made more tractable by looking upon them as problems in or closely related to the nature and operation of channels. This last circumstance makes channels an appropriate topic for a symposium honoring Dean Grether, so much of whose professional work has concerned itself with social issues in marketing.

TRACING FLOWS THROUGH CHANNELS

Member agencies of marketing channels are easily seen, but the channel itself is very difficult to trace out in the marketplace. The Bureau of the Census has no great difficulty (other than the great labor involved) in finding large numbers of establishments that sell goods. It readily classifies them (with significant but partly compensating errors) into two categories: (1) those that sell what they themselves produce (i.e.,

*In preparing this paper I have benefited from discussions with faculty members and students at Louisiana Tech University, the University of Texas, the University of Alabama, and the University of Minnesota, as well as from comments on it in its original form by Professor Louis P. Bucklin.

extract, process, or manufacture); and (2) those that resell to third parties goods extracted or made by others. The category of resellers, taken in the aggregate, is the distribution industry. The Bureau sets itself the task of finding all of these resellers and obtaining from each one data concerning its organization and operation as well as some of its relations with other agencies, including suppliers, other resellers, and users. These data are converted into masses of statistics that can be published in public reports. From these can be derived rudimentary and narrowly limited descriptions of marketing channels.

Difficulties arise when one tries to trace out channels more precisely in order to manage and control them. Various assumptions underlie the effort, of which at least two are germane here:

1. What the agencies do can be summarized into a list of the "functions" they perform or the "activities" in which they engage. For example, they transport and store goods; they buy and sell goods, thus assuming or transferring to others the benefits, responsibilities, and risks that go with ownership; they seek out the capital needed to finance these processes and bring it into the system; they collect and disseminate market information; and so on. All this is familiar enough and calls for no particular comment here.
2. What they do in performing these functions can conveniently be described as participating in an assortment of "flows." For example, physical products may flow from factory to warehouse to retail store; the ownership of or title to these goods may flow from seller through one or more resellers to the final user; capital flows in the form of credit from banks directly to consumers or indirectly to them through finance companies, wholesalers, and retailers; information about a product flows from manufacturers through advertising media to consumers; and so on. All this, too, is familiar enough.

In practice, as I have said, the flows are often very complex and extremely difficult to trace. The agencies involved keep incomplete and often fleeting records concerning them. Many managers do not think at all about channels as a concept. If they do think about them, they are apt to dismiss them as an invention of ingenious but impractical academic minds. The situation has changed somewhat since 1966, when Mallen, one of the most distinguished of present day writers on channels, concluded that even academic writers had done little work on the channel as a concept. On this subject, he said, "there is a desert of scholarly contributions." (Mallen, 1967, p. ix.) A decade later he found a somewhat different situation (Mallen, 1977, p. xviii):

. . . a new universe of concepts, theories, hypotheses, and empirical findings has arisen in the channel field (but) except for the relatively few channel scholars, these concepts generate bewilderment, to whatever extent they are recognized, among students, marketing practitioners and even marketing scholars.

So he undertook to write a book that would show the practitioners in marketing how they can organize and administer a system of channel management. How successful he has been in reaching practitioners cannot yet be determined. The thesis I shall support here holds that the spread of computerization into retailing, and particularly into the checkout or "front-end" areas, will give support to the effort.

PUBLIC POLICY RELEVANCE OF TRACING
CHANNEL FLOWS

The opportunities opening up are not limited to business managers, whose basic interest lies in maximizing profits. They also apply to the analysis of social problems raised by marketing. For illustration of the significance of channel analysis in working with such problems, we can turn to the section on "Legal Developments in Marketing" published in successive issues of the Journal of Marketing. Most of these notes have to do with matters in the broad range of antitrust; but other aspects of government activity come up from time to time. A continually changing concept of what "competition" is and how it can be preserved in the give and take of business underlies many of these developments. For example, in any given market, who competes with whom? Conventionally, we answer this question by designating such entities as "firms," "agencies," and "enterprises" that are in direct rivalry with one another or whom we want to be in such rivalry. The boundaries of such entities do not always correspond closely with the boundaries of the problems under surveillance. The question I raise here is whether in this context competitors can best be seen not as "firms," say, but rather as segments of channels or even as complete channels. The same sort of thinking can enter fruitfully into efforts to delimit the boundaries of "markets" within which competition is to be stimulated or restrained, as the case may be.

Resale price maintenance, a subject to which Dean Grether made important contributions in his early days as a scholar in marketing (Grether, 1935 and 1939) can also be visualized as a problem of choosing among channels. When a manufacturer or other owner of a brand maintains resale prices, he reduces or eliminates intrabrand competition among the resellers of his product, who vie with each other for the patronage of buyers who want that particular brand. Simultaneously, he stimulates aggressive interbrand competition among resellers of brands other than his own. Social evaluation of what is done must take account not only of what happens at the channel level where sellers and resellers compete directly with each other for shares in intermediate markets, but also at the consumer level, where complete channels struggle with each other for the patronage of final users.

"Price discrimination" has been defined to mean many things. Narver's paper in this book develops this subject in detail. To some, it can mean charging different buyers of a product different prices even though each buyer is at precisely the same level in each of the several flows within a given channel. Alternatively, it can mean charging the same nominal price to customers who are at different levels in one or more flows. In fact, the concept of "price" itself has little meaning if stated simply as so many dollars per unit of a product unless the product is described carefully, and this may mean primarily specifying its location in the various flows through the channel.

Definitions of products in connection with other aspects of the antitrust and related laws also can use channel concepts. Some writers define a channel as beginning when materials and parts are incorporated in a product offered for sale and as ending either when it itself is incorporated in another product or reaches an ultimate consumer. The consumer is served by a succession of channels thus defined, each of which is a complex assortment of flows. As we shall see shortly, there is also merit in an alternative view that treats everything that happens to a product when it moves from elemental raw material to finished product as taking place in a single channel.

The definition of a product is crucial in still other ways. When does an assortment of parts become an assembled product? Attaching parts to a given assembly and refusing to sell either the assembly without the parts or the unassembled parts without the assembly may be interpreted as unlawful full-line forcing or a tying contract. "Untying" such an arrangement not only opens the market to other manufacturers of the parts in question, but may make it necessary for whoever manufactures the parts to find or organize a new channel for them. If a telephone company requires that all the equipment and attachments its customers want shall be made by its own manufacturing subsidiary and installed by its own workmen, there is a vertical foreclosure that may be unlawful. Here again, loosening this foreclosure by order of public authorities is forcing the creation of new channels by the subsidiary in question. Can optometrists combine with other optometrists as professional men to formulate and enforce standards for advertising eye examinations without simultaneously getting into trouble for conspiring with the same optometrists as retailers of eyeglasses to regulate the marketing of eyeglasses? Firms of this type really operate in two different channels at once that call for different treatment by the authorities.

Farm cooperatives enjoy exemptions from the antitrust laws under the Capper-Volstead Act. Are integrated producers of broiler chickens "farmers" under the terms of this act? The Supreme Court has ruled that they are not. In effect, they use chicks and feeds bought from farmers, perhaps through the same cooperative, to "manufacture" broilers. Without regard to the applicability of any law, this decision illustrates how it may be extremely difficult to determine when changes in ownership do and when they do not result in the closing of one channel and the opening of another.

Who among those in the various flows of marketing is responsible for deceptive or false advertising? Who should pay for corrective advertising if it is ordered? Who should pay penalties imposed and damages assessed in civil suits filed by competitors or consumers? It has been held that not only the manufacturer who, in common parlance, "does" the advertising, but also advertising agencies, advertising media, and even individual performers in television, may be held jointly responsible. Are resellers further down the channel also to be held liable? If so, when and how does each member of the channel learn before the fact that a coming campaign is deceptive, that he probably will be one of the parties held responsible, and how large his share of the responsibility will be? An intricate and difficult channel analysis may be needed to settle such questions.

In some circumstances, a firm that is accused of unfair or predatory pricing may defend itself by asserting that it is merely meeting competition. What channels may he use in obtaining information as to the prices his competitors are charging? Suppose a potential customer says that a competitor has offered a better deal. Can the first would-be seller investigate what the competitor really is charging or even call him directly on the telephone and ask for verification? The matter has not been resolved and there seems to be disagreement in the lower courts.

Examples of this sort could be multiplied almost indefinitely, but these are enough to make the situation clear. The analysis of channel structures and their operation can play a significant role in working with many of the social problems raised by marketing. With this thought in the background we can now turn to a more specific consideration of the nature and functions of channels and the effects computerization may have on them.

MEASURING CHANNEL ACTIVITIES

The oldest publication cited by Bartels in his History of Marketing Thought is Crowell's report on the distribution of farm products published in 1901 (Bartels, 1976; Crowell, 1901.) One can conveniently date the formal study of marketing channels from that report. Crowell does not use the term explicitly, but he implies the concept when he describes the agencies intervening between farmer and user, tells what they do, and reports some of the charges they make for the services they perform. From this modest beginning, interest in channels has grown steadily – at first slowly, then in a rush. Recent years have seen a flood of books, articles, and fugitive publications pouring into the field.

Interest has burgeoned in spite of the fact that the channel has always been a difficult subject to study, to teach, and to apply to managerial problems. Much of what it does is not easily displayed in action or subject to observation and measurement. In contrast, anyone who takes the trouble to do so can readily observe production (i.e., extraction, processing, and fabrication) in action. He can, for example, watch a cotton farmer prepare his soil, plant his seed, cultivate his fields, harvest his crop, and take it in truckloads to a nearby gin. He can then watch others separate the seed from the fiber and change each of these into a succession of intermediate products and eventually into consumable goods. The processes he watches are physical, noisy, and frequently spectacular, as in the familiar assembly lines that put parts flowing in from many places into an automobile. The intangible aspects of production can be related quite easily to the tangible product.

Showing anyone what marketing does is much more difficult. Transportation and storage, it is true, can be observed easily, so it has not been difficult to separate out a field of logistics in which physical activity can be seen and to which impressively complex mathematical analyses can be applied. The superficial aspects of advertising, display, auctions, commodity exchanged, and planned shopping centers also are easy to see. What lies at the heart of marketing, however, all the buying, selling, and controlling, is not concerned with tangible objects but with intangibles – relations among people, among objects, and between objects and people. It does not always lend itself readily to physical observation.

It is particularly difficult to satisfy the observer at the end of the assembly line who says, "Now show me one of the marketing channels you have been talking about." There is no corresponding assembly line, although the entire marketing process has sometimes been described as a gigantic sorting process that alternately assembles and disperses products until they arrive in wanted assortment at the place of consumption. If there were such a physical establishment to be observed, much of it would have to be seen as a "disassembly" line (a term used in packing houses), since the ultimate objective is to divide commercial lots of goods into smaller units for individual consumption.

The available statistics we have on channels are derived largely from the Bureau of the Census, which offers counts of establishments, a term it has invented for its purposes. It assigns such establishments to the distribution industry if their major activity is concerned with buying and reselling goods made by others and consumed by others. A great deal of marketing activity is done by firms and establishments that are primarily manufacturers, so that classifications are imprecise and sometimes uncertain. Rigorous detailed analyses often are impossible. Most of the information made available has to do with large blocks of the distribution industry. Only very limited and very broad generalizations can be made about the relations of these blocks to each other.

Given these circumstances, it is hardly surprising that the channel concept has turned out to be little used in the management of business. McVey, in his classic article published two decades ago, said that manufacturers tend to think of the firms to whom they sell simply as their market, not as the first units in a channel to be controlled and managed as a whole (McVey, 1960). Intermediate traders or resellers similarly tend to think of themselves as buying goods from sources of supply and reselling them to their own customers. They are not, in this view, parts of an extended organization set up to serve the suppliers (once or twice removed) of firms from whom they buy or the customers (once or twice removed) of the resellers to whom they sell, so they look upon their relations with suppliers and customers as aspects of their own programs of purchasing or selling. Like many other generalizations about marketing, these are only partly true. Significant exceptions are to be found (Moore and Eckrich, 1976), but there is no gainsaying the fact that the channel concept is primarily an academic one used in armchair research rather than a tool to be used in empirical research or by managers in their day-to-day operations.

In the light of these difficulties, why has the concept of the channel managed to live so long and to be so persistent? One reason is that, vague and uncertain though they may be, the channels talked about in textbooks are useful instruments for academic people in formalizing intuitive judgments as to what goes on in marketing. By using hypothetical data about imaginary firms, we can come up, or so we believe, with tables and charts that give us a better understanding of what goes on in the real world than we can come to by any other nonquantitative technique.

THE TRANSVECTION CONCEPT

Computerizations, particularly in retailing, bids fair to change matters significantly. To see why this is so, we can look first at a more precise concept of the channel. This embodies an idea derived from Alderson's concept of transvection (Alderson and Martin, 1965). Consider a single unit of usable goods delivered to a consumer. It starts as a small pile of materials taken from one or more sources. This material is subjected to a series of processes, often complex and extensive, that change its form, its location, and the identity of those who own and control it. When it has passed as a consumable good into the consumer's possession and control at the place and time when he wants to use it, it has finally been, in the broadest sense of the term, produced.

The end product may be a simple one, such as an ounce or two of roasted and ground coffee that is ready for some consumer's percolator, having been made from a few beans provided, probably months before, by a small tree in southern Brazil. At the other extreme, it may be a very complicated product that begins with an assortment of many materials drawn from many sources. Through an intricately complex set of processes, these are converted into an automobile in our consumer's garage or the house of which the garage is a part (Cox and Goodman, 1956).

The combination of processes by means of which materials are converted into an individual unit of consumable goods ready for use is, in Alderson's terminology, a transvection. We know by intuition or common sense that transvections as thus described are actual, largely physical occurrences. We are not looking at abstract notions of what happens in a hypothetical world. We know that we could not drink a cup of coffee, ride in an automobile, or live in a house, without passing materials through a succession and combination of events that add up to a transvection. We know that, in principle, any such transvection should be observable from end to end. Its parts should be countable and measurable.

The qualifier in principle needs to be inserted because in practice observation of a full transvection may be extremely difficult and laborious. Records describing the steps, one after another, through which the product passes as it comes into being may be evanescent. Some of them disappear almost before they have appeared. But they are there and available, however fleetingly, for permanent recording and analysis if we can devise computerized sampling and storing mechanisms for the purpose and are satisfied that the results will be worth the effort.

One reason why the idea of a transvection is useful in the study of channels is that we can base upon it a definition of what we may call the basic channel. Every part of every transvection is performed by some agency. Usually several and often a great many agencies participate in the process of performing one transvection. These are not a chaotic, haphazard, or even random assortment of entitities. They fit into both a structure and a sequence through which the overall task is performed.

We could say that marketing includes everything that is done in a transvection to and for materials from the time they leave the farm, forest, or mine until ultimate users begin consuming the products made from them. Students of agricultural marketing have long followed this convention as regards farm products. Virtually all other students of marketing follow a different convention. They differentiate marketing from production, which is done not only at the farms, mines, and so on, but also by processors along the way to market. In abstract economic terms, the distinction is between establishments that produce form utility and those that produce space, time, or possession utility. In less formal terms, extractors (including farmers) and processors (often called producers, suppliers, or manufacturers) are differentiated (and differentiate themselves) from distributors, resellers, and other marketers.

In substance this represents an effort to separate extraction and physical processing from the full transvection. It leads to the following definition:

> The basic channel of marketing is the combination and sequence
> of agencies that jointly perform one transvection, except for
> activities concerned with extraction and processing.

In the conventional usages of marketing this definition is denominated as institutional. It concentrates its interest upon agencies or establishments and what they do. Starting with such a definition opens the way to efforts to answer such questions as: How has the overall task of producing a transvection been divided among channel members? To what extent and in what ways do the members of the channel make sure that everything necessary for the completion of the transvection is in fact done and done well? Of the value accrued through the transvection and delivered to the consumer, how much is contributed by each agency? This question can be put the other way around: Of the price paid by the final user, how much goes to each agency involved? Can the performance of the channel be improved by reallocating responsibilities and powers among its members? Can it be improved by changing the temporal sequence in which the various chores are performed or the places at which they are performed?

The ideas thus far discussed can lead to a more effective use by students of the armchair reasoning that has played a large part in the studies they do make of channels. Anyone who wants to do so is still free to use whatever verbalizations he likes in describing channels. He can readily construct charts based upon hypothetical data derived from his imagination or such empirical knowledge as he may have, fragmentary and faulty though it may be.

More importantly, however, he now begins to find an alternative making its appearance. Circumstances have brought into his view the possibility that he can subject his reasoning to empirical tests. He already knows, as we have seen, that every unit of consumables had to originate somewhere as a specific set of materials extracted at a specific set of places. Everything done to convert these materials from their original condition to one in which they enter into consumption as finished goods has been done at specific places and times by specific agencies. These events have fallen into a specific sequence and been performed within a specific period. At every stage of its progress, the item has been owned by someone and been in the possession of someone for operational purposes. Specific agencies have performed all the facilitating services required. There thus emerges into his view a set of entities performing a set of activities that are in principle observable, countable, and measurable.

ROLE OF POINT-OF-SALE COMPUTERS

What makes this view of the channel particularly promising just now is the development of small computers and their spread throughout the business world. These may make do-able in practice what we have described as do-able in principle. Most significant for our purposes is the appearance of so-called front-end computers. In an increasing number of retail stores, such a computer records information about the smallest detail of the business – the purchase by a customer of an individual item of goods. It thus stands at the end of innumerable transvections, which it summarizes for the immediate purpose of telling the customer and the checkout operator how much is to be paid for the goods in question.

The information can be passed along to various memories and further computers where it can be stored and subjected to analyses of many sorts. The uses made of it may vary widely in practice, but the basic fact remains that where such a point-of-sale system exists, it brings with it the beginning of a possibility that we can set up for analysis a multitude of identifiable transvections about which a good deal of information has been recorded.

The greatest advance in this kind of computerization seems to have been made in retail food stores where the possibility of recording for future analysis individual sales transactions is made easier by the establishment of a standardized system for classifying products called the Universal Product Code (UPC). UPC has been worked out with the cooperation of practically all of the major manufacturers of products sold in supermarkets in the United States and Canada (Stern and El-Ansary, 1977, pp. 466-474). A recent estimate indicates that some 80 percent of the packaged goods distributed through supermarkets are covered.

The outward evidence of UPC is a cryptic symbol that appears on the packages. It is a combination of lines of varying widths, separated by spaces of varying widths, and a block of numbers. Encoded in them is a range of information about the specific product and its source.

Whether read by optical scanner or entered by the sales clerk on a keyboard, the information contained in the UPC symbol is transferred into the computer. The first output comes from what may be called a sophisticated cash register. It lists each item by name, brand, and price on a sales slip for the customer, and computes the change. The information encoded in the symbol is passed into memories for storage and such analysis as may be made of it subsequently.

How far transvections thus entered into the records can be traced back toward their points of origin remains to be seen. Thus far, use of these devices seems to have been concentrated upon improving the internal operations of the enterprises making the records. In particular, they have been used to speed the checkouts, to reduce errors in listing and recording items and prices both on consumers' tapes and in the store's records, to provide more accurate and more timely data for use in managing inventories, to facilitate the use of logistical procedures and controls, and to evaluate the effects of advertising and other promotions on sales. Combined with field surveys, they can show variations in the response of different groups of customers to the stores, their products, and their policies. Manufacturers now have opportunities to buy from the stores data showing how well the goods they make are moving through stores to consumers.

The use of electronic systems at successive levels of a channel can open up new possibilities for observing, analyzing, and perhaps eventually controlling the flows of ownership, information, promotion, physical possession, financing, and so on, of which we have already spoken. Appropriate sampling techniques would provide a much better opportunity than we have thus far had for observing, counting, and measuring successive steps in at least large sections of these transvections. It should carry both analysis and control far beyond what was possible at the beginning of this century for Crowell or even half a century ago, when a few students tried briefly and ineffectually to work with so-called "invoice traces" in mapping out where particular units of goods in particular markets came from, how they got there, where they went next, and what happened to them as they advanced. It should also make possible research instruments much more precise than the intellectual axes Goodman and I (together with several colleagues) used two decades ago in our efforts to trace the materials used in constructing a house from their points of origin to the building site (Cox and Goodman, 1956). This should lead to the formulating of realistic models of channels that can be tested by empirical investigations.

There are, of course, many practical difficulties to be overcome in installing automated retail checkouts in individual stores and in getting access for channel research to the data produced. One is the high starting cost. Many firms cannot provide the sophisticated managerial techniques required to obtain and use effectively the masses of data envisioned. Governmental restrictions may be imposed because of objections raised by some consumers or their spokesmen against some parts of the system. An example is the substitution of shelf pricing for item pricing. Perhaps the stores will be reluctant to make the records available to researchers. Even if individual stores are willing to do so, other members of channels must be persuaded to cooperate in research or managerial ventures that require a pooling of data.

Perhaps nonprofit or governmental agencies that can keep data confidential may be required. They could start with a survey such as the experimental census of distribution for 1926 taken in 1927 (Retail and Wholesale Trade in Eleven Cities, 1928). The data obtained in this survey were of some immediate interest for their own sake, but the primary achievement was to test procedures for taking a full census and to determine that they worked.

Although the first task to be performed in the empirical study of channels may well be to trace out individual basic channels as fully as possible, the underlying objective should be to assemble either sample or census data from which generalizations can be developed as guides to future action and research. Thus, one would classify the basic channels traced by empirical research into types identified by the sorts of agencies that compose them, the sequences in which the component agencies appear, the combinations of flows they carry out, their comprehensiveness, their vertical reach through levels of channels, and their horizontal reach over the kinds of products and geographic areas. The extent to which particular channels are used over and over is of much interest, as are the frequency of such recurrences, the persistence of channel types, and their life expectancy. Emphasis can be put on segments of channels, rather than upon complete channels, if this is expedient or desirable, and upon either single or multiple flows. The classification of channels by the kinds of end-products they deliver can take many forms and serve many purposes. The measures and analyses made possible by the computers can continue to use the concept of establishments developed by the Census Bureau as the basic units to be measured or devise others if it seems desirable.

THE CHANNEL AS A UNIT OF COMPETITION

Success in developing the channel concept as a basis for empirical research will carry with it some important consequences for our understanding of what market competition is and how it operates. One consequence is particularly important for those who look at the implications of channel analysis for social policy. In popular discussion, we are likely to think of the term competition as denominating rivalry among individual sellers and resellers for the patronage of buyers who seek or can be induced to seek particular goods or products. Breyer in a little known paper (Breyer, 1965) suggested that what would-be sellers offer to consumers should be visualized not as products but as propositions. The proposition, he says, is "a concept that embraces the entire offer made to the consumer as an integrated whole. This is the essential form in which the offer generally exists in the consumer's mind." It is composed of the physical product, plus "accompanying services" (such as installation, credit, delivery, and warranties), "adjunctive elements" (such as trading stamps, giveaways, and consumer contests), statements of quantities offered, and the formal price.

Efforts to understand and control channels as social or economic institutions must keep in mind the fact that the proposition the consumer buys is produced by the entire channel, not the agency that stands at the end of the transvection. Would-be members of the basic channel presumably compete with each other vigorously for positions in the channel. That is, retailers compete strongly, even savagely, with other retailers, wholesalers with other wholesalers, and so on, for opportunities to make contributions to the transvection, even though they have never heard the term. Up the line in the transvection, suppliers correspondingly fight strongly for access to facilities and services provided by the resellers.

However, even when their parts in the propositions they help to produce have been assured, the battle is only half won. True success can be achieved only at the end of the transvection. Having fought against each other on their way into the transvection, the successful members of the channel must now cooperate with each other, knowingly or not. Only by working jointly can they win against competing transvections in the struggle to capture the patronage of the ultimate users.

Although common sense should tell everyone that all this is true, it is often (perhaps one should say commonly) overlooked in discussions of channels and how they can be managed or controlled. Exceptions are to be found, of course, among manufacturers of branded and strongly promoted consumer goods. Such firms put great emphasis upon what we have long called "pull" merchandising. Those who advertise less aggressively or not at all to final consumers have to rely more upon "push" merchandising. The "push" merchandiser emphasizes getting the goods into the hands of his immediate customers, who, together with succeeding and facilitating members of the channel, are expected to push them the rest of the way. The two systems are not mutually exclusive, since heavy advertisers also use push techniques in their battles for acceptance into resellers facilities, as exemplified in the facings on display shevles of stores that must be allocated to suppliers.

Underlying any efforts that may be made to understand, manage, or control channels are two further concepts that have been touched upon lightly in the literature but not brought into full recognition. These are what we may call the critical point of competition and the channel as a unit of competition.

The critical point of competition is the transaction that embodies the final bargain made between buyers and sellers in moving a particular unit of goods into consumption. All the marketing efforts exerted at all levels of the channel meet their critical test here in that the transvection toward which everything has been moving does or does not take place. Despite its importance, the explicit concept of the critical point of competition has received little attention from either businessmen or academicians. Except for some advertising and related efforts in point-of-sale merchandising by large companies, the emphasis in selling continues to be placed primarily on solving problems with customers viewed separately as targets of marketing rather than as parts of a coordinated whole.

The concept of the channel as an entity to be managed in itself rather than an agglomeration of entities (Cox, 1958) is not strongly established. In much of the literature, the term channel is little more than a collective designation of various agencies intervening between producers (or more specifically manufacturers) and consumers. This is true even though a good deal has been written recently under the general title of vertical marketing systems. (Bucklin, 1970; Moyer, 1978.) Much of what writers call the management of channels is really a process of selecting target customers at one or more points in the channel and trying to persuade them to buy the goods in question.

A careful reading of what has been written in this area also indicates that the management of channels is commonly confused with managing the captain's or the leader's own staff in their dealings with channel members. A good deal has been written about channel leaders, but we are left without a very clear picture of who they are, if they exist at all, and what they do in their role as leaders.

Inherent in the discussion of this range of problems is a distinction between managed and unmanaged channels. Mallen draws a clear distinction between the two. (Mallen, 1977, chapters 7 and 8 and appendix 8A.) On the one hand, the channel may be "a sequence of loosely connected markets," whose members view themselves as merely buying from or selling to one another. Into this picture, Mallen says in substance, management does not enter. Members are not interested in controlling the policies of their fellow members. Social analysis of what takes place is likely to be done primarily in economic terms. It considers the structures of the markets and puts emphasis upon degrees of monopoly and monopsony, either of which may in any given case be simple, successive, or bilateral.

As against this view, the channel can be treated as "an interacting political-social system." Here, channel members see themselves as buying or selling <u>through</u> rather than <u>from</u> or <u>to</u> one another. Doing this opens room for concepts of management in channels. The approach is more academic than managerial and leads to descriptions of what is happening in terms derived from sociology and political science rather than from economics. It operates with such concepts as cooperation, conflict, roles, communication, power, and leadership.

What some students see as being required in this situation is an injection of more management. Shaw, perhaps the most imaginative of the early writers on marketing, established an attitude that still appeals to many students when he exclaimed in exasperation, "Our whole system of distribution is in chaos!" (Shaw, 1915, p. 118). This opinion implies that a higher degree of order and system must be introduced into an essentially anarchic situation by someone, perhaps a higher authority or a channel leader. Who this leader is to be and how he is to be selected are left unspecified.

Another way to look at these things is to differentiate market controls from administrative controls as alternative forms of management. It may literally be true to say that channels controlled by competition in open markets are unmanaged, but lack of management does not automatically imply lack of control. Those brought up in the traditions of classical and neoclassical economics will probably feel that the discipline of a truly competitive market is likely to be more effective than the discipline of administered systems, no matter how well devised and operated.

Looking upon the channel as a unit of competition has important implications for judgments made as to the social performance of marketing and, more specifically, of judgments clustered under the rubric of antitrust. In a purely competitive economy as visualized in traditional economics, things would presumably work out so that competition at the end of the channel, being reflected back through the states of the channel (each level of which would be purely competitive), would optimize the contribution made at each level to the proposition eventually offered to the consumer. This does not mean that each element considered separately is optimized. In a system, there is always a danger of suboptimizing. Herein lies the rub for public policy. Our antitrust enforcement policy usually looks at the nature of competitive structure, conduct, and performance at that level. At some level it may find monopoly and assume, as a result, nonoptimal resource allocation. However, from the standpoint of the total channel system, a monopoly may provide better resource allocation than competition. The unit of analysis ought to be the channel system and the controlling consideration should be the optimizing of the joint product of the transvection.

In practice, a far from perfect result must be expected because of lags and frictions. It would be extraordinarily difficult to determine in particular how checks and goads introduced by governmental action affect the situation at the final decision points. This is a formidable problem in its own right. We cannot consider it fully here, so I content myself with merely suggesting that a full exploration of the world of channels and the critical transactions in which they end can throw important new light on this troublesome problem.

Exploration of the points I have tried to make here can best be left to future papers. For the moment, we must be satisfied with what the computer is doing for us in facilitating use of a channel system for study and management. With improved data and methods of handling it, we can expect great steps to follow in efforts to advance our understanding of marketing as an academic discipline and as a subject of administrative or governmental control.

16 The Theory of Interregional Marketing
Ronald Savitt

Although E.T. Grether is best known for his work in the area of marketing and public policy, some of his earlier work represented important contributions to the development of marketing theory. The writings in marketing theory integrated concepts from economics and helped to develop the burgeoning marketing literature. These ideas have been valuable in understanding the marketing system, especially the nexus between marketing and public policy.

As an economist, Grether has always been interested in the functioning of markets and the performance of firms. His analysis of market forces has concentrated on understanding the barriers which affect competition among firms. Underlying his analysis of competition has been the theoretical perspective of interregional marketing. There is a common theme in much of his writing which shows a great understanding of the multidimensional nature of firms. The problems of marketing organization from the standpoint of microanalysis, he has remarked, consist of three substantive issues:

> (1) how to obtain and maintain effective access to the materials, supplies, capital, labor, etc., essential for the operation of the enterprise; (2) how to gain and maintain access to the customers whom it supplies; and (3) which of the complex relationships and activities essentially should it bring within direct control and operation of the enterprise itself, and which should it leave to the spontaneous process of the market. (Grether, 1966, Marketing and Public Policy, p. 80)

The theory of interregional marketing which pervades his analysis of public policy issues was put forward in two separate works. The first discussion is found in "A Theoretical Approach to the Analysis of Marketing" (Grether, 1950); the second is found in Marketing in the American Economy (Vaile, Grether, and Cox, 1952). The present discussion extends the theory and applies it to a specific problem in public policy, the definition of "relevant geographic market." The paper proceeds by stating the integrated theory and then proposing how it might be used to fully understand the spatial dimensions of firms and regions.

INTERREGIONAL MARKETING

Background

The theory of interregional marketing is at the same time a theory of trade and a theory of location. It explains why a firm locates at a specific point in time and space, why trade takes place between that point and other points, and what the market boundaries (the region) are for that firm. It provides management with direction with regards to trade potential and location possibilities (Douglas, 1975, p. 44). Further, interregional marketing offers new dimensions for those concerned with antitrust and regulation to better understand marketing behavior in so far as any definition of market based on the theory demands the inclusion of a wide range of variables.

The theory of interregional marketing has been greatly influenced by the work of Edward Hastings Chamberlain and Bertil Ohlin and the environment in which Grether found himself in California in the 1930s and 1940s. The regional elements in the theory are based on Ohlin's work in interregional trade; the issues of competitive behavior stem from Chamberlain's basic ideas regarding monopolistic competition. The theory, however, is more than the integration of the concepts of these two economists in so far as Grether brought his own analytic powers to bear on the issues of marketing organization.

From Ohlin, Grether drew upon the wider concept of "the market" than that that had pervaded the earlier economic literature. Ohlin clearly suggested the degrees to which such analysis must go:

> ... the geographical distribution of productive factors is important. Industrial activity must be adapted to the varying supply of such factors in different places; for only to a limited extent can the supply itself be adapted to the demands of various industries. ... This fact alone would necessitate a general analysis of the space aspect of the price mechanism.

> The one-market doctrine evidently needs a superstructure for the consideration of the geographical or territorial aspects of pricing, i.e., the location of industry, and of trade between places and districts of various types. (Ohlin, 1933, p. 4)

Hence, the spatial dimensions of a market are not solely limited to something approaching the "sales territory" but include buying as well and, as shall be developed later, potentially the entire set of marketing functions. As Grether argued, the essence of interregional marketing "takes the form of specific goods and services bought and sold by individual enterprises under the conditions of their environment. The device of economic region allows one to focus attention upon resource utilization and other factors that lie at the basis of our whole structure of production and marketing." (Grether, 1950, Theory in Marketing, p. 118)

Within the concept of the region, Grether refined and then applied Chamberlain's monopolistic competition and developed it as enterprise differentiation (Alderson, 1965, p. 197). Basically, it stated that the spatial and temporal behavior of firms within a region, between regions, or among regions, is a function not only of the transport gradient assumptions of pure competition, but also a function of the degree to which Chamberlainian selling costs affect behavior. Grether's approach is to clearly examine what might be termed "active behavior," the differentiation in products, services, and space, rather than accept the passive assumptions of economics. The firm is described as a dynamic, competitive entity; "Its 'variation' may refer to an alteration in the quality of the product itself — technical changes, a new design, or better materials; it may mean a new package or container; it may mean more prompt or courteous service, a different way of doing business, or perhaps a different location." (Chamberlain, 1933, p. 71)

The Core of the Theory

The core of the theory is an attempt to understand the behavior of the firm in a marketing perspective; it could almost be considered a theory of marketing strategy.

The behavior of the firm should be investigated not only in a price and marketing sense, but under the conditions of its physical and social environment, in its determination of its location, its spatial out reach in selling and buying, and its relationship in the marketing channel with suppliers on the one hand and buyers on the other. (Grether, 1950, Theory in Marketing, p. 117)

The existing economic structures can not be taken as given to explain marketing organization and behavior. "Because the marketing system is an integral part of that economic structure — both determining and determined — it must be explained in terms of the broad economic function as well as in terms of its relationship to a given economic organization." (Grether, Theory in Marketing, 1950, p. 117) All of the factors which affect a firm's behavior must be understood; as Ohlin stated: "Nothing less than a consideration of all the elements that constitute the price mechanism — the system of mutual interdependence — can adequately explain the nature of interregional trade." (Ohlin, 1933, p. 29)

Ohlin's definition or statement of the region is at the core of Grether's: a region is defined as a relatively large geographic area with the following characteristics: (1) it has more than one center of economic control; (2) it has greater internal homogeneity than would be present if merged with other contiguous areas; (3) it exports a characteristic group of products to other areas; and (4) it imports the characteristic products of other areas (Vaile, Grether, and Cox, 1952, p. 488). The purpose of defining a region is to focus "analysis on the products and services characteristic of the region in export and import trade." (Grether, 1950, Theory in Marketing, p. 119)

The intensity of interregional marketing, the focus on the active behavior in the performance of all the marketing functions, depends primarily on four elements. These are the relative inequality of the regions with respect to supplies of factors of production, the relative prosperity of regions, the strength of reciprocal demands among regions, and the relative effectiveness of internal competition within regions. When competition is active and effective, there should normally be a stronger basis for interregional marketing than when competition is docile (Vaile, Grether, and Cox, 1952, p. 509). Competition is active to the extent that firms engage in rivalry which leads to enterprise differentiation. Because marketing goes beyond the conditions of pure competition, new assumptions had to be taken into consideration. Under pure competition, firms will only engage in interregional trade if they can recover their transport costs. Under Grether's assumptions, sellers will be willing to absorb such costs; implicitly, the economies of larger sales resulting from greater market opportunities will allow these costs to be covered. To the extent that demand elasticities vary among firms, regions, or nations, then price discrimination arising from enterprise differentiation will allow them to cover costs.

Interregional marketing takes into consideration the effects of numerous factors in the determination of market areas. While it concentrates primarily on the definition of market areas for the individual firm by incorporating buying and selling functions, the level of analysis can be shifted to other functions as well as to the regions themselves. Grether, as Ohlin, did not accept the proposition that specialization was the cause of interregional trade (marketing). Rather, "trade is caused by the uneven distribution of the factors and their lack of divisibility, and it tends to reduce the disadvantages caused thereby." (Ohlin, 1933, p. 58) Further, the vertical dimension of the marketing channel was incorporated; "The essence of marketing and hence marketing organization and the unique area of professional marketing literature is found in vertical, internal relationships and transactions." (Grether, 1966, Marketing and Public Policy, p. 81) This becomes especially important since "The analysis of hierarchies in the marketing channel takes on new meaning in the perspective of a distinction between local and home marketing and interregional marketing." (Grether, 1950, Theory in Marketing, p. 120)

The Theory's Importance

The theory is important for four major reasons. First, the theory is an important integration of the works of two major economists whose ideas might not have been taken into marketing. By doing this, Grether created a framework for the emerging discipline of marketing and a boundary between economics and marketing which allowed for the "possibility for the development of 'theory in marketing' by an extension of both micro- and macroeconomic theory." (Grether, 1967a, p. 320) Secondly, the theory introduced in a systematic fashion geographic analysis into marketing. Marketing theory should analyze "the behavior of the firm (or the region as a trading unit) as it adjusts to horizontal spatial relationships to industrial, regional, and national groups." (Lockley, 1964, p. 53) Thirdly, the theory provides an expansive, comprehensive view of the firm which is the basis of general marketing strategy especially in the area of diversification and growth. Finally, the theory adds considerable dimension to the definition of "relevant geographic market" in antitrust and regulation matters. This aspect is discussed in greater detail in the next section.

INTERREGIONAL MARKETING AND PUBLIC POLICY

The theory of interregional marketing is implicitly applied in much of Grether's writings on public policy. It can be seen in the systematic approach to the evaluation of cases and specific decisions. This section of the paper provides an extension of the theory to the problem of defining "relevant geographic market" which comes to the front in many areas, especially mergers. The discussion begins with a brief review of the links between interregional marketing and competition; the theory is extended by developing propositions which are consistent with the basic framework. This latter serves as the basis for considering alternative approaches to present definitions of "relevant geographic market."

Interregional Marketing and Competition

It is fair to state that the theory provides more than a powerful taxonomy for understanding marketing behavior because of the focus on the linkages between marketing and the environment. Within it is found a normative direction for the nature of competition. "In doing this he (Grether) obviously has in mind the idea that by the means of a rational marketing structure uninhibited by trade barriers and other entranched trade practices a much stronger economy could be developed." (McGary, 1953) This point is clearly made by Grether:

A critical issue to the maintenance of a strong pro competitive policy is the extent to which competitive forces are effective over geographical areas. The high relative wealth of the United States is often explained in terms of effective competition in our great, internal free trade area. Undoubtedly, this model has been the most important single economic influence behind the European Common Market conceptualization. (Grether, 1967b, p. 238)

The degree to which firms and regions engage in rivalry is the determinant of the benefits of competition. Namely, as firms more actively pursue markets, the larger markets should provide lower costs at the same time that consumers are provided with greater choice. Barriers which are constructed to eliminate rivalry – that is, eliminate the expansion of markets – should be eliminated. That does not mean that firms should have unbridled power at all times in the exploitation of markets. The absence of artificial barriers should encourage the type of competitive process that Grether develops.(1) He argues that the geographic marketing under monopolistic competition has a special, critical significance in the national endeavor to maintain and promote competition. There are dangers that systematic price structures, for example, established "overtly, or implicitly under competition among the few, could subvert or even stifle the basic forces and adjustments of surplus and deficit . . . between regions. Clearly, this outcome could not and should not be tolerated in the name of preserving competition." (Grether, 1966, Marketing and Public Policy, p. 73) In order to know about such effects, substantial analysis as directed by the theory is required. "Marketing decisions and therefore the significance of govern- ment constraints vary greatly, depending on whether the interests are merely local, regional, national, or international." (Grether, 1966, Marketing and Public Policy, p. 94)
How the market might be defined using Grether's approach and views of the competitive process is taken up in a subsequent section. Before that discussion is presented, however, some elaboration of the theory of interregional marketing is introduced.

The Theory Extended

Instead of viewing the firm as a relatively simple element in the interaction of supply and demand, the firm can be related to the market transaction in more complex terms. In order for exchange to take place, all of the marketing functions must be performed by some combination of agencies that are located in some orderly space and time relation- ship. For simplicity, assume the case of a single buyer and seller. Instead of describing the geographic extent of the market in terms of only the sales function, the "sales territory," consider the extent of the market for all of the marketing functions. As in fig. 16.1, the geographic areas of each of the functions can be described. In that figure, three areas for three separate functions are shown. What is important to note is that each has its own space and that none of them are congruent. The locational patterns for each of the functions varies; hence, there is already a more complex and realistic definition of the market than the "sales territory" approach.

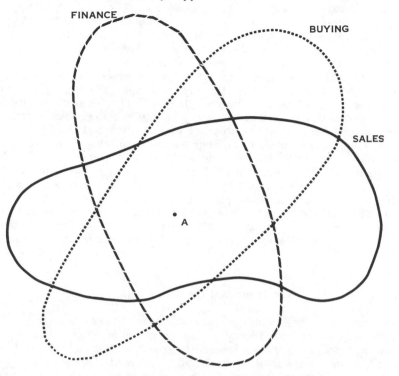

Fig. 16.1. Geographic areas of marketing functions.

This approach illustrates only one dimension; more must be included. Recall that the theory is also concerned with the inclusion of vertical relationships; that is, those which have a temporal dimension as well as spatial. The traditional illustration of the channel in the marketing literature is to show the channel in a vertical dimension; it is an attempt to show the flow characteristics between and among various members of the channel. That description is somewhat unfortunate because it often implies a difference in the spatial location of the various agencies. Channel members or agencies performing different functions may be located at the same point in space or they may be located at very different places. Regardless of their location in time or in space, they are part of the out-reach of any firm and, as shown earlier, the performance of the functions by a firm has an important effective on the boundaries for the firm. The center principle of this argument is that a firm's market cannot be defined solely by a single function which is based on the location of customers in regard to a location of the firm. Of course, the problem becomes more complex when a firm has several branches, because it is all too easy to accept the simple fitting descriptions like a jig-saw puzzle. The individual pieces fit together, but none alone gives a good idea of the total.

The problem is not of conceptual complexity but of the ability to fully illustrate the dimensions of the region for a firm. Fig. 16.2 attempts to give some insights into this. The planes at each end of the three dimensional figure represent the out-reach of selected marketing functions. The distance between them represent time or vertical dimensions. It is clear that the figure shows a fairly regular set of characteristics which may be unreal; however, it does show one more level of complexity. More analytical exercises using n-dimension space are required but beyond the scope of the present discussion.

A composite figure of the regions for competing firms for each of the marketing functions, or at least for the important ones, could be constructed.   That would be a highly fluid figure over time as firms engage in competition with one another. This differentiation will not only have the spatial characteristics of shifting the physical location; that is, more branches, but also by readjusting the performance of the various functions. Time can be affected to the extent that changes are made in vertical relationships − integration by merger or contract, for example.

The "Relevant Geographic Market"

The concept of "relevant geographic market" takes new and grander dimensions under the theory of interregional marketing. It allows a more detailed analysis than presently considered − one, as Grether has noted, that "should involve the total pattern of competitive relationships in relation to the given sub-market under scrutiny." (Grether, 1967b, p. 240) The market is thus defined in multidimensional terms including time and space.

The definition of the "relevant geographic market" in economic or legal terms certainly does not meet the criteria suggested previously. Carl Kaysen and Donald F. Turner, in their important book on antitrust policy, indicated the difficulties that are present in such analysis. They began their definition using the traditional economic proposition regarding the cross-elasticities; namely, "Two products belong to the same market if a small change in price or (product) causes a significant diversion in relatively short time of the buyers' purchases or the sellers' production from one product to another." (Kaysen and Turner, 1959, p. 27) They go on to point out how difficult it was to develop geographic market definitions from Department of Commerce data. They employed relatively simple rules which required quantum leaps in faith. They assumed that firms were in national markets when all of the production of the product was concentrated geographically, "and thus all sellers are capable of operating in national markets so far as the geographic structure of industry goes." (Kaysen and Turner, 1959, p. 28)

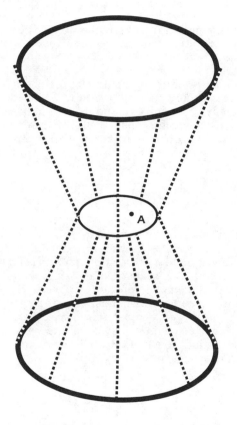

Fig. 16.2. Regional dimensions for a firm.

A less satisfactory approach was given by the United States' Supreme Court when, in effect, Justice Black suggested that there was no critical element in defining the "relevant geographic market." In the Pabst case, he suggested that:

> The language of this section requires merely that the Government prove the merger has substantial anticompetitive effect somewhere in the United States – "in any section" of the United States. This phrase does not call for the delineation of a "section of the country" by meters and bounds as a surveyor would lay off a plot of ground.(2)

In one sense, the concept of geographic market is not to be considered relevant as it relates to any specific market. While it is expected that business management, economists, and policy makers will have different interests and viewpoints about behavior, it seems unreasonable to suggest "relevant geographic market" can be accepted in such terms. The nature of the element which is to be preserved, namely competition, loses all meaning in that approach.

Will It Work?

The critical issue is whether an extended view of "relevant geographic market" will be accepted. The answer is that some change should be considered. A likely candidate for a basis for reformulation of the concept is the theory of interregional marketing. It will not be an easy task. The theory is a complex one. Much work is required just to formalize the measures to be used in operationalizing the theory and its application to the study of competition in a vertical, interregional channel system. However, it is a beginning theoretical structure that takes into consideration a wider set of elements than any of the available alternative approaches.

NOTES

(1) Grether has written extensively on artificial price barriers. See: Resale Price Maintenance in Great Britain, University of California Press, 1935; Price Control Under Fair Trade Legislation, Oxford University Press, 1939; Price Control Under Fair Trade Legislation; Report of The Federal Trade Commission on Resale Price Maintenance, U.S. Government Printing Office, 1945.

(2) United States v. Pabst Brewing Co. et. al., 384 U.S. 547 (1966), p. 549.

17 Relevant Geographic Markets in Coal: Analysis and Delineation

David L. Huff
Reed Moyer

Section 7 of the Clayton Act outlaws mergers "where in any line of commerce in any section of the country, the effect of such acquisition may be substantially to lessen competition, or to tend to create a monopoly." "Line of commerce" is synonymous with the relevant product market. "Section of the country" is construed to be the relevant geographic market. Thus, before the court can rule on the effect of an acquisition on competition and in some other antitrust cases, it must come to grips with the relevant product and geographic market issues.

How one defines relevant markets in energy is especially pertinent in view of increased concern over the degree of competition in that sector. This article focuses on the delineation and evaluation of relevant markets in coal. The antitrust implications of heightened merger activity in the coal industry and the movement of oil firms into coal – leading to legislative proposals for horizontal divestiture – make such a focus particularly appropriate. Although we address the issue of relevant product market definition in coal, our attention concentrates mostly on the relevant geographic market.

We approach the issue in two ways. First, we review the significant court cases that have shaped the legal conception of relevant markets in coal. We then describe a procedure for delineating geographic boundaries of coal markets that builds on and improves a technique that is prominently cited in the literature on coal markets.

PRODUCT MARKETS

Before dealing with the geographical market definition issue, one must determine the extent to which coal distinguishes itself from other fuels. Is coal a unique product or does it compete directly with other fuels? The answer is that "it depends." It depends first upon the time frame under consideration. Coal and its primary competitors – natural gas, petroleum, uranium, and geothermal steam – possess some common

239

characteristics. In the short run (i.e., with given fuel-consuming facilities), the consumers of each fuel may be limited or barred completely from shifting to alternative forms of energy. The long run, however, may allow such changeovers.

Another complication centers on the existence of various submarkets for coal. In the steel market, for example, there is no acceptable substitute for coking coal in the steel-making process. Production processes in industrial markets may also dictate a particular fuel. The glass industry's need for gas is a case in point. Other industrial users requiring a boiler fuel technically may substitute one fuel for another, but are limited by supply availability (especially with natural gas) and the need to retrofit fuel burning and storage facilities.

Developments in the conversion of coal to synthetic fuels offer potential interfuel competition in a variety of end-use markets. On-site gasification of coal, the conversion of coal to pipeline quality gas for residential and commercial markets, and the liquefaction of coal as an oil substitute would open up areas of interfuel competition in the electric utility, industrial, commercial, and household fuel consumption (e.g., gasoline) markets. But these are speculative developments with a long time horizon.

The electric utilities offer the greatest scope for fuel interchangeability, and since this is coal's leading market, it is the area where we focus our attention in defining relevant markets. Short-run interfuel competition exists in two forms. Some power plants are capable of burning coal, oil, or gas, or a combination of the three fuels. But fuel availability and government regulations and statutes discouraging the use of oil and natural gas as boiler fuels limit this form of competition. Boiler fuels compete in this market in a second, indirect way in the short run via load dispatch; that is, in the degree to which various units in an electric utility system are used and the order in which they are called on. The opportunities for interfuel competition through load dispatch policies, however, also are limited. The greatest scope for interfuel competition in the electric utility market exists in the long run in the fuel selection process when new power plants are constructed. The limited availability and high cost of oil and natural gas leave coal pitted against uranium. The near disaster at Three Mile Island, however, may have weakened, if only temporarily, the competitive threat of this fuel source.

What yardstick have the courts used to measure the degree of and extent of competition among similar products? In Brown Shoe, the Supreme Court held that "The outer boundaries of a product market are determined by the reasonable interchangeability of use or the cross-elasticity of demand between the product itself and substitutes for it."(1) No specified degree of cross-elasticity was deemed to constitute a threshold amount; thus, a low cross-elasticity between two products did not necessarily prevent including them in the same line of commerce. Brown Shoe set out criteria for judging the extent of cross-elasticity which have formed the standards for delineating product market boundaries in subsequent antitrust cases.

The courts have ruled inconsistently on the question of relevant product markets in recent coal cases. In Tampa Electric, the court assumed, without deciding, that coal and not boiler fuel in general (which could have included alternative fuels) constituted the line of commerce, since the case was decided on other grounds.(2) In Kennecott Copper, the Federal Trade Commission held coal to be the relevant product market "separate and distinct from other fuels," and cited some of the Brown Shoe criteria as precedent.(3) A district court in General Dynamics held "energy" to be the relevant product market, finding persuasive evidence that large fuel buyers, especially in the electric utility industry, compare the relative cost and availability of several energy sources before buying a particular fuel.(4) On review, the Supreme Court avoided a ruling on this issue, although the minority decision argued in favor of coal as the relevant product market.

GEOGRAPHIC MARKETS

Having determined the status of the relevant product market issue, we turn now to our principal area of concern: relevant geographic market determination.   In the Philadelphia Bank case, the court defined a geographic market as a "locality in which the seller operates and to which the purchaser can practically turn for supplies."(5) In that case and others the courts have looked to the following factors as determinants of market boundaries:(6)

- "Importance of industry recognition of the area as a separate economic entity."(7)
- "Impact of transportation costs on delivered price and of other economic considerations in supplying geographically diffuse consumers."(8)
- "The advantage of service and convenience in a local area."(9)
- "Special factors differentiating consumers in one area from other consumers."(10)
- "Common economic and competitive factors of an area which distinguish it from other areas, such as distinctive advertising and marketing programs, distribution systems, public bidding patterns, labor rates, and costs of raw materials."(11)

The antitrust cases involving coal view the geographic market definition issue inconsistently. In Kennecott Copper, the Court agreed with the F.T.C., which pressed the case, that the "nation as a whole constitutes a relevant geographic market, based . . . on the Commission's analysis that the large coal companies compete with each other throughout the United States."(12) Kennecott, which owned a small quantity of western coal reserves, sought to acquire Peabody Coal Company, the country's largest coal producer. Testimony revealed that prior to the acquisition, Kennecott had planned a de novo entry into coal mining, probably on a large scale. Evidence also showed that

Peabody operated mines in a number of states and sold coal over a wide geographical area. Some of Peabody's largest competitors also operated over a wide area and competed directly with Peabody in several markets. This pattern evidently convinced the Commission and the Court that coal operators competed nationally, notwithstanding the existence of high transportation charges that limit the geographical scope of most mines. Thus, whether the market is viewed as being national or regional seems to hinge partly on whether analysis centers on the company or on the individual mine.

In General Dynamics, the district court rejected the Justice Department's regional view of the market and settled on the defendant's position that not one, but ten, separate geographic coal submarkets existed.(13) The case involved an acquisition by General Dynamics of United Electric Coal Companies, a prominent Illinois operator. A General Dynamics' subsidiary was also a major Illinois coal producer.

The Justice Department saw the market encompassing one of two possible areas: the state of Illinois or the sales region covered by mines operating in the Eastern Interior Coal Region, a large midwestern coal basin of which Illinois is a part. This market area included Illinois, Indiana, and parts of Wisconsin, Minnesota, Iowa, Missouri, Kentucky, and Tennessee. It is interesting to note that the government here, in contrast to its position in Kennecott, sought to narrow the geographical scope of the market. Its narrower scope allowed it to point to an area in which concentration ratios had increased fairly sharply in the years immediately preceding the merger and to stress the further increase in concentration that General Dynamics' acquisition would create. Decisions in Von's Grocery, Pabst Brewing Co., and Continental Can Co. provided strong support for the government's position that such increases in concentration constituted a substantial lessening of competition in violation of Section 7 of the Clayton Act.(14)

The lower court accepted the defendant's contention that the relevant geographic market consisted of the utility and nonutility sales areas served by four I.C.C. freight rate districts in Illinois, the Commonwealth Edison Co. plants, and the Metropolitan Chicago Interstate Air Quality Control Region – ten separate markets. Whether such a definition conforms with the Brown Shoe holding that geographic markets must "correspond to the commercial realities of the industry and be economically significant" is open to question.(15) On appeal, the Supreme Court supported the lower court's position without addressing the issue of the relevant geographic market since it found other bases for upholding the district court's position. In a strong dissent, however, the minority rejected the lower court's conception of the relevant market.

The Tampa Electric case offers the clearest view of the Supreme Court's definition of relevant geographic markets for coal. In the Court's review of the Kennecott decision, rather than focus attention on the relevant geographic market definition issue, it accepted the F.T.C.'s position on this issue and directed its attention elsewhere. In Tampa Electric, however, geographic market definition formed the centerpiece of the Court's decision.

The original action in the case was brought by Nashville Coal Company which sought release from an onerous coal supply contract with Tampa. It had contracted to supply 2,250,000 tons of coal annually from a western Kentucky mine to Tampa Electric's proposed new generating station. Before the plant opened, Nashville brought suit on antitrust grounds, arguing that the requirements contract violated Section 3 of the Clayton Act. The 6th District Court of Appeals found for Nashville, but the Supreme Court reversed, and stressed the failure of the lower court to define the relevant market adequately.

The lower court had found that in the early years of the new generating station's existence, its consumption of coal under the challenged contract would exceed the total coal consumption in Florida in the year the contract was consummated. The court saw this condition representing a violation of the "quantitative substantiality" rule laid down in the Standard Stations case which dealt with the requirements contract issue.(16)

The Supreme Court, however, denied that the relevant market consisted of Florida, or even as Nashville conceded, Florida and Georgia combined.(17) Instead, it uncritically accepted Tampa Electric's contention that producers in eight states – Alabama, Kentucky, Tennessee, Virginia, West Virginia, Illinois, Ohio, and Pennsylvania – could supply its needs competitively. These producers marketed 250 million tons of coal annually; hence, Tampa's requirements represented less than 1 percent of the relevant market. Viewed in this light, the Court found the contract not to violate the "quantitative substantiality" rule.

The Court may have erred on several counts. First, it failed to narrow the relevant product market to include only coal capable of competing in the boiler fuel market. It overstated the 250 million ton output figure by the tonnage of metallurgical and other specialized coals whose quality and cost rendered them effectively ill-suited to serve Tampa's boiler fuel requirements. Second, and more important, shipping records failed to bear out the contention that Tampa could be served by coal mines as distant as those in Pennsylvania. Even if the market were broadened to include both Florida and Georgia, shipping data reveal that electric utilities in these states were supplied coal from mines in Alabama, Tennessee, and Kentucky in the early years of the period covered by the contract. Producers in the other five states alleged to constitute the relevant market failed to ship a single ton to the Florida-Georgia electric utility market.(18) If one accepts the notion that trade flow data are important, if not conclusive, indicators of the ability to compete, one ought to question the validity of the Court's finding on the geographic market issue.

An analysis of the three coal cases reveals several things. First is the absence of a pattern in the courts' definition of a relevant geographic market. Second – and related – in resolving the relevant geographic market issue, the nature of the cases brought against the defendants determined whether attention focused on the supplying region or the market areas where demand was generated. In General Dynamics, the supply region was a given, and attention centered on the markets generating demand for coal from that region. In Tampa Electric, the Court sought to determine the producing districts that might supply coal to a given locus of demand. Kennecott pays some attention both to supply and demand patterns, but it fails to trace trade flows in the systematic way necessary to insure that supply and demand factors get adequately built into determination of the relevant geographic market.

NEW DATA NEEDS

In coal, as in other markets, a network of transactions links suppliers with demand points. The typical product market, however, finds consumers so diffused that it is infeasible to map the network by isolating each transaction. Instead, buyers and sellers are grouped into geographical units for which transaction data exist. The state often becomes the unit of analysis. (Where markets are national in scope, attention focuses on the entire country.)

Coal studies, including those defining relevant geographic markets, generally utilize state data. This is understandable since much of the published production, consumption, and distribution data take this form. One wonders, however, whether the state is the appropriate unit of analysis in coal. It is questionable also whether relevant geographic markets can be adequately delineated without simultaneous consideration of supply and demand elements.

Raising these two issues is particularly appropriate in analyses of the electric utility coal market. Widespread use of large, long-term contracts gives this market a unique character. The spatial configuration of many markets may resemble the ripple pattern caused by dropping a pebble in still water. This conventional configuration is replaced in the electric utility coal market by a contractual network; that is, a fairly small number of point-to-point linkages. Delineating markets this way requires a finer grained analysis than the state data permit. Thus, the balance of this article outlines a procedure for delineating coal markets by adapting a new data base to a revised version of a prominent method for defining such markets.

DELINEATING GEOGRAPHIC MARKET AREAS

An attempt to formulate an objective procedure for delineating geographic market areas was made by Elzinga and Hogarty.(19) Hogarty utilized this procedure in delineating geographic energy markets, including bituminous coal.(20) The distinctive feature of this procedure is that both supply and demand elements were considered simultaneously. Thus, trade flows into and out of an area had to be examined. In order for an area to qualify as a distinct geographic market, two criteria had to be met: (1) none or only a small portion of the product is shipped into the area from outside — Hogarty refers to this as the "little in from outside" or LIFO criterion; and (2) none or only a small proportion of the product is shipped out of the area – this is referred to as the "little out from inside" or LOFI criterion. Hogarty used 75 and 90 percent as weak and strong standards respectively for the LIFO and LOFI criteria.

The steps suggested by Elzinga and Hogarty for delineating geographic market areas are indicated below.

1. Identify the product's major producing centers (areas). If only one major producing center exists but the product is sold nationally, then the market is obviously national in scope.
2. Organize the product's shipments data in terms of both production origin and consumption destination. Typically, the latter will be available in political units such as states, and for most purposes this is adequate.
3. Taking each producing area one at a time, calculate the minimum area (e.g., minimum number of states) required to account for at least 75 (90) percent of shipments from the producing area. This will satisfy the weak (strong) form of the LOFI criterion. Designate this area as a hypothetical market area (HMA).
4. Of total shipments to destinations within the HMA, do 75 (90) percent or more of the shipments originate from the designated producing area? If so, the weak (strong) form of the LIFO test is met. As long as only one producing center exists within the HMA, the LOFI test is met through step 3. Given more than one producing center, however, the LOFI test must be repeated. If the LIFO test is not met, then re-draw the HMA, determining the minimum area necessary to absorb 75 (90) percent of the shipments from producing centers located within the new HMA. If there is no sub-national area satisfying this criterion, the market is (at least) national in scope.
5. If both the LOFI (step 3) and LIFO (step 4) criteria are satisfied, the HMA comprises a distinct geographic market area. Assuming this area is less than national in size, the final step consists of calculating total consumption within this area to get market size in terms of volume.(21)

A modified form of the Elzinga and Hogarty procedure is utilized in this study to delineate geographic market areas for western bituminous and lignite coal used by utility plants. The study area was limited to the western portion of the U.S. and comprised the following 17 states:

Arizona	New Mexico
California	North Dakota
Colorado	Oklahoma
Idaho	Oregon
Kansas	South Dakota
Montana	Texas
Nebraska	Utah
Nevada	Washington
	Wyoming

We chose this part of the United States because it is more manageable for a pilot study. Fewer mines and fewer users of coal are located in this area than in the eastern portion of the United States. Furthermore, western coal production has come to have increasing importance in recent years because of its generally lower sulfur content compared to eastern coal. Estimates are that 93 percent of the lower sulfur coal in this country is located west of the Mississippi River.

NATURE OF THE DATA

Only coal used by electric utilities was considered in this study. Sales to utilities represent the largest domestic market for American coal. The market for steam coal is expected to expand even further in the future. By 1985, coal is projected to account for 78 percent of domestic consumption.(22)

Data that were used for the delineation of western regional coal markets were reported shipments of coal to all utility plants in the United States during the month of January, 1976. These data are reported to and compiled by the Federal Power Commission and consist of the types of fuel used by utility plants as well as the supplier of the particular fuel.(23) For coal, if the reporting process is complete for a particular utility plant, the listed entry will include the supplying company's name, the mine from which the coal was procured, the county of production, the coal district and state of production, the class of coal (lignite, bituminous, sub-bituminous, or anthracite), the method of mining (strip or underground), the quantity delivered, the price, and various aspects related to the quality of the coal, including Btus per ton, sulfur content, and ash content. With a complete set of data, it would be possible to construct a matrix indicating the point of origin and point of destination of coal shipments. The cell entries in the matrix would reflect the transaction (in tons).

Unfortunately, such a data matrix could not be constructed for this analysis. Data for many of the utility plants that received coal shipments were not totally complete. In many cases, the supplier, the mine, and/or the county of production were not included. In all cases, the producing district and state of origin were reported. As a consequence, a county-to-county matrix was constructed representing the smallest geographic unit for which complete data (with a few exceptions that will be mentioned below) could be compiled. The county of location for production, if not given, could usually be determined adequately on the basis of the mine name or the company name. When the mine name, but not the county, was given, the Keystone Coal Industry Manual, which lists mines and counties of location, provided one source for cross-referencing.(24) In those cases where only the mining company was given, the county would be determined since a particular company only operated one mine in a given district and state. Thus, the county of location could be assumed. In other cases in which utility plants received coal under contract, additional cross-referencing was done on the basis of data reported in the February issue of Fuel Price Analysis. If the February issue contained a listing including the county of production, and if the listing in January was also a contract for coal of the same quality, the January entry was deemed to have originated from the same mine. In a few additional cases, comparisons of the sulfur and ash content as well as Btu ratings permitted the identification of additional entries through cross-referencing with the Keystone Coal Industry Manual and Fuel Price Analysis issues.

In two cases, it was necessary to use larger geographic areas for the analysis. Big Horn and Rosebud Counties in Montana were combined since it was not possible to allocate mine entries with respect to their locations in either one or the other of these countries in all cases. Colorado mines located in District 16 produced a relatively small amount of coal that was shipped to utility plants during the month of January. In most cases, the county of production was not specified and the various cross-referencing procedures were inadequate to identify the locations of the mines. As a result, all counties comprising District 16 in Colorado were combined as a single geographic entry for the analysis.

Since production data were organized on a county basis with the above exceptions, counties were also used as the consumption units. In cases where there were two or more utility plants located in a county that received coal shipments, the flows were aggregated.

An algorithm was formulated based on Elzinga and Hogarty's methodology for assigning countries to particular markets. The algorithm was designed to overcome weaknesses in their approach. Using county data eliminated the need to "force" certain production statistics into a geographical configuration that would put both production and consumption data on a common basis.

The Elzinga and Hogarty methodology suffers from another deficiency: a lack of precision. Their approach allows a given geographic market to be allocated to more than one regional market even though both the LIFO and LOFI test have been met. A small producing and consuming area might be added to a number of regional markets and could meet the strong test criteria in both cases. The Elzinga and Hogarty procedure provides no means for assigning such an area to one and only one market area. In addition, they do not indicate how the original areas to be tested are formed into candidate market areas.

Our approach corrects these deficiencies through the use of county data with an algorithm designed to insure that a given county would always be assigned to the same market. The choice of starting point will not affect the areal extent of the final markets. The flow diagram shown in fig. 17.1 depicts the sequential steps in the algorithm.(25)

RESULTS

Eleven geographic market areas (GMAs) were identified for bituminous coal (see table 17.1). They are composed both of producing and

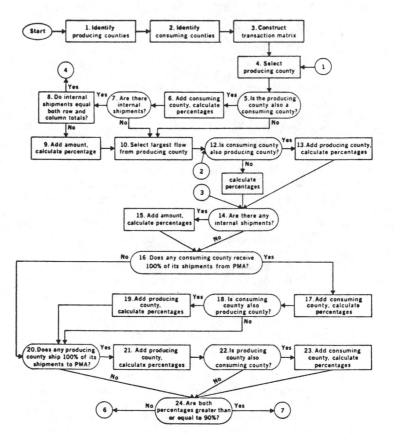

Fig. 17.1. Flowchart depicting steps in delineating regional coal markets.

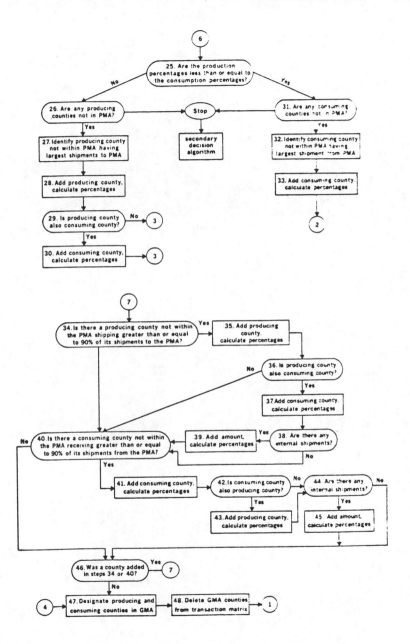

Fig. 17.1. (Cont.)

Table 17.1. Geographic Market Areas for Bituminous and Sub-bituminous Coal (90 percent criterion)

Geographic Market Area Number	County	State	Status
1	Lewis	Washington	P,C
	Thurston	Washington	P
2	Sweetwater	Wyoming	P,C
3	Converse	Wyoming	P,C
4	Linn	Kansas	P,C
	Bates	Missouri	P
5	San Juan	New Mexico	P,C
6	Montrose	Colorado	P,C
7	Wyandotte	Kansas	C
	Crawford	Kansas	P
	Nowata	Oklahoma	P
	Haskel	Oklahoma	P
	Craig	Oklahoma	P
8	Emery	Utah	P,C
	Carbon	Utah	P,C
	Salt Lake	Utah	C
	Utah	Utah	C
	Clark	Nevada	C
	Coconino	Arizona	C
	Navajo	Arizona	C
	Sevier	Utah	P
	McKinley	New Mexico	P
9	El Paso	Colorado	C
	Denver	Colorado	C
	Mesa	Colorado	C
	Fremont	Colorado	P,C
	Routt	Colorado	P,C
	Mofatt	Colorado	P
	La Plata	Colorado	P

Geographic Market Area Number	County	State	Status
10	Clay	Missouri	C
	Jackson	Missouri	C
	Woodbury	Iowa	C
	Douglas	Kansas	C
	Shawnee	Kansas	C
	Douglas	Nebraska	C
	Lake	Illinois	C
	Lake	Indiana	C
	Tazewell	Illinois	C
	Will	Illinois	C
	Itasca	Minnesota	C
	Ramsey	Minnesota	C
	Hennepin	Minnesota	C
	Sherburne	Minnesota	C
	Rosebud/Big Horn	Montana	P,C
	Yellowstone	Montana	C
	Columbia	Wisconsin	C
	Cook	Illinois	C
	St. Louis	Minnesota	C
	Cherokee	Kansas	P,C
	Greene	Missouri	C
	Lancaster	Nebraska	C
	Sarpy	Nebraska	C
11	Bourbon	Kansas	P
	Le Flore	Oklahoma	P
	Rogers	Oklahoma	P
	Carbon	Wyoming	P
	Lincoln	Wyoming	P,C

P = Producing county
C = Consuming county

consuming countries, as indicated in table 17.1. Seven of these markets were local in scope. They consisted of one mine (located in one county or in two contiguous counties) that supplied coal to one consuming county. In some cases, the mines were captive mines owned by a particular utility plant under contract. In six of these seven GMAs (1, 2, 3, 4, 5, and 6), the production from the producing counties was shipped to a sole consuming county. In some cases, the producing county and consuming county were the same. In the seventh GMA (11), the producing county shipped a small percentage of its production to other counties.

The other four geographic market areas were considerably larger. GMA 7 consisted of Wyandotte County, Kansas (Kansas City) as the sole consumption county with various Kansas and Oklahoma counties supplying the coal. GMA 8 consisted of parts of Utah, Nevada, Arizona, and New Mexico (see fig. 17.2).(26) The one county in Nevada that was part of this GMA was a consuming county. The one county in New Mexico was solely a producer. Counties in Utah and Arizona included both producers and consumers, and in some cases a county was both a producer and a consumer. GMA 9 was restricted to Colorado (see fig. 17.3) It consisted of various producing counties supplying utility plants in Denver and other communities in the state. In some cases, the producing counties were also consuming counties. GMA 10 was the largest, in terms of the number of counties included as well as the total level of coal shipments (see fig. 17.4). It comprised major producing counties in Wyoming and Montana with additional counties in Kansas and Oklahoma supplying smaller levels of production. The consuming area included counties in nine states including Cook County, Illinois (Chicago), Hennepin County, Minnesota (Minneapolis), Clay and Jackson Counties, Missouri (Kansas City), and Lake County, Indiana (Gary).

GEOGRAPHIC MARKET AREAS FOR LIGNITE COAL

There were six geographic market areas for lignite (see table 17.2). GMAs 1, 2, and 3 consisted of mines supplying a utility plant in the same county.   There were no shipments from mines located in other counties, nor did these mines make coal shipments to utility plants located in other counties. In GMAs 4 and 5, coal was shipped exclusively from one producing county to a single neighboring consuming county. In GMA 6, a number of mines located in a two-county area supplied coal to utility plants in four consuming counties.   The consuming counties included both production counties. One hundred percent of the production and consumption was accounted for within these four counties. The lignite markets were very limited geographically. Lignite's low Btu content and its tendency to crumble relatively easily when exposed to air makes long distance shipments uneconomical.

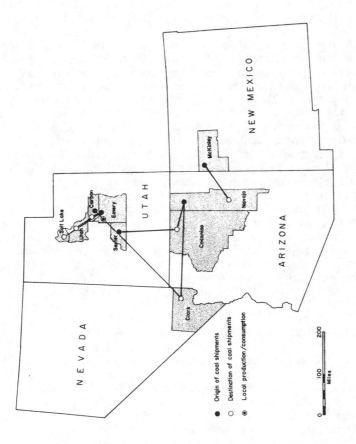

Fig. 17.2. Geographic market 8: an example using the LOFI and LIFO criteria.

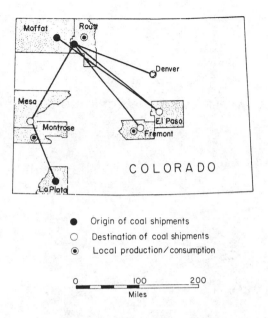

- ● Origin of coal shipments
- ○ Destination of coal shipments
- ◉ Local production∕consumption

0 ——— 100 ——— 200
Miles

Fig. 17.3. Geographic market 9: an example using the LOFI and LIFO criteria.

Table 17.2. Geographic Market Areas for Lignite

Geographic Market Area Number	County	State	Status
1	Freestone	Texas	P,C
2	Titus	Texas	P,C
3	Richland	Montana	P,C
4	McHenry	North Dakota	C
	Ward	North Dakota	P
5	Roberts	South Dakota	C
	Bowman	North Dakota	P
6	Mercer	North Dakota	P
	Oliver	North Dakota	P
	Morton	North Dakota	C
	Otter Tail	Minnesota	C

P = Producing county
C = Consuming county

GEOGRAPHIC MARKET 10:

AN EXAMPLE USING THE LOFI AND LIFO CRITERIA

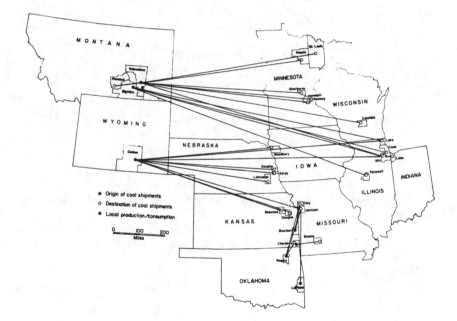

Fig. 17.4. Origin of coal shipments and destination of coal shipments.

OTHER GEOGRAPHIC MARKET AREAS

A number of producing counties in the western portion of the United States were not allocated to a distinct market area in the West. All the consuming counties in the western part of the United States were supplied with western coal as well as some points in the East. The District 16 Colorado mines mentioned previously shipped mainly to consumption points in the Midwest that also received large shipments of eastern coal. Thus, these counties would seem to be part of a large eastern market or a smaller midwestern regional market. Two counties in Wyoming had major shipments outside the study area. They shipped to points in Iowa that also received Iowa coal. These two counties might be part of a localized market consisting of themselves and producing counties in Iowa and consumption points in Iowa.

All areas met both the LIFO and LOFI criteria at the 90 percent levels of the geographic market. The areal extent of the different markets was highly variable. Some contained only one county, while the largest included counties in 11 different states. In terms of total transactions, the markets ranged from less than ten thousand tons to over two million tons. The market areas did not form contiguous areas. The larger ones were disjointed. The counties included in a particular GMA were at times not even those closest to each other. In some cases, the producing counties shipped past nearer consumption points (or the consumption points order the coal from more distant points). Some of the smaller markets are more or less "nesting" within the larger ones.

The spatial pattern that would be expected if the market were working perfectly would be that all utility companies would purchase coal from the nearest suppliers in order to minimize transport costs. Thus, there would be no cross shipments. While beyond the scope of this study, factors that alter this pattern include:

1. product differences and local variations in environmental standards
2. differential transport rates
3. availability of transportation facilities
4. long-term contracts between coal suppliers and utility companies (nearby mines might not have been in existence when the contract was made)
5. joint ownership of coal deposits and rail facilities (given that such a ocmpany would maximize its overall profits, it may be in its interest to sell coal to more distant markets)

Among these factors cited, the one that has great potential for anti-competitive behavior is rail transportation. This is particularly true if a railroad does not have any competition in a given geographical area. The potential is accentuated if the railroad also owns significant quantities of coal deposits. Thus, it may be in the public interest to establish federal policies that would:

1. encourage alternative means of transporting coal
2. regulate the leasing of federally controlled lands in different geographic areas in order to ensure competition among different railroad companies
3. facilitate extending new rail lines to coal lands currently isolated.

CRITICAL EVALUATION

One might object that market configurations depend upon historical data which, in most instances, reflect a limited number of long-term contracts. Shipments from production point A to consumption point B imply that producer at point C was excluded because he was noncompetitive. But another reason suggests itself. He may have lost out because the user at point B elected to have a single supplier. The consumer may benefit from the use of a single, large supplier due to the potential for scale economies in coal production, from more efficient use of burning equipment designed for a single fuel, etc. Thus, an expansion of demand at a given consuming point could change the market's configuration as potentially competitive suppliers, excluded from earlier contract awards, become successful bidders. In other words, with so few buyers and sellers, the potential for substitution of coal from other mines is more important than the historic pattern.

The reply to this criticism is the fact that most relevant geographic market delineations, including these derived by Elzinga and Hogarty, are based on historical data. These studies presume that the relevant factors affecting competition among potential suppliers, including coal quality, costs, transportation charges, etc., have been reflected in the shipment patterns. However, narrowing the unit of analysis as we have done may reduce stability of the market configurations for the reason outlined above and because minor changes in market conditions may lead to major shifts in market shapes. The shape and size of coal markets as large as some of those envisaged by Elzinga and Hogarty – e.g., eastern Appalachia – are less likely to be altered by a freight rate change that opens up a market to a previously noncompetitive supplier than is the case with small submarkets. That kind of development could reduce the LIFO measure a few percentage points, but if the 90 percent limit were unaffected, the market shape would remain unchanged. But such a development might substantially alter the configuration of a market limited in extent and tonnage, as are many of those listed in table 17.1.

CONCLUSION

It must be emphasized that the results of this study are only preliminary since they deal with data reported for a limited time period. Nonetheless, the available data permit a geographic market delineation in coal that takes account of some unique market conditions in the industry. Previous studies which used states as the unit of analysis may have assumed more uniformity of coal quality, production costs, demand conditions, and distribution facilities within each state than is warranted by the facts. Thus, though the western Kentucky and eastern Kentucky coal fields lie in the same state, market conditions require that producers in these two fields sell their output to different parts of the country. Analysis at the state level obscures such conditions. Disaggregating the data to a smaller unit of analysis, as we have done using county data, overcomes problems of this sort. Changing the unit of analysis may sharply alter the scope and configuration of geographic market areas, as this study has also shown. Which unit of analysis is the more appropriate for this or other product markets is a suitable subject for further investigation.

NOTES

(1) Brown Shoe Co. v. United States, 370 U.S. 294 (1962), at 325.

(2) Tampa Electric v. Nashville Coal Co., 5L.Ed.2d 580 at 588.

(3) Kennecott Copper Corp. v. Federal Trade Commission 467 Fed. Reporter 2d 67, at 70.

(4) United States v. General Dynamics Corporation 341 F. Supp. 534 (1972).

(5) United States v. Philadelphia National Bank, 374 U.S. 321 at 359.

(6) Summarized in Herbert S. Sanger, Jr. and William E. Mason, The Structure of the Energy Markets: A Report of TVA's Antitrust Investigation of the Coal and Uranium Industries, Tennessee Valley Authority, June 14, 1977, p. 58.

(7) Philadelphia Bank, p. 361.

(8) Federal Trade Commission v. Procter and Gamble Co., 386 U.S. 568 (1967).

(9) Philadelphia Bank, p. 358.

(10) United States v. Pabst Brewing Co., 384 U.S. 546.

(11) United States v. Kimberly Clark Corp., 246 F. Supp. 439.

(12) Kennecott Copper, p. 71.

(13) United States v. General Dynamics Corporation.

(14) United States v. Von's Grocery Company, 384 U.S. 270 (1966); United States v. Continental Can Company, 378 U.S. 441 (1964); and Pabst Brewing Company, op. cit.

(15) Brown Shoe, pp. 336-37.

(16) Standard Oil Company v. United States, 337 U.S. 293 (1949). Standard's requirements contracts with independent dealers were held to injure competition because the gallonage accounted for a "substantial" share of commerce in the relevant geographic market. Such contracts ran afoul of Section 3 of the Clayton Act which declared illegal contracts conditioned on the agreement by the purchaser not to deal in the goods of the seller's competitors "where the effect of such . . . contract . . . may be substantially to lessen competition. . . ." (38 Stat. 731 (1914).)

(17) During administration of the Guffy Act in the late 1930s, Georgia and Florida were combined into one consuming district for reporting purposes.

(18) For an elaboration of this analysis, see Reed Moyer, "Requirements Contracts and Energy Transportation Developments in Coal," Southern Economic Journal, April 1965, pp. 331-41.

(19) K. Elzinga and T. Hogarty, "The Problem of Geographic Market Delineation in Antimerger Suits," Antitrust Bulletin, 18:1 (Spring 1973), 45-81.

(20) Thomas F. Hogarty, "The Geographic Scope of Energy Markets: Oil, Gas and Coal," in Thomas P. Duchesneau, Competition in the U.S. Energy Industry (Cambridge: Ballinger Publishing Company, 1975), 1978-218; and Kenneth G. Elzinga and Thomas F. Hogarty, "The Problem of Geographic Market Delineation Revisited: The Case of Coal," The Antitrust Bulletin (Spring 1978), pp. 1-18.

(21) Elzinga and Hogarty, "The Geographic Scope of Energy Markets: Oil, Gas, and Coal," 202-203.

(22) S.S. Penner and L. Icerman, Energy: Volume II, Nonnuclear Energy Technologies (Reading, Mass.: Addison-Wesley Publishing, 1975), 67. Cf. Saalbeck, United States Bituminous Coal Markets, 31; George F. Deasy and Phyllis R. Griess, "Local and Regional Differences in Long Term Bituminous Coal Production Prospects in Eastern United States," Annals of the American Association of Geographers, 37:2 (June 1967), 519.

(23) The data obtained by the Federal Power Commission were, in turn, compiled and published by McGraw-Hill, in Fuel Price Analysis, 1:1 (January 1976).

(24) <u>1974 Keystone Coal Industry Manual</u> (New York: McGraw-Hill, 1974).

(25) The algorithm was developed and reported initially in Hossein Askari, David L. Huff, George Kozmetsky, and James M. Lutz, <u>Industrial Classification, Regional Market Structure and Divertiture</u> (Austin, Texas: Institute for Constructive Capitalism, Graduate School of Business, University of Texas, 1977).

(26) This contrasts with the Elzinga-Hogarty result of a southwestern submarket comprised of producers in New Mexico and consumers in New Mexico, Nevada, and Arizona.

References

This bibliography is divided into two sections. In the first are listed, in alphabetical order, all of the references cited in the book except those by E.T. Grether. In the second section are almost all of the published works of E.T. Grether in chronological order. References to Grether cited in the text may be found in the second section rather than the first.

Abegglen, James C. 1971. Dynamics of Japanese Competition. United States International Economic Policy in an Interdependent World. Vol. II. Washington: U.S. Government Printing Office, pp. 153-182.

Adams, Walter and Lanzillotti, Robert F. 1963. The Reality of Administered Prices. Administered Prices: A Compendium on Public Policy. U.S. Senate A-T Subcommittee.

Adams, William James. 1970. Firm Size and Research Activity: France and the United States. Quarterly Journal of Economics 84: 386-409, August.

Adelman, M.A. 1963. A Commentary on "Administered Prices." Administered Prices: A Compendium on Public Policy. U.S. Senate Antitrust Subcommittee.

_____. 1959. Differential Rates and Changes in Concentration. Review of Economics and Statistics 41: 68-69, February.

_____. 1958. Pricing by Manufacturers. Delbert A. Duncan (ed.). Conference of Marketing Teachers from Far Western States (University of California).

_____. 1951. The Measurement of Industrial Concentration. Review of Economics and Statistics 33: 269-296, November.

Administered Prices: A Compendium on Public Policy. 1963. U.S. Senate Antitrust Subcommittee, 88th Cong.

Aitchison, J. and Brown, J.A.C. 1957. The Lognormal Distribution. Cambridge, Mass.: Harvard University Press.

Alchian, Armen. 1959. Costs and Outputs. Moses Abramovitz et al. The Allocation of Economic Resources. Stanford, Cal.: Stanford University Press.

_____. 1963. Reliability of Progress Curves in Airframe Production. Econometrica 31: October.

Alderson, Wroe and Martin, Miles W. 1965. Toward a Formal Theory of Transactions and Transvections. Journal of Marketing Research 2: 117-127, May.

_____. 1965. Dynamic Marketing Behavior. Irwin. P. 197.

Aldrich, Howard. 1978. Centralization Versus Decentralization in the Design of Human Service Delivery Systems: A Response to Gouldner's Lament. R.C. Sarri and Y. Hasenfeld (eds.). The Management of Human Sciences. New York: Columbia University Press.

Areeda, Phillip and Turner, Donald F. 1978. Antitrust Law: An Analysis of Antitrust Principles and their Application. Boston: Little, Brown and Company. 3 volumes.

_____. 1975. Predatory Pricing and Related Practices Under Section 2 of Sherman Act. Harvard Law Review 88: 697-733.

_____. 1977. Williamson on Predatory Pricing. Yale Law Journal 87: 1337-1352.

Arndt, Johan. 1979. On the Political Economy of Marketing Systems: Untapped Potentials of an Institutional Approach to Marketing. Working Paper, Bergen: Norwegian School of Economics and Business Administration.

Baer, Stafford. 1970. Managing Modern Complexity. The Management of Information and Knowledge. Papers presented to the 11th Meetings of the Panel on Science and Technology Committee on Science and Astronautics, U.S. House of Representatives. Washington: Government Printing Office.

Bailey, D. and Boyle, S.E. 1971. Optimal Measure of Concentration. Journal of the American Statistical Association 66: 702-706, December.

Bailey, Martin J. 1959. Discussion American Economic Review. 49: 459-461, May.

Bailey, Martin Neil. 1972. Research and Development Costs and Returns: The U.S. Pharmaceutical Industry. Journal of Political Economy 80: 70-85, January/February.

Bain, Joe S. 1956. Barriers to New Competition: Their Character and Consequences in Manufacturing Industries. Cambridge, Mass.: Harvard University Press.

_____. 1970. Changes in Concentration in Manufacturing Industries in the United States 1954-1966. Review of Economics and Statistics 52: 411-416, November.

_____. 1959. Industrial Organization. New York: Wiley.

Balderston, F.E. and Hoggatt, A.C. 1962. Simulation and Market Processes. Berkeley: University of California Inst. of Bus. and Econ. Res.

Bartels, Robert. 1976. The History of Marketing Thought. Columbus, Ohio: Grid, Inc.

Becker, Gary S. 1965. A Theory of the Allocation of Time. The Economic Journal. 75, September.

Bell, Daniel. 1979. Communications Technology – For Better or For Worse. Harvard Business Review 57: 20-22 May/June.

————. 1976. Welcome to the Post-Industrial Society. Physics Today. February: 46.

Blair, John M. 1959. Administered Prices: A Phenomenon in Search of a Theory. American Economic Review May.

————. 1972. Economic Concentration: Structure, Behavior and Public Policy. New York: Harcourt Brace.

Bock, Betty. 1975. From Administered Pricing to Concentrated Market Pricing. The Conference Board Record.

Bork, Robert. 1978. The Antitrust Paradox. New York: Basic Books.

The Boston Consulting Group, N.d. Cross Sectional Experience Curves. Boston. (pamphlet).

————. 1968. Perspectives on Experience. Boston.

Boyle, Stanley, 1973. The Average Concentration Ratio: An Inappropriate Measure of Industry Structure. Journal of Political Economy 81: 414-426, March/April.

———— and Sorenson, Robert L. 1971. Concentration and Mobility: Alternative Measures of Industry Structure. Journal of Industrial Economy 19: 118-132, April.

Breyer, Ralph F. 1965. Proposition Formation and Programmed Marketing. Philadelphia: Mimeographed by the author.

Bucklin, Louis P. (ed.). 1970. Vertical Marketing Systems. Glencoe, Ill.: Scott, Foresman & Co.

Buzzell, Robert D., Gale, Bradley T. and Sultan, Ralph G.M. 1974. Market Share, Profitability, and Business Strategy. Cambridge, Mass.: Marketing Science Institute (Working Paper), August.

Capon, Noel and Lutz, R.J. 1979. A Model and Methodology for the Development of Consumer Information Programs. J. of Marketing 43: 58-67.

Carman, James M. 1980. Paradigms for Marketing Thought. J.N. Sheth (ed.). Research in Marketing. Vol. 3. Greenwich, Conn.: JAI Press.

Carter, C.F. and Williams, B.R. 1959. The Characteristics of Technically Progressive Firms. Journal of Industrial Economics 7: 87-104, March.

Carter, Colin. 1979. A Test of the Efficient Marketing Hypothesis. Ph.D. dissertation, Dept. of Agr. and Res. Econ., University of California, Berkeley.

Chamberlain, Edward Hastings, 1933. The Theory of Monopolistic Competition. 8th Edition. Cambridge, Mass.: Harvard University Press.

Champernowne, D.G. 1953. A Model of Income Distribution. Economic Journal 63: 318-351, June.

Collins, Norman R. and Preston, Lee E. 1969. Price-Cost Margins and Industry Structure. Review of Economics and Statistics 51: 271-286, August.

Comanor, William S. 1967. Market Structure, Product Differentiation and Industrial Research. Quarterly Journal of Economics 81: 639-657, November.

_____. 1965. Research and Technical Change in the Pharmaceutical Industry. Review of Economics and Statistics 47: 182-187, May.

_____. 1964. Research and Competitive Product Differentiation in the Pharmaceutical Industry in the United States. Economica 31: 372-384, November.

_____ and Scherer, F.M. 1969. Patent Statistics as a Measure of Technical Change. Journal of Political Economy. 77: 392-398, May/June.

_____ and Wilson, Thomas A. 1969. Advertising and the Advantages of Size. American Economic Review 59: 87-98, May.

Computer Technology and Communications. 1979. Intermedia 2, No. 6 (May).

Consumers' Association of Canada. 1969. A Community Information Network (Mimeographed).

Cooper, Arnold C. 1964. R&D is More Efficient in Small Companies. Harvard Business Review 42: 75-83, May/June.

Cootes, Joseph. 1977. Aspects of Innovation: Public Policy Issues in Telecommunications Development. Telecommunications Policy 1: 196, June.

Cox, Reavis and Goodman, Charles S. 1956. Marketing of Housebuilding Materials. Journal of Marketing 21, 36-61, July.

_____. 1958. The Channel of Marketing as a Unit of Competition. W. David Robbin (ed.). Successful Marketing at Home and Abroad. Chicago: American Marketing Association. pp. 208-212.

Critchlow, Robert V. 1970. Technological Changes in the Printing and Publishing Industry. Monthly Labor Review 93: 3-9, August.

Crowell, John Franklin, 1901. Report of the Industrial Commission on the Distribution of Farm Products. 56th Congress, H.R. Doc. No. 494. Washington: Government Printing Office.

Cyert, R.M. and March, J.G. 1955. Organizational Structure and Pricing Behavior in an Oligopolistic Market. American Economic Review March: 129-139.

Dansby, R.E. and Willig, R.D. 1979. Industrial Performance Gradient Indexes. American Economic Review 69: 249-260, June.

Delombre, J. and Bruzelius, B. 1977. Importance of Relative Market Share in Strategic Planning – A Case Study. Long Range Planning 10, August.

Devine, D.G. and Marion, B.W. 1979. The Influence of Consumer Price Information on Retail Pricing and Consumer Behavior. Amer. J. Agr. Econ. 61: 228-237.

Douglas, E.J. 1969. Apparent and Real Levels of Concentration in Australian Manufacturing Industry. Economic Record 45: 251-257, June.

_____. 1970. Apparent and Real Levels of Concentration: A Reply. Economic Record 46: 124-127, March.

Douglas, Edna. 1975. Economics of Marketing. New York: Harper & Row.

Eisgruber, L.M. 1978. Developments in the Economic Theory of Information. Amer. J. of Agr. Econ. 6: 901-905.

Elainga, Kenneth G. and Hogarty, T.F. 1973. The Problem of Geographic Market Delineation in Antimerger Suits, Antitrust Bulletin 18: 45-81, Spring.

_____. 1978. The Problem of Geographic Market Delineation Revisited: The Case of Coal, Antitrust Bulletin 23: 1-18, Spring.

Fama, E. 1970. Efficient Capital Markets: A Review of Theory and Empirical Work. J. Finance 25: 383-417.

Fellner, William. 1951. The Influence of Market Structure on Technological Progress. Quarterly Journal of Economics 65: 556-577, November.

Figlewski, S. 1979. Market Efficiency in a Market with Heterogeneous Information. J. Pol. Econ. 86: 581-597.

Fisher, F.M. 1966. Community Antenna Television Systems and the Regulation of Television Broadcasting. American Economic Review 56: 320-329, May.

_____ and Temin, P. 1973. Returns to Scale in Research and Development: What Does the Schumpeterian Hypothesis Imply? Journal of Political Economy 81: 56-70, Jan./Feb.

Fornell, Claes. 1976. Consumer Input for Marketing Decisions: A Study of Corporate Departments of Consumer Affairs. New York: Praeger Press.

Fruhan, William E., Jr. 1972. Pyrrhic Victoric in Fights for Market Share. Harvard Business Review 100. September/October.

Goldschmid, H.J., Mann, H. Michael, and Weston, J. Fred. 1974. Industrial Concentration: The New Learning. Boston: Little, Brown and Company.

Gorham, Michael. 1978. Public and Private Sector Information in Agricultural Commodity Markets. Economic Review. Federal Reserve Bank of San Francisco, 30-38. Spring.

Gort, M. and Hogarty, T.F. 1970. New Evidence on Mergers. Journal of Law and Economics 13: 167-184.

Grabowski, Henry G. 1966. The Determinants and Effects of Industrial Research and Development. Econometric Research Program: Research Memorandum No. 82. Princeton, N.J.: Princeton University.

_____. 1968. The Determinants of Industrial Research and Development: A Study of the Chemical, Drug, and Petroleum Industries. Journal of Political Economy 76: 292-306, March/April.

_____ and Mueller, Dennis. 1970. Industrial Organization: The Role and Contribution of Econometrics. American Economic Review 60: 100-108, May.

Grether, David M. 1974. Correlations with Ordinal Data. Journal of Econometrics 2: 241-246, September.

_____. 1976. On the Use of Ordinal Data in Correlation Analysis. American Sociological Review 41: 908-912, October.

Griliches, Zvi. 1958. Research Costs and Social Returns: Hybrid Corn and Some Related Innovations. Journal of Political Economy 66: 419-431, October.

Grossman, S.J. 1977. The Existence of Futures Markets, Noisy Rational Expectations and Informational Externalities. Review of Economic Studies 44: 431-439.

Hall, Marshall and Tideman, Nicolaus. 1967. Measures of Concentration. Journal of the American Statistical Association 62: 162-168, March.

Hamberg, D. 1963. Invention in the Industrial Research Laboratory. Journal of Political Economy 71: 95-115, April.

_____. 1964. Size of Firm, Oligopoly, and Research: The Evidence. Canadian Journal of Economics and Political Science 30: 62-75, February.

_____. 1959. Production Functions, Innovations, and Economic Growth. Journal of Political Economy 67: 238-245, June.

_____. 1966. R&D: Essays on the Economics of Research and Development. New York: Random House.

Hamermesh, R.G., Anderson, M.J., Jr., and Harris, J.E. 1978. Strategies for Low Market Share Businesses. Harvard Business Review 58: 95-102. May/June.

Hart, P.E. 1957. On Measuring Business Concentration. Bulletin of Oxford University Institute of Economics and Statistics 19: 225-251, August.

Hart, P.E. 1961. Statistical Measures of Concentration vs. Concentration Ratios. Review of Economics and Statistics 43: 85-86, February.

_____ and Prais, S.J. 1956. The Analysis of Business Concentration: A Statistical Approach. Journal of the Royal Statistical Society 18: 150-181, February.

Hause, John C. 1977. The Measurement of Concentrated Industrial Structure and the Size Distribution of Firm. Annals of Economic and Social Measurement 6: 73-108, Winter.

Hayami, Y. and Peterson, W. 1971. Social Returns to Public Information Services: Statistical Reporting of U.S. Farm Commodities. American Econ. Rev. 61: 561-572.

Hedley, Barry. 1976. A Fundamental Approach to Strategy Development. Long Range Planning December: 2-11.

Hexter, J. Lawrence and Snow, John W. 1970. An Entropy Measure of Relative Aggregate Concentration. Southern Economic Journal 36: 239-243, January.

_____. 1971. An Entropy Measure of Relative Aggregate Concentration: Reply. Southern Economic Journal 37: 112-114, July.

Hirsch, W.Z. 1956. Firm Progress Ratios. Econometrica 24.

Hirschleifer, J. 1971. The Private and Social Value of Information and the Reward to Inventive Activity. Amer. Econ. Rev. 61: 561-572.

_____. 1962. The Firm's Cost Function: A Successful Reconstruction? Journal of Business 36: 235-254, July.

Horowitz, I. 1962. Firm Size and Research Activity. Southern Economic Journal 28: 298-301, January.

_____. 1971. Numbers-Equivalents in U.S. Manufacturing Industries: 1954, 1958, and 1963. Southern Economic Journal 37: 396-408, April.

Horvath, Dezso and McMillan, Charles. 1978. Industrial Planning in Japan. Faculty of Administrative Studies, York University, Toronto: Industrial Strategy Working Paper.

Howe, J.D. and McFetridge, D.G. 1976. The Determinants of R&D Expenditures. Canadian Journal of Economics 9: 57-71, February.

Hunt, H. Keith. 1978. Consumer Satisfaction and Dissatisfaction and the Public Interest: Conceptualization, Measurement Problems and Application. J.F. Cady (ed.). Marketing and the Public Interest. Marketing Service Institute.

Jones, Mary Gardiner. 1976. Aspects and Characteristics of the Future Information Society. ICSU AB, Symposium on Information Demand and Supply for the 1980's. National Academy of Science, June.

_____. 1977. Governmental Priorities in the Delivery of Consumer and Citizen Information. Paper prepared for 1977 Lecture Series for Regulation, Graduate School of Management, Northwestern, November.

Jones, Linder and Weil. 1973. Panel Report to the Committee on Scientific and Technical Information. Consequences of Uniqueness in Knowledge Banks. The Honeywell Computer Journal 7: 13.

Kalecki, M. 1945. On the Gibrat Distribution. Econometrica 13: 161-170, April.

Kamien, M.I. and Schwartz, N.L. 1975. Market Structure and Innovation: A Survey. Journal of Economic Literature 13: 1-37, March.

Kaysen, C. and Turner, D.F. 1959. Antitrust Policy: An Economic and Legal Analysis. Cambridge, Mass.: Harvard University Press.

Kendall, M.G. 1943. The Advanced Theory of Statistics. London: Griffith.

Khinchin, A.I. 1957. Mathematical Foundations of Information Theory. New York: Dover Publications.

Kilpatrick, Robert W. 1967. The Choice among Alternative Measures of Industrial Concentration. Review of Economics and Statistics 49: 258-260, May.

_____. 1976. The Validity of Average Concentration Ratios as a Measure of Industry Structure. Southern Economic Journal 42: 711-714, April.

Kobayashi, Takao. 1979. Informational Efficiency of Competitive Prices: An Intertemporal Analysis. Graduate School of Business Administration, Harvard University, Working Paper HBS 79-8: January, 31 pp.

Kottke, Frank J. 1971. An Entropy Measure of Relative Aggregate Concentration: Comment. Southern Economic Journal 37: 109-112, July.

Kryzanowski, L. 1978. Misinformation and Regulatory Actions in the Canadian Capital Markets: Some Empirical Evidence. Bell J. Econ. 9: 355-368.

Kuznets, Simon. 1962. Inventive Activity: Problems of Definition and Measurement. The Rate and Direction of Inventive Activity: Economic and Social Factors. National Bureau for Economic Research. Princeton, N.J.: Princeton University Press. pp. 19-43.

Lecraw, Donald J. and Thompson, Donald N. 1978. Conglomerate Mergers in Canada: A Background Report. Ottawa: Supply and Services, Canada. Government of Canada, May.

Leonard, W.N. 1971. Research and Development in Industrial Growth. Journal of Political Economy 79: 232-256, March/April.

_____. 1973. Reply. Journal of Political Economy 81: 1249-1252, September/October.

Leuthold, R.M. and Hartmann, P.A. 1979. A Semi-Strong Form Evaluation of the Efficiency of the Hog Futures Market. Amer. J. Agr. Econ. 61: 482-489.

Levy, Ferdinand K. 1968. The Allocation, Characteristics, and Outcome of the Firm's Research and Development Portfolio: Comment. Journal of Business 41: 89-93, January.

Lockley, Lawrence C. 1964. An Approach to Marketing Theory. Cox, Reavis, Alderson, Wroe and Shapiro, Stanley J. (eds.). Theory in Marketing. Homewood, Ill.: Richard D. Irwin.

Loeb, P.D. and Lin, V. 1977. Research and Development in the Pharmaceutical Industry: A Specification Error Approach. Journal of Industrial Economics 26: 45-51, September.

McCallum, B.T. 1972. Relative Asymptotic Bias from Errors of Omission and Measurement. Econometrica 40: 757-758, July.

McGary, E.D. 1953. Some New Viewpoints in Marketing. Journal of Marketing 18: 36, July.

McGee, John S. 1958. Predator Price Cutting: The Standard Oil of New Jersey Case. Journal of Law and Economics 1: 137-169, October.

McMillan, C.J. 1978. The Changing Competitive Environment of Canadian Business. Journal of Canadian Studies 13: 38-47, Spring.

McVey, Philip. 1960. Are Channels of Distribution What the Textbooks Say? Journal of Marketing 24: 61-65, January.

Maddala, G.S. 1965. Productivity and Technological Change in the Bituminous Coal Industry, 1919-1954. Journal of Political Economy 73: 352-365, August.

Mallen, Bruce E. 1977. Principles of Channel Management. Toronto and Lexington, Mass.: D.C. Heath. Chapters 7 and 8 and Appendix 8A.

_____. 1967. The Marketing Channel: A Conceptual Viewpoint. New York: John Wiley & Sons. P. ix.

Mansfield, Edwin. 1962. Entry, Gibrat's Law, Innovation and the Growth of Firms. American Economic Review 52: 1023-1051, December.

_____. 1969. Industrial Research and Development: Characteristics, Cost, and Diffusion of Results. American Economic Review 59: 65-71, May.

_____. 1964. Industrial Research and Development Expenditures — Determinants, Prospects, and Relation of Size of Firm and Inventive Output. Journal of Political Economy 72: 319-340, August.

_____. 1968. Industrial Research and Technological Innovation. New York: W.W. Norton.

_____. 1966. National Science Policy: Issues and Problems. American Economic Review 56: 476-487, May.

_____. 1963b. Size of Firm, Market Structure, and Innovation. Journal of Political Economy 71: 556-576, December.

_____. 1963a. The Speed of Response to Firms of New Techniques. Quarterly Journal of Economics 78: 290-311, May.

Markham, Jesse W. 1965. Market Structure, Business Conduct, and Innovation. American Economic Review 55: 323-332, May.

Mason, R.H. and Goudzwaard, M.B. 1976. Performance of Conglomerate Firms: A Portfolio Approach. Journal of Finance 31: 39-48, March.

Mayer, R. and Nicosia, F. 1976. Consumer Information: Sources, Audiences, and Social Effects. in R.N. Katz (ed.), Protecting the Consumer Interest. Cambridge, Ma.: Bellinger Publishing Co.

Maynes, E. Scott. 1975. The Local Consumer Information System: An Institution to be? in Proceedings of the Second Workshop in Consumer Action Research. Berlin: Wissenschaftszentrum.

Means, Gardiner. 1935. Industrial Prices and Their Relative Flexibility. U.S. Senate Document 13, 74th Cong, 1st Session, Washington.

Miller, Richard A. 1967. Marginal Concentration Ratios and Industrial Profit Rates: Some Empirical Results of Oligopoly Behavior. Southern Economic Journal 34: 259-267, October.

_____. 1971. Marginal Concentration Ratios as Market Structure Variables. Review of Economics and Statistics 53: 289-293, August.

_____. 1972. Numbers Equivalent, Relative Entropy, and Concentration Ratios: A Comparison Using Market Performance. Southern Economic Journal 39: 107-112, July.

Minasian, Jora R. 1962. The Economics of Research and Development. The Rate and Direction of Inventive Activity: Economic and Social Factors. National Bureau for Economic Research. Princeton: Princeton University Press. pp. 93-141.

Montgomery, W. David and Quirk, James P. 1974. The Market for Innovations. Social Science Working Paper No. 60. Pasadena: California Institute of Technology, October.

Moore, James R. and Eckrich, Donald F. 1976. Marketing Channels from a Manufacturer's Perspective: Are They Really Managed? American Marketing Association Educators' Conference.

Moulton, K.S. et al. 1974. The Feasibility of Measuring Benefits of the California Federal-State Market News Service. Berkeley: University of California Division of Agricultural Sciences.

_____ and Padberg, D.I. 1976. Mandatory Public Reporting of Market Information. Marketing Alternatives for Agriculture. New York: The State College of Agriculture at Cornell.

Moyer, Mel S. 1978. Managing Vertical Marketing Systems. Arch G. Woodside et al. Foundations of Marketing Channels. Austin, Texas: Lone Star Publishers.

Nadler, G. and Smith, W.D. 1963. Manufacturing Progress Functions for Types of Processes. International Journal of Production Research 2: 115-135, June.

Narver, John C. 1979. Attributes, Constraints, and Consumer Choice. Unpublished manuscript.

_____. 1978. 'Effective Price' and Market Analysis. John F. Cady (ed.). Marketing and the Public Interest. Marketing Science Institute.

National Research Council. 1978. Telecommunications for Metropolitan Areas: Opportunities for the 1980's. National Academy of Sciences, Washington, D.C.

Needham, D. 1975. Market Structure and Firms' R&D Behavior. Journal of Industrial Economics 23: 241-255, June.

Niehans, Jurg. 1958. An Index of the Size of Industrial Establishments. International Economic Papers 8: 122-132.

Nightingale, J. 1970a. Apparent and Real Levels of Concentration in Australian Manufacturing Industry: A Comment. Economic Record 46: 120-123, March.

_____. 1970b. Apparent and Real Levels of Concentration: A Rejoinder. Economic Record 46: 590-591, December.

Nuts and Bolts of the Economy: Background Papers. 1978. London: Chief Secretary to the Treasury, H.M. Government. Chapter 2: Productivity, June.

Ohlin, Bertil. 1933. Interregional and International Trade. Cambridge, Mass.: Harvard University Press.

Ornstein, S.I.; Weston, J.F.; Intriligator, M.D., and Shrieves, R.E. 1973. Determinants of Market Structure. Southern Economic Journal 39: 612-625, April.

Parker, Edward B. 1976. Social Implications of Computer of Telecoms Systems. Telecommunications Policy, December.

Phillips, Almarin. 1966. Patents, Potential Competition, and Technical Progress. American Economic Review 56: 301-310, May.

Prais, S.J. 1958. The Statistical Conditions for a Change in Business Concentration. Review of Economics and Statistics 40: 268-272, February.

Ramsey, J.B. 1974. Classical Model Selections Through Specification Error Tests. P. Zaremba (ed.). Frontiers in Econometrics. New York: Academic Press.

_____. 1970. Models, Specification Error, and Inference: A Discussion of Some Problems in Econometric Methodology. Bulletin of the Oxford University Institute of Economics and Statistics 32: 301-318.

_____. 1969. Tests for Specification Error in Classical Linear Least-Squares Regression Analysis. Journal of the Royal Statistical Society, Series B, 31: 350-371.

Rapp, William V. 1977. Japan: Its Industrial Policies and Corporate Behavior. Columbia Journal of World Business 12: 38-48, Spring.

Rausser, G.C. and Just, R.E. 1979. Agricultural Commodity Price Forecasting Accuracy: Futures Markets Versus Commercial Econometric Models. Department of Agricultural Economics, University of California, Berkeley, Working Paper No. 66, May, 56 pp.

Report of the Royal Commission on Corporate Concentration. 1978. Ottawa, Canada: Government of Canada, Department of Supply and Services. 449 pp.

Retail and Wholesale Trade in Eleven Cities. 1928. Washington: Chamber of Commerce of the United States.

Review of Monopolies and Mergers Policy: A Consultative Document. 1978. London: Her Majesty's Stationery Office, May.

Robinson, Bruce and Lackhani, Dhet. 1975. Dynamic Price Models for New Product Planning. Management Science: 1113-1122, June.

Roland, Jon. 1949. Microtechnology for the Masses. The Futurist Review: 29, June.

Rosenberg, J.B. 1976. Research and Market Share: A Reappraisal of the Schumpeter Hypothesis. Journal of Industrial Economics 25: 101-112, December.

Rothschild, M. 1973. Models of Market Organization with Imperfect Information: A Survey. J. Pol Econ.: 1283-1308, December.

Rumelt, Richard P. 1974. Strategy, Structure, and Economic Performance. Graduate School of Business Administration, Harvard.

Rutenberg, David P. 1978. Umbrella Pricing. Kingston, Ontario: Queen's University School of Business, Working Paper, January.

Sallenave, Jean-Paul. 1976. Experience Analysis for Industrial Planning. Boston: Lexington Books.

Sanders, B.S. 1962. Some Difficulties in Measuring Inventive Activity. The Rate and Direction of Inventive Activity: Economic and Social Factors. National Bureau for Economic Research. Priceton, N.J.: Princeton University Press.

Scherer, F.M. 1965a. Corporate Inventive Output, Profits, and Growth. Journal of Political Economy 73: 290-297, June.

_____. 1965c. Firm Size, Market Structure, Opportunity, and the Output of Patented Inventions. American Economic Review 55: 1097-1125, December.

_____. 1970. Industrial Market Structure and Economic Preference. Chicago: Rand McNally and Co.

_____. 1967. Market Structure and the Employment of Scientists and Engineers. American Economic Review 57: 524-531, June.

_____. 1976. Predatory Pricing and the Sherman Act: A Comment (and replies). Harvard Law Review 89: 868-903.

_____. 1965b. Size of Firm, Oligopoly, and Research: A Comment. Canadian Journal of Economics and Political Science 31: 256-266, May.

Schmalensee, Richard. 1977. Using the H-Index of Concentration with Published Data. Review of Economics and Statistics 59: 186-193, May.

Schmookler, Jacob. 1954a. Invention, Innovation, and Competition. Southern Economic Journal 20: 380-385, April.

_____. 1954b. The Level of Inventive Activity. Review of Economics and Statistics 36: 183-190, May.

_____. 1957. Inventors Past and Present. Review of Economics and Statistics 39: 321-333, August.

_____. 1959. Bigness, Fewness, and Research. Journal of Political Economy 67: 628-635, December.

_____. 1962. Economic Sources of Inventive Activity. Journal of Economic History 22: 1-19, March.

_____. 1965. Technological Change and Economic Theory. American Economic Review 55: 333-347, May.

_____ and Brownlee, Oswald. 1962. Determinants of Inventive Activity. American Economic Research 52: 165-176, May.

Schoeffler, Sidney; Buzzell, Robert D., and Heany, Donald F. 1974. Impact of Strategic Planning and Profit Performance. Harvard Business Review 52: 137-145, March/April.

Schumpeter, J. 1942. Capitalism, Socialism, and Democracy. New York: Harper & Row.

Scitovsky, Tibor. 1950. Ignorance as a Source of Oligopoly Power. American Economic Review 40.

Shalit, S.S. and Sankar, U. 1977. The Measurement of Firm Size. Review of Economics and Statistics 59: 290-298, August.

Shaw, Arch W. 1915. Some Problems in Market Distribution. Cambridge, Mass.: Harvard University Press.

Sherman, Roger. 1974. The Economics of Industry. Boston: Little, Brown.

Shrieves, R.E. 1978. Market Structure and Innovation: A New Perspective. Journal of Industrial Economics 26: 329-347, June.

Simon, Herbert A. and Bonini, Charles P. 1958. The Size Distribution of Business Firms. American Economic Review 48: 609-617, September.

Skeoch, L.A. and McDonald, B.C. 1976. Dynamic Change and Accountability in a Canadian Market Economy. Ottawa: Queen's Printer.

Smith, Adam. 1776. Wealth of Nations. Modern Library Edition.

Stelzer, Irwin M. 1956. Technological Progress and Market Structure. Southern Economic Journal 23: 63-73, July.

Stern, Louis W. and El-Ansary, Adel. 1977. Marketing Channels. Englewood Cliffs, N.J.: Prentice-Hall.

_____ and Reve, T. 1980. Distribution Channels as Political Economics. Journal of Marketing forthcoming.

Stigler, George J. 1964. A Theory of Oligopoly. Journal of Political Economy 72: 44-61, February.

_____. 1961. The Economics of Information. Journal of Political Economy 69.

_____ and Kindahl, James K. 1970. The Behavior of Industrial Prices. National Bureau of Economic Research.

Sullivan, Lawrence A. 1977. Handbook of the Law of Antitrust. St. Paul, Minn.: West Publishing Company.

Theil, Henri. 1967. Economics and Information Theory. Chicago: Rand McNally.

Thompson, Donald N. 1979. Mergers, Effects, and Competition Policy: Some Empirical Evidence. Robert Pritchard (ed.). Canadian Competition Policy. Toronto: University of Toronto Press.

Thompson, Gordon. 1979. Memo from Mercury, Information Technology is Different. Background Paper for the Institute for the Future's Workshop on Teletext and View Data in the U.S., Monterey, California.

Thorelli, Hans B. 1977b. Strategy Plus Structure Equals Performance. Bloomington, Ind.: Indiana University Press.

_____ and Thorelli, Sarah V. 1977a. Consumer Information Systems and Consumer Policy. Cambridge, Mass.: Ballinger Press.

Tilton, John E. 1973. Research and Development in Industrial Growth: A Comment. Journal of Political Economy 81: 1245-1252, September/October.

Tucker, K.A. and Yamey, B.S. 1973. Economics of Retailing. Penguin.

Tyler, Michael. 1979. Electronic Publishing: A Sketch of the European Experience. Background Paper for the Institute for the Future's Workshop of Teletext and View Data in the U.S., Monterey, California.

Villard, Henry H. 1958. Competition, Oligopoly, and Research. Journal of Political Economy 66: 483-497, December.

Wasson, Chester R. 1978. Dynamic Competition Strategy and Product Life Cycles. Third Edition. Austin, Texas: Austin Press.

Watson, D.S. and Holman, M.A. 1970. The Concentration of Patent Ownership in Corporations. Journal of Industrial Economy 18: 112-117, April.

Weiss, L. 1969. Quantitative Studies of Industrial Organization. M.D. Intriligator (ed.). Frontiers of Quantitative Economics. Amsterdam: North-Holland. pp. 362-403.

_____. 1977. Stigler, Kindahl and Means on Administered Prices. American Economic Review 67: 610-619, September.

Weston, J. Fred. 1972. Pricing Behavior of Large Firms. Western Economic Journal 10: March.

Whitehead, Alfred N. 1967. Science and the Modern World. Glencoe, Ill.: The Free Press.

Wickens, M.R. 1972. A Note on the Use of Proxy Variables. Econometrica 40: 759-762, July.

Williamson, Oliver E. 1965. Innovation and Market Structure. Journal of Political Economy 73: 67-73, February.

_____. 1975. Markets and Hierarchies: Analysis and Antitrust Complications. New York: Free Press.

_____. 1977. Predatory Pricing: A Strategic and Welfare Analysis. Yale Law Review 87: 284-340.

Wilson, R.W. 1977. The Effect of Technological Environment and Product Rivalry on R&D Effort and Licensing of Inventions. Review of Economics and Statistics 59: 171-178, May.

Worley, James S. 1961. Industrial Research and the New Competition. Journal of Political Economy 69: 183-186, April.

Wright, T.P. 1936. Factors Affecting the Cost of Airplanes. Journal of the Aeronautical Sciences 3.

Yamey, Basil S. 1972. Predatory Price Cutting: Notes and Comments. Journal of Law and Economics 15.

Zald, M.N. 1970. Power in Organizations. Nashville, Tenn.: Vanderbilt University Press.

Grether Bibliography

Special Sales in Retail Merchandising. Nebraska Studies in Business, No. 19, (April, 1927). 37 pp.
"Pros and Cons of Sales Events," Business, 8 (July), pp. 32-37.

1928

"Trade Marks and Differential Gain," The Ronald Forum, (May), pp. 67-74. (Abstract of paper read before the Pacific Collegiate Economic and Commercial Conference, Vancouver, B.C., December 29, 1927.)
"When the Retailer Advertises," Business, 9 (January 1, 1928), pp. 20-21, 45.

1929

"Training for Purchasing," The Pacific Purchasor, 11 (August), pp. 5, 23.
"The Class Room and the Purchaser," The Pacific Purchasor, 11 (September), pp. 24, 27, 28.
"The Purchaser and the Buyer's Market," The Pacific Purchasor, 11 (October), pp. 5, 33, 34.
"No Decision Debates," The Gavel, 11 (January), p. 14.
Review of: The California and Hawaiian Sugar Refining Corporation of San Francisco, California, by Boris Emmet. Stanford Business Series, No. 2. The American Economic Review, 19, (June), pp. 285-286.
Review of: Sales Management Fundamentals, by R.C. Hay. The American Economic Review, 19, (June), p. 295.

275

1930

"Trends in the Wholesale Grocery Trade in San Francisco," Harvard
    Business Review, 8 (July), pp. 443-451.
"The Teaching of Economic Theory," The Balance Sheet (Sup.), (Sep-
    tember, 1930), pp. 13-15. (Paper read before the Pacific Economic
    Association at the University of California at Los Angeles, Decem-
    ber 28, 1929.)
"Looking Backward," The Pacific Purchasor, 12, (January), p. 10.
"Why Study Economics?" The Credit News, 1, (April), p. 17.
"Purchasing Executives Become Professors," The Purchasing Agent, 19
    (April), pp. 354, 405.
"An Academic Definition of Merchandising, Marketing, and Distribu-
    tion," Printer's Ink, 151, (May 22), p. 36.
"Financing the Consumer — Installment Credit," The Credit News, Vol.
    2, (September-October), pp. 12-20.
"Speaker's Ideals," The Gavel, 12 (January), p. 23.
"Market Research in California," Proceedings of the Semi-Annual
    Conference of California Economic Research Council (December 12,
    1930), pp. 5, 6.
"Trends in Distribution," (Abstract of Paper), Bulletin of the National
    Association of Cost Accountants, 11 (January 1, 1930), pp. 606-607.
Review of: The Elements of Marketing, by Paul D. Converse. (New
    York: Prentice-Hall, 1930). Journal of Farm Economics, 12 (Oc-
    tober), pp. 631-632.

1931

Consumer Attitudes Toward Chain and Independent Dealers. The Com-
    monwealth, Part Two, 7 (July 14, 1931), pp. 185-214, 235, 238.
"Combination and Scattering of Food Purchases," Retail Grocers Ad-
    vocate, 36 (August 7, 1931), p. 13.
"What Does the Consumer Think About the Chains?" I. Western Busi-
    ness, 5 (November), pp. 4, 16.
"What Does the Consumer Think About the Chains?" II. Western
    Business, 5 (December), p. 6.
"Are Purchasing Executives Different?" Pacific Purchasor, 13 (Decem-
    ber), pp. 7, 29.
Review of: Marketing Principles, by John F. Pyle. Journal of Farm
    Economics, 13, (October), pp. 631-632.

1932

"Market Factors Limiting Chain Store Growth," Harvard Business
    Review, 10 (April), pp. 323-331.
"Consumer Food Purchases from Chain and Independent Dealers,"
    Journal of Home Economics, 24, (May), pp. 436-437.

"The Wholesale Poultry Business in San Francisco," Journal of Farm Economics, 14 (October), pp. 630-639.

"The Census of Wholesale Distribution," Bulletin of the National Association of Marketing Teachers, 1932 Series, (February, 1932), pp. 13-20. (Paper presented before the annual meeting of the Association at Washington, D.C., December 28, 1931.)

"The Problem of Marketing Technology. Report of the Committee on Definitions." Bulletin of the National Association of Marketing Teachers, 1932 Series, (October), pp. 1-13. (With R.S. Alexander, G.R. Collins, M.T. Copeland, and J.W. Wingate.)

"Two Cities Handle Three-Fourths of California's Wholesale Trade," Western Business, 5 (February), p. 5.

"What Do They Think of the Chains?" Retail Ledger, 27 (March), p. 6.

"Big Sales Means Small Expenses in California's Wholesale Trade," Western Business, 5 (March), pp. 6, 7.

"What Does the Consumer Think of Chains and Independents?" Boston Retail Bulletin, Vol. 6, pp. 1-2.

"Exhibit 19," Abstract of Hearings on Unemployment Before the California State Employment Commission (August), pp. 221-223.

Review of: Economic Stabilization in an Unbalanced World, by Alvin H. Hansen. (New York: Harcourt, Brace, and Company, 1932). Journal of Farm Economics, 14 (April), pp. 363-366.

1933

"A Unique Clearing House System for Member Accounts," Journal of Retailing, 9 (October, 1933), p. 86.

"Report of the Committee on Definitions, September, 1932-September, 1933," Bulletin of the National Association of Marketing Teachers, 1933 Series, No. 4, (November), pp. 1-18. (With R.S. Alexander, G.R. Collins, H.R. Tosdal, and J.W. Wingate.)

Review of: The Paradox of Plenty, by Harper Leech. (Whittlesey House, New York and London, 1932). The University of California Chronicle, 35 (January), pp. 193-195.

Review of: Economics, Principles and Problems, by Lionel D. Edie (Thomas Y. Crowell Company, New York). Journal of Farm Economics, 15 (January), pp. 186-187.

Review of: The Crisis of Capitalism in America, by M.J. Bonn. (The John Day Company, New York). The University of California Chronicle, 35 (January), pp. 209-212.

Review of: The Means to Prosperity, by John Maynard Keynes. (New York: Harcourt Brace, 1933). American Economic Review, 23 (June), pp. 347-349.

1934

"Effects of Price Maintenance Upon Large Scale Retailing," Journal of Retailing, 9 (January), pp. 97-101.

"Alfred Marshall's Role in Price Maintenance in Great Britain," The Quarterly Journal of Economics, 48 (February), pp. 348-352.

"Trends in the Wholesale Meat Business of San Francisco," Journal of Business, (University of Chicago), 7 (April), pp. 124-132.

"Resale Price Maintenance in Great Britain," The Quarterly Journal of Economics, 48, (August), pp. 620-644.

1935

Resale Price Maintenance in Great Britain: With an Application to the Problem in the United States. University of California Publications, 11, pp. vi and 257-334.

Essays in Social Economics in Honor of Jessica Blanche Peixotto. Berkeley, California, University of California Press, p. 363. (Acted as Chairman of the Editorial Committee.)

"John Ruskin – John A. Hobson" in Essays in Social Economics in Honor of Jessica Blanche Peixotto. Berkeley, California, University of California Press, pp. 145-164.

"Resale Price Maintenance and the Consumer," The American Marketing Journal, 2 (July), pp. 144-149.

"Definitions of Marketing Terms." Consolidated Report of the Committee on Definitions. The National Marketing Review, Vol. 1, No. 2 (Fall), pp.   148-166. (With R.S. Alexander, G.R. Collins, M.T. Copeland, J.W. Wingate, H.R. Tosdal, Wroe Alderson, and P.D. Converse.)

"Resale Price Maintenance Under the California Fair Trade Law." Papers and Proceedings of the 14th Annual Conference of the Pacific Coast Economic Association (December), pp. 19-26.

Review of: Institutional Economics: Its Place in Political Economy, by John R. Commons. (New York: The Macmillan Company, 1934). California Law Review, 23 (September), pp. 649-651.

1936

Restriction of Retail Price Cutting with Emphasis on the Drug Industry, (with Mark Merrell and Sumner S. Kittelle). Washington, D.C., Work Materials No. 57, Division of Review, National Recovery Administration, Trade Practice Studies Section, (March), pp. xi, 430 processed.

"The Changing Status of Independent Local Wholesaling in San Francisco, 1900-1930," The American Marketing Journal, 3 (April), pp. 131-148.

"Experience in California with Fair Trade Legislation Restricting Price Cutting," California Law Review, 24 (September), pp. 640-700.
"Fair Trade Legislation in California." Proceedings of the San Francisco Conference on Distribution, (February 6), pp. 52-60.
Review of: Fundamentals of Industrial Marketing, by R.F. Elder. (New York: McGraw-Hill, 1933). American Economic Review, 26 (March), pp. 125-126.

1937

"Fair Trade Legislation Restricting Price Cutting," Journal of Marketing, 1 (April), pp. 344-354.
"Solidarity in the Distributive Trades in Relation to the Control of Price Competition," Law and Contemporary Problems, Vol. IV, No. 3, (June), pp. 375-391. (Symposium dealing with Price Discrimination and Price Cutting.)
Review of: Determination of Confusion in Trade Mark Conflict Cases, by Neil H. Borden. Harvard University Graduate School of Business Administration, Business Research Studies, No. 16, (December, 1936), 34 pp. in the California Law Review, 25 (May), p. 567.
Review of: Wholesaling Principles and Practice, by T.N. Beckman and N.H. Engle. (New York: The Ronald Press Company, 1937). The Journal of Marketing, 2 (July), pp. 85-87.

1938

"Why Most Retail Prices Will Escape Control Under Fair Trade," Printer's Ink, 182 (February 17), pp. 11-14, 102-106.
"Price Maintenance Laws Left Their Impression on the Year's Business," Retailing, Home Furnishings Edition, 10 Section 2, (December 26, 1938), p. 13.
"Legislatures, Courts, and Price Cutting," The M.B.A. Club Reporter, 2, (November 18, 1938), pp. 1 and 3.
Review of: Sales Analysis from the Management Standpoint, by D.R.G. Cowan. (Chicago: University of Chicago Press, 1938). American Economic Review, 38, (June), p. 363.
Review of: Business and the Robinson-Patman Law, edited by Benjamin Werne. (New York: Oxford University Press, 1938). Brooklyn Law Review, 8 (October), pp. 124-127.

1939

Price Control Under Fair Trade Legislation. New York: Oxford University Press, (1939), pp. x, 517.
"The Future of Super-Markets," The Wharton Review, 7 (March), pp. 8, 9, 22, 23.

"Effects of the Robinson-Patman Act Upon the Distributive Pattern." Papers on Price Policy. Conference on Price Research. 11 pp. (Mimeographed for private circulation.)
"The Specific Effects of the Robinson-Patman Act," American Economic Review, 29 No. 1, Part 2 (March), pp. 105-107.

1940

"Round Table on Price Control Under 'Fair Trade' Legislation," American Economic Review, 30 No. 1, Part 2, Sup. (March), pp. 112-117.
"Marketing Legislation," in Marketing in our American Economy. Annals of the American Academy, 209 (May), pp. 165-175.
Review of: The Control of Competition in Canada, by Lloyd G. Reynolds. (Harvard Studies in Monopoly and Competition). (Cambridge: Harvard University Press, 1940). Journal of Political Economy, 48 (December), pp. 908-920.

1941

"Current Trends Affecting Pricing Policies," Journal of Marketing, 6 (January), pp. 222-223.
"Tax Policy and Price Fixing as Economic Controls for Defense Mobilization," (with M.M. Davisson), Annals of American Academy of Political and Social Science, 214, (March), pp. 148-156.
"Effects of Weighting and of Distributive Price Controls Upon Retail Price Comparisons," Journal of Marketing, 6 (October), pp. 166-170.
Review of: Fair Trade: With Special Reference to Cut-Rate Drug Prices in Michigan, by Edgar H. Gault. Journal of Political Economy, 49 (April), pp. 312-313.
Review of: Government Price Fixing, by Jules Backman. Journal of Political Economy, 49 (August), pp. 633-634.
Review of: Unfair Competition, by J.P. Miller, Journal of Marketing, 6 (October), pp. 193-194.
Review of: Public Regulation of Competitive Practices in Business Enterprise, by Myron W. Watkins. Journal of Political Economy, 49 (December), pp. 931-933.

1942

"Price Policy Trends, 1941." In "Significant Current Trends in Marketing," Journal of Marketing, 6, Part 2, (April), pp. 16, 17.
Review of: Unfair Competition: A Study in Criteria for the Control of Trade Practices, by John Perry Miller. Journal of Political Economy, 50 (February), pp. 142-143.
Review of: Agricultural Price Analysis, by Geoffrey S. Shepherd. The Journal of Marketing, 6 (April), Part I, pp. 415-416.

Review of: War Time Price Control, by George P. Adams, Jr. The Annals of the American Academy, 224, (November), pp. 223-224.

Review of: Distribution Cost Analysis, by Donald R. Longman. American Economic Review, 22 (December), pp. 881-883.

1943

"Locality Price Differentials in the Western Retail Grocery Trade," (with Ralph Cassady, Jr.), Harvard Business Review, 21 (Winter Number), pp. 190-206.

"Price Control and Rationing Under the Office of Price Administration: A Brief Selective Appraisal," Journal of Marketing, 7 (April), pp. 300-318.

Review of: The Anglo-American Trade Agreement, by Carl Kreider. The Annals of the American Academy, 229 (September), p. 185.

1944

"Long Run Postwar Aspects of Price Control," Journal of Marketing, 8 (January), pp. 296-301.

"Geographical Price Policies in the Grocery Trade, 1941: A Note," Journal of Marketing, 8 (April), pp. 417-422.

Review of: Price Making in a Democracy, by Edwin G. Nourse. The Management Review, 33, (September), pp. 326-327.

1945

"Education for Purchasing," Pacific Purchasor (February, 1945), p. 9.

"Should Industry Move West?" (With E.A. Mattison, A.R. Heron, P.J. Raver, and J.H. McBurney.) Northwestern University, The Reviewing Stand, 5 (September 9), pp. 1-12.

1946

"Marketing Problems and Prospects of Western Manufacturers," in Marketing in The West. New York, Ronald Press, pp. 41-55.

The Steel and Steel-Using Industries of California. (With the collaboration of R.A. Gordon, F.L. Kidner, D. Gordon Tyndall, and J.T. Nichols.) Sacramento, California, State Reconstruction and Reemployment Commission, pp. viii, 408.

"The Changing Structure of the American Economy," American Economic Review, 36 (May, 1946), pp. 84-87. (Discussion before meeting of American Economic Association, January 25, 1946.)

"California's Industrial Destiny. California's Inescapable Future as a Great Manufacturing Area." California Monthly (September), pp. 14, 15, 41, and 47.

Testimony in the Case, Aetna Portland Cement Co. et al vs. Federal Trade Commission, Transcript of Record, Vol. 19, pp. 14379-14542.

Review of: Principles of Business Organization, by William R. Spriegel and E.C. Davies. The Annals of the American Academy, Vol. 246, (July), p. 163.

1947

"The Federal Trade Commission vs. Resale Price Maintenance," Journal of Marketing, 12 (July), pp. 1-13.

"Content and Research Uses of Price Control and Rationing Records," American Economic Review, 37, (May), pp. 650-666, 757-760. (Report of the Subcommittee on Research Use of OPA Records, R.B. Heflebower, J.K. Galbraith, E.T. Grether, E.S. Mason, A.C. Neal, and J.D. Summer.)

"Industrial Boom Ahead," Western Advertising, (March), pp. 50, 52.

"Future of the West," Western Metals, (March), pp. 42-45.

"Realty Courses Ready – University of California Plan Summarized," California Real Estate Magazine, 27, (July), p. 7.

"Western Metals Forum," (with others). Western Metals (August), p. 30.

"Western Metals Forum," (with others). Western Metals (September), p. 29.

"Western Metals Forum," (with others). Western Metals (October), p. 28.

Review of: Light Metals Monopoly, by Charlotte Muller. The United States Quarterly Book List, 3 (March), pp. 50-51.

1948

"Delivered Pricing and the Far West," in Delivered Pricing and the Future of American Business. Washington, D.C., Second 1948 Economics Institute, Chamber of Commerce of the United States, (December 9 and 10, 1948), pp. 160-170.

"The Postwar Market and Industrialization in California," Journal of Marketing, 12 (January), pp. 311-316.

"The Relationship of the Professional Schools and Colleges to the University," (with others). Proceedings of the University of California Third All-University Faculty Conference, Davis Campus (February 9-11, 1948), pp. 31-34.

"Rejoinder to 'In Defense of Fair Trade'," Journal of Marketing, 13 (July), pp. 85-88.

"Western Metals Forum," (with others). Western Metals (March), p. 28.

Review of: The Basis and Development of Fair Trade, by the National Wholesale Druggists' Association. The Journal of Marketing, 12 (January), pp. 409-411.

Review of: Open Markets, by Vernon H. Mund. The United States Quarterly Book List, 4 (September), p. 303.

1949

Proceedings of the Governor's Conference on Employment. Sacramento, (December 5 and 6, 1949), 346 pp. Published by the California Department of Employment. (Acted as General Chairman of the Conference, edited the Proceedings, and wrote the Foreword.)

"Preparedness for War and General Economic Policy," American Economic Review, Vol. 39, No. 3 (May, 1949), pp. 366-377. (Papers and Proceedings of the 61st Annual Meeting of the American Economic Association, Cleveland, Ohio, December 27-30, 1948.)

"Radically Different Economic Steps Needed If War Came Soon," The Commonwealth, Vol. 25, No. 9 (February 28, 1949), pp. 43-44. (Abstract of address before the Club, February 18, 1948, on "National Security Planning.")

"Maybe Down, Not Out," The Reporter (June 21, 1949), pp. 11-14.

Central Valley Project Studies: Economic Effects. Problem 24, U.S. Department of the Interior, Bureau of Reclamation (1949), pp. xviii, 278. (Participated as a committee member.)

Central Valley Project Studies: Indirect Beneficiaries. Problem 12, U.S. Department of the Interior, Bureau of Reclamation (1949), pp. 102-166. (Participated as a committee member.)

Review of: The Basing Point System, by Fritz Machlup. The United States Quarterly Book List 5, (June), pp. 196-197.

Review of: The Basing Point System - An Economic Analysis of a Controversial Pricing Practice, by Fritz Machlup. The Journal of Marketing, 14 (October), pp. 480-482.

1950

"A Theoretical Approach to the Analysis of Marketing," in Theory in Marketing: Selected Essays, edited by W. Alderson and R. Cox. Chicago: Richard D. Irwin, Inc., pp. 113-124.

"Economic Development and the Business Manager." General Management Series No. 146, American Management Association, pp. 18-24. (Paper presented before the West Coast General Management Conference of the American Management Association, San Francisco, January 18-20, 1950.)

"The Study of Economics in Schools of Business," American Economic Review, Vol. XL, No. 5, Part 2 (December, 1950), pp. 107-124. (With H.R. Bowen, E.J. Brown, R. Meriam, L.L. Watkins, and J.B. Woosley. Report of the Committee on the Undergraduate Teaching of Economics and the Training of Economists.)

"The Steel Industry of the West," (I) Western Advertising (November, 1950), pp. 47-48, 83-84.

"Must Use Resources Effectively if California to Progress," The Commonwealth, Vol. 26, No. 8 (February 20, 1950), pp. 31, 37. (Excerpts from speech given before Commonwealth Club, February 10, 1950, on the Governor's Conference on Employment.)

"Security and Economic Resources," in International Cooperation for World Economic Development, (1950), pp. 75-79. (Address before Conference on International Cooperation for World Economic Development, University of California, Berkeley, March 16 and 17, 1950.)

Review of: Citrus Fruit Rates, by T.C. Bigham and M.J. Roberts. The United States Quarterly Book Review, 6, (September), p. 316.

1951

"'Fair Trade' Price Regulation in Retrospect and Prospect," in Changing Perspectives in Marketing, edited by Hugh C. Wales with Foreword by Herbert Hoover. Urbana, Illinois, University of Illinois Press, (1951), pp. 197-227.

"The Steel Industry of the West," (II) Western Advertising (January, 1951), pp. 50-52, 56, 58.

"The Consequences of the Abrogation of Tenure: An Accounting of Costs." Interim Report of the Committee on Academic Freedom to the Academic Senate, Northern Section of the University of California (February 1, 1951), 59 pp. (With J.R. Caldwell, W.R. Dennes, R.A. Nisbet, and W.M. Stanley, Chairman).

1952

Marketing in the American Economy, with Roland S. Vaile and Reavis Cox. New York, The Ronald Press Co.

"Fair Trade Pricing Reappraised," in Marketing: Current Problems and Theories. Bloomington, Indiana, University of Indiana Business Report No. 16, (December), pp. 80-94.

"The Cigarette Industry's Price Policies," The Journal of Business of The University of Chicago, 25 (October), pp. 264-266.

"Statement of Resale Price Maintenance Under Fair Trade Regulation," in Study of Monopoly Power, Hearings Before the Anti-trust Subcommittee of the Committee on the Judiciary, House of Representatives, 82nd Congress, Serial No. 12, pp. 552-561 (U.S. Government Printing Office, Washington, D.C.)

Review of: Industrial Pricing and Marketing Practices, by Alfred R. Oxenfeldt. (New York: 1951, 602 pp.) The Journal of Marketing, No. 3, Part 1, (January), pp. 375-376.

Review of: Managerial Economics, by Joel Dean. (New York: Prentice-Hall, 1951). The American Economic Review, 42 (June), pp. 452-455.

Review of: The Nature of Competition in Gasoline Distribution at the Retail Level, by Ralph Cassidy, Jr., and Wylie L. Jones. (Berkeley: University of California Press, 1951). The Journal of Marketing, 17 (October), pp. 204-205.

1953

Instructor's Manual for Marketing in the American Economy, with R.S. Vaile and Reavis Cox. (New York: Ronald Press)

A Source Book on Unemployment Insurance in California. California Department of Employment, (September 28, 1953), 400 pp. (Prepared under the joint auspices of the California Department of Employment and the Institute of Industrial Relations of the University of California. Foreword by E.T. Grether).

"The Two Structures: Faculty Self-Government and Administrative Organization." Report of Sub-Committee No. 1 of Eighth All-University Faculty Conference, 1953. Published in The Faculty and Educational Policies (with others), pp. 7-13.

"Faculty Participation in University Government," California Monthly (April), pp. 10, 11, 39, 40, 41.

1954

"The Regulation of Competition: An Analysis of the Historical Development and Outlook for the Future," in The Role and Nature of Competition in our Marketing Economy, University of Illinois Bulletin, 51, (June), pp. 16-29. (Edited by Harvey W. Huegy).

"Aging and the National Economy," Journal of Gerontology, 9, (July), pp. 354-358.

"What the Chains Did," with D.A. Revzan, in The Year Book of Agriculture, (1954), U.S.D.A., pp. 64-67.

"Industries We Need – And What To Do About It?" Part I, California Real Estate Magazine, 35 (December) pp. 10, 26.

Review of: The Iron and Steel Industries of the South, by H.H. Chapman et al. The United States Quarterly Book Review, 10, (March), pp. 76-77.

Review of: A History of the Graduate School of Business, Columbia University, by Thurman W. Van Metre. The Journal of Higher Education, (November), pp. 451-452.

Review of: Industry in the Pacific Northwest and the Location Theory, by Edwin Joseph Cohn, Jr. The United States Quarterly Book Review, (December), p. 527.

Review of: Basing Point Pricing and Regional Development, by George W. Stocking. The United States Quarterly Book Review, (December), pp. 531-532.

1955

Report of the Attorney General's National Committee to Study the Antitrust Laws, U.S. Government Printing Office, Washington, D.C., (March 31, 1955), 14, 393 pp. (Was a member of this committee).

"Enlarging the Supply of Qualified Candidates for Faculty Positions In Business Administration," in Faculty Requirements and Standards in Collegiate Schools of Business, pp. 60-80. (Proceedings of a Conference on Professional Education for Business, October 27-29, 1955, Arden House, New York, 1955, 216 pp.)

"Industries We Need – And What To Do About It," Part II, California Real Estate Magazine, 35 (January), p. 11.

Review of: The Marketing of Automotive Parts, by Charles N. Davisson et al. The United States Quarterly Book Review, (March), p. 85.

1956

"External Product and Enterprise Differentiation and Consumer Behavior," in Consumer Behavior and Motivation, edited by Robert H. Cole, University of Illinois Bulletin, 53, (February), pp. 82-103.

"Economics in the Curricula of Schools of Business," American Economic Review, 46 (May), pp. 575-577.

"Roland S. Vaile," The Journal of Marketing, 20, (April), pp. 333-335.

"California's Industrial Potentials," California, (June), pp. 21, 30, 31.

Review of:
Distribution's Place in the American Economy Since 1869, by Harold Barger.
Retail Trading in Britain, 1850-1950, by James B. Jefferys.
Productivity in the Distributive Trade in Europe, Wholesale and Retail Aspects, by James B. Jefferys, Simon Hausberger, and Goran Lindblad.
The American Economic Review, 46 (December), pp. 1020-1027.

1957

"The Proper Interpretation of 'Like Grade and Quality' Within the Meaning of Sec. 2(a) of the Robinson-Patman Act," (with Ralph Cassady, Jr.) Southern California Law Review, 30, (April), pp. 241-279.

"Evaluating Our Industrial Development Programs," Seventh Annual Bay Area Management Conference on Industrial Expansion in the Bay Area (February 27, 1957), p. 13-18.

"The Economics of Space: A Review Article," Journal of Marketing, 26 (January), pp. 369-375.

1958

"Pioneers in Marketing: Edwin Griswold Nourse," Journal of Marketing, Vol. 22, No. 4 (April, 1958), pp. 417-419.

"Marketing and Public Policy," Proceedings of the Conference of Marketing Teachers from Far Western States, (September 8, 9, 10, 1958), pp. 200-209.

Review of: <u>Selling in Our Economy: An Economic and Social Analysis of Selling and Advertising</u>, by Harry R. Tosdal. <u>The American Economic Review</u>, 48 (September), pp. 729-731.

1959

"Organization for Industrial Development in California," <u>California Management Review</u>, 1 (Winter), pp. 20-28.

"Economic Analysis in Anti-Trust Enforcement," <u>The Anti-Trust Bulletin</u>, 4 (January-February), pp. 55-76.

"Anti-Trust Policy in the U.S.," <u>Hearings Before the Joint Economic Committee, Congress of the United States, 86th Congress, First Session</u> (September 23, 1959), pp. 2115-2119, 2128, 2131-2132, 2134-2141, 2144, 2147, 2150-2153.

"Handelsutbilding," <u>Ekonomen</u> (Stockholm, Sweden), 15, (October 10, 1959), pp. 24-30.

"California's Economic and Industrial Future," <u>Proceedings of the Third Annual State-wide Industrial Development Conference</u>, San Nateo (February 18, 1959), pp. 3-8.

1960

Statement before the California Water Commission, December 5, 1958. Investigation of Alternative Aqueduct Systems to Serve Southern California, Appendix 1, Economic Demand for Imported Waters, Bulletin No. 78, State Diversion Projects, March, 1960, pp. 243-247.

"National Goals in Air Pollution Research," Report of the Surgeon General's Ad Hoc Task Group on Air Pollution Research Goals, U.S. Department of Health, Education, and Welfare, Public Health Service, August, 1960, pp. v, 39. (Was a member of the ten-man task group that prepared this report.)

Review of: <u>Cost Justification</u>, by Robert F. Taggart. <u>Journal of Marketing</u>, 24 (January), pp. 119-120.

Review of: <u>New Forces in American Business</u>, by Dexter Merriam Keezer and Associates. <u>The Accounting Review</u>, 35 (April), pp. 382-383.

Review of: <u>The Price Discrimination Law: A Review of Experience</u>, by C.D. Edwards. <u>Annals of the American Academy</u>, 33 (September), pp. 171-172.

1961

"The Environment of the Bureau in Relation to Its Organization Goals, Policies, and Programs," <u>Selected Papers From the Workshops in Research Methods</u>, Colorado University, <u>Bureau of Economic and Business Research</u>, University of Illinois, September, 1961.

"Modern Management and Marketing," Marketing Series, No. 13, Japan Marketing Association, (Tokyo), April, 1961, pp. 22-27.

Review of: A Moral Philosophy for Management, by B.M. Selekman. Journal of Business, 34 (October), pp. 511-512.

1962

"Competition as a Dynamic Process," California Management Review, 4 (Summer), pp. 72-84.

Review of: Pricing Power and the Public Interest: A Study Based on Steel, by Gardiner C. Means. The Annals of the American Academy of Political and Social Science, 344 (November), p. 194.

1963

"Models of Value Theory and Antitrust: Comments," in Models of Markets, edited by A.R. Oxenfeldt. (New York, Columbia University Press), pp. 137-143.

"The Impacts of Present Day Antitrust Policy on the Economy," (Address before Antitrust Section of the American Bar Association, August 13, 1963, Chicago, Illinois), pp. 292-336.

"Consistency in Public Economic Policy with Respect to Private Unregulated Industries," American Economic Review, 53 (May), pp. 26-37.

1964

"Federal Trade Commission," Encyclopaedia Britannica, 1964, pp. 142-143.

"Fair Trade Laws," Britannica Senior, Vol. 18, 1964, pp. 469-470.

"Explanatory Notes On 'A Scholar's Dedication'," California Management Review, 6 (Spring), p. 4.

Review of: Development of Marketing Theory, by George Schwartz. Journal of Marketing Research, 1 (May), pp. 78-79.

Review of: Business Aspects of Pricing Under the Robinson-Patman Act, by Albert E. Sawyer, U.C.L.A. Law Review, 11 (July), pp. 904-916.

1965

"An Emerging Apologetic of Managerialism: Theory in Marketing, 1964," Journal of Marketing Research, 2 (May), pp. 190-195.

"Public Policy Affecting the Competitive Market System in the United States," in Marketing and Economic Development, pp. 533-537. (Proceedings, 1965 Fall Conference, American Marketing Association.)

"Public Policy Affecting the Competitive Market System in the United States," in Marketing Thought Leaders, A.M.A., 1965, pp. 77-101.
Review of: Cost Justification: The Thomasville Chair Co., by Herbert F. Taggart. Supplement No. 1, (Ann Arbor, Bureau of Business and Economic Research, University of Michigan, 1964). The Accounting Review, (July), p. 721.

1966

The American Association of Collegiate Schools of Business, 1916-1966 (with A. Kroeger, L.C. Lockley, O. MacKenzie, J.T. Wheeler, and C.J. Dirksen). Homewood, Illinois, Richard D. Irwin, Inc., 1966, pp. IX, 296. Also, sole author of Chapter IV, "The Development of the AACSB Case Curriculum," pp. 146-157.
Marketing and Public Policy, (Englewood Cliffs, New Jersey, Prentice-Hall, Inc., 1966).
"Sharp Practice in Merchandising and Advertising," in Ethics in America: Norms and Deviations. The Annals of the American Academy of Political and Social Science, 363, (January), pp. 108-116.
"Higher Education for Business: A Look Back," in Proceedings: The American Association of Collegiate Schools of Business, Golden Jubilee Meeting, April 25-29, 1966, pp. 1-10.
"Role of the Senate of the University of California," Proceedings of the First Annual Faculty Assembly of State University of New York, October 24-26, 1965, Albany, New York, February, 1966, pp. 12-16.
Review of: On Competition in Economic Theory, by P.W.S. Andrews. The American Economic Review, 56 (December), pp. 1263-1264.

1967

Chapter 15. "Chamberlin's Theory of Monopolistic Competition and the Literature of Marketing," in Monopolistic Competition Theory: Studies in Impact. Essays in Honor of Edward H. Chamberlin, edited by Robert E. Kuenne (New York: John Wiley & Sons, Inc., 1967a), pp. 307-329.
"Pricing Practices and Antitrust," in Prices: Issues in Theory, Practice, and Public Policy, edited by A. Phillips and O.E. Williamson (Philadelphia, University of Pennsylvania Press, 1967b), pp. 228-246.
"Impact of Government Upon the Market System," (with R.J. Holloway), Journal of Marketing, 31, (April), pp. 1-5. (Commentary by Seymour Books, pp. 5-7).
"From Caveat Emptor to An Emerging Caveat Venditor: Whither?" A.M.A., 1967 Winter Conference Proceedings Series, No. 26, in Changing Marketing Systems, pp. 174-177.
"The Critical Problems of Business Management in the Next Decade," in Industrial California Prepares for the 1970's, University of Santa Clara, 1967, 8 pp.

"School and Department of Business Administration," in The Centennial Record of the University of California, Verne Stadtman, ed., University of California Printing Department, 1967, pp. 70-71.

1968

"Galbraith Versus the Market: A Review Article," Journal of Marketing, 32, (January), pp. 9-13.
Review of: Marketing in A Competitive Economy, by Leslie W. Rodger. Journal of Marketing, 32 (January), pp. 100-101.

1969

"Business Responsibility Toward the Market," California Management Review, 12 (Fall), pp. 33-42.

1970

"Industrial Organization: Past History and Future Problems," American Economic Review, Papers and Proceedings of the 82nd Annual Meeting, New York, December 28-30, 1969, 60 (May), pp. 83-88.
"Antitrust Policy Is Still Vital," Reading #48, P.A. Samuelson, Readings In Economics, 6th ed. (McGraw-Hill Book Co., New York, 1970, pp. xvi, 464), pp. 230-234.
"From Caveat Emptor to an Emerging Caveat Venditor: Whither?" pp. 21-28 in Marketing and Society: The Challenge, ed. by R.J. Lavidge and R.J. Holloway (Irwin, Homewood, Illinois).
"Impact of Government Upon the Market System," E.T. Grether and Robert J. Holloway, pp. 116-123, Introduction to Marketing: Readings in the Discipline, ed. by Edward M. Mazze (Chandler Publishing Co., Scranton, Pennsylvania).
Review of: The Rise of American Cooperative Enterprise, 1620-1920, by Joseph G. Knapp, Journal of Marketing, 34 (April), p. 106.

1971

"Business Responsibility Toward the Market," pp. 27-37 in Perspectives in Marketing Management Readings, ed. by F.D. Sturdivant et al. (Glenview, Illinois: Scott, Foresman and Company) 382 pp.
"Introduction: Contractual Marketing Systems — Some Observations," pp. xv to xxi in Donald N. Thompson, Contractual Marketing Systems (Lexington, Massachusetts, Heath Lexington Books).
"Improving the Measurement of Industrial Concentration: Recent Departures," Discussion, 1971 Proceedings of the Business and Economic Statistics Section, American Statistical Association, pp. 152-154.

1972

"Impact of Government Upon the Market System" (with Robert J. Holloway) in Louis E. Boone, Management Perspectives in Marketing (Dickenson Publishing Co., Inc., Encino and Belmont, California), pp. 414-21.

"From Caveat Emptor to an Emerging Caveat Venditor: Whither?" pp. 352-358 in Consumerism, Viewpoints From Business, Government, and the Public Interest. Ralph M. Gaedecke and Warren W. Etcheson (San Francisco, Canfield Press (Harper & Row)).

1973

"The Environment and Integrity of Marketing and Public Policy: An Overview," pp. 391-398 in Public Policy and Marketing Practices, ed. by Fred C. Allvine, Proceedings of Workshop on Public Policy and Marketing Practices, Northwestern University, American Marketing Association.

"Business Responsibility Toward the Market," pp. 321-356 in W. Lazer and E.J. Kelley, Social Marketing: Perspectives and Viewpoints (Irwin, 1973); (Reprinted from the California Management Review, Fall 1969), pp. 33-46.

"Efficiency in Antitrust Resource Allocation," Journal of Contemporary Business, 2 (Autumn), pp. 95-107.

"Foreword" to Dinoo J. Vanier, Market Structure and the Business of Book Publishing (Pitman, New York), p. v.

1974

Review of: J.G. Knapp, The Advance of American Cooperative Enterprise: 1920-1945. Journal of Marketing, 38 (April), p. 111.

Pioneers In Marketing, ed. by J.S. Wright and Parks B. Dimsdale, Jr. (Publishing Services Division, School of Business Administration, Georgia State University, 1974). Reprinted:
Edwin G. Nourse, by E.T. Grether, pp. 91-93
Roland S. Vaile, by E.T. Grether, pp. 147-150

"Impact of Government Upon the Market System," E.T. Grether and Robert J. Holloway, pp. 111-116 in The Environment of Marketing Management, 3rd ed., by R.J. Holloway and R.S. Hancock (New York: John Wiley & Sons, Inc., 1974); (Reprinted from Journal of Marketing, April 1967).

"Foreword" to Ralph Cassady, Jr., Exchange By Private Treaty (University of Texas, 1974, Bureau of Business Research, Graduate School of Business, The University of Texas at Austin, pp. xix to xxi, xxiv, 287).

"Competition Policy in the United States – Looking Ahead," California Management Review, 17 (Summer).

"Marketing and Public Policy: A Contemporary View," Journal of Marketing, 38 (July).

1975

Review of Pioneers In Marketing, edited by John S. Wright and Parks B. Dimsdale, Jr. (Atlanta: School of Business Administration, Georgia State University, 1974, 16 pp.), Journal of Marketing, 39, (July) p. 116.

"Remembering Bob Sproul," California Monthly, November 1975, page 6.

1976

"The Journal of Marketing: The First Forty Years," Journal of Marketing, 40 (July), pp. 63-69.

"Competition Policy in the United States: Looking Ahead," reprinted as No. 21 in Focus: Microeconomics, Annual Editions Reader, pp. 81-88 (The Dushkin Publishing Group, Inc.).

"Competition Policy in Our Democracy — Whither?" pp. 87-105 in Public Policy and Marketing Thought, Proceedings from the Ninth Paul D. Converse Symposium, edited by Alan R. Andreasen and Seymour Sudman, American Marketing Association, Chicago, Illinois.

1977

"The Genesis of the Cal Business School: Reminiscences by Dean E.T. Grether (Emeritus)." Decision, (Fall), pp. 6-11.

"Four Men and A Company: Levi Strauss Since World War I," California Management Review, 20 (Fall), pp. 14-20.

1978

"Perspectives of Marketing: Past, Present and Future" with Reaves Cox and W.T. Tucker. Working Paper 78-46, The University of Texas, Austin, Graduate School of Business, May, 1978, pp. 1-40.

Marketing and the Public Interest. Proceedings of the Symposium Conducted by the Marketing Science Institute in Honor of E.T. Grether, June 8-10, 1977, edited by John F. Cady, July, 1978, Report No. 78-105, pp. ix, 311. "Marketing and the Public Interest: Perspectives on the Issues," pp. 1-13, by E.T. Grether.

Review of Charles Schultze's The Public Use of Private Interest (Washington, D.C., The Brookings Institution, 1977, 93 pp.) Journal of Marketing, 42 (October), pp. 103-104.

"Competition," pp. 185-188 in Encyclopedia of Professional Management. Lester R. Bittel, Editor-in-Chief (McGraw-Hill).

Index

List of Participants

ROLAND A. ARTLE
Ekon. Dr., Stockholm School of Economics, 1959
Professor, Schools of Business Administration
University of California, Berkeley

FREDERICK E. BALDERSTON
Ph.D., Princeton University, 1953, Economics
Professor and Associate Dean, Graduate School of Business Administration
University of California, Berkeley

JAMES M. CARMAN
Ph.D., University of Michigan, 1963, Business Administration
Professor, Schools of Business Administration
University of California, Berkeley

EARL F. CHEIT
LL.B., Ph.D., University of Minnesota, 1955, Economics
Professor and Dean, Schools of Business Administration
University of California, Berkeley

REAVIS COX
Ph.D., Columbia University, 1932
Professor Emeritus, Wharton School of Commerce and Finance
University of Pennsylvania

DAVID M. GRETHER
Ph.D., Stanford University, 1969, Economics
Professor of Economics, California Institute of Technology

RICHARD H. HOLTON
Ph.D., Harvard University, 1952, Economics
Professor, Schools of Business Administration
University of California, Berkeley

DAVID L. HUFF
Ph.D., University of Washington, 1960, Business Administration
Professor, Graduate School of Business
University of Texas, Austin

MARY GARDINER JONES
J.D., Yale University, 1948
U.S. Federal Trade Commissioner, 1964-1973
Adjunct Professor of Business Administration, University of Illinois
Vice President – Consumer Affairs, Western Union Telegraph Company,
    Washington, D.C.

KIRBY S. MOULTON
Ph.D., University of California, Berkeley, 1970, Business Administration
Economist, Cooperative Extension Service, and on Giannini Foundation
    of Agricultural Economics, University of California, Berkeley

REED MOYER
Ph.D., University of California, Berkeley, 1962, Economics
J.D., Michigan State University, 1978
Lecturer, Schools of Business Administration
University of California, Berkeley

JOHN C. NARVER
Ph.D., University of California, Berkeley, 1965, Business Administration
Professor, School of Business Administration
University of Washington

FRANCESCO M. NICOSIA
D. Econ. and Commerce, University of Rome, 1950
Ph.D., University of California, Berkeley, 1962, Business Administration
Professor, Schools of Business Administration
University of California, Berkeley

ALMARIN PHILLIPS
Ph.D., Harvard University, 1953, Economics
Professor of Economics and Law, University of Pennsylvania

LEE E. PRESTON
Ph.D., Harvard University, 1958, Economics
Professor of Business Administration
University of Maryland

RONALD SAVITT
Ph.D., University of Pennsylvania, 1967, Marketing/Industrial Organiza-
tion
Professor, Department of Marketing and Economic Analysis
Faculty of Business Administration and Commerce
University of Alberta, Edmonton, Alberta, Canada

DONALD N. THOMPSON
Ph.D., University of California, Berkeley, 1967, Business Administration
Professor, Faculty of Administrative Studies, York University
Downsview, Ontario, Canada

HANS B. THORELLI
LL.B., Ph.D., University of Stockholm, 1954
E.W. Kelley Professor of Business Administration, Indiana University

SARAH V. THORELLI
M.A., University of Alabama; Ph.Lic., University of Stockholm, Politi-
cal Science
Freelance researcher in organization management and consumer affairs

DONALD F. TURNER
Ph.D., Harvard University, 1947, Economics
LL.B., Yale University, 1950
Assistant U.S. Attorney General for Antitrust, 1965-1968
Professor, Harvard Law School, 1954-1979
Private practice, Washington, D.C.

OTHER PARTICIPANTS AT THE CONFERENCE

L.P. BUCKLIN
University of California, Berkeley

LAWRENCE A. FOURAKER
Harvard University

CLARK KERR
Carnegie Council on Policy Studies in Higher Education
University of California, Berkeley

MARK S. MASSEL
Economic consultant

DAVID A. REVZAN
University of California, Berkeley

LAWRENCE SULLIVAN
University of California, Berkeley